I WANT TO CHANGE BUT I DON'T KNOW HOW!

I WANT TO CHANGE BUT I DON'T KNOW HOW!

Tom Rusk M.D. & Randy Read M.D.

PRICE STERN SLOAN, INC.
Los Angeles

SEVENTH PRINTING — FEBRUARY 1988

Published by Price Stern Sloan, Inc.
360 North La Cienega Boulevard, Los Angeles, California, 90048

ISBN: 0-8431-0491-0

"Just what the world needs,
another self-help book. . ."

ACKNOWLEDGEMENTS

For all those without whom there never would have been a first edition, let alone a third: Jeanne, Jan, Betty, Rosemary, Pat, Kathy, Sandy, Kitty, Emily, Ruth, and Woody.

Special love and appreciation go to Judy and Mallory. Therapists themselves, they helped refined the manuscript while tolerantly accepting episodes of crankiness. Living with an "author" is a heroic feat.

And, finally, much thanks and love to my daughter Natalie Rusk, whose help was invaluable in the mammoth task of revising.

INTRODUCTION

When Randy Read and I self-published I WANT TO CHANGE BUT I DON'T KNOW HOW *in 1978, with an initial print run of 3000 books, we certainly didn't anticipate ever having to revise it. Now, thanks to our publishers, Price/Stern/Sloan, who bought the rights to the book in 1980, I have the responsibility of writing this introduction to the third edition.*

Randy and I wrote this book to help people who truly wish to change, and to assist counselors as they guide others in mastering their own lives. I did this revision with the same aim in mind, and have reorganized the book for easier use, as well as edited it to include updated material.

Randy Read did not participate in this revision; he died tragically in 1983 at the age of thirty-four. Randy was the smartest person I have ever known. We had an extremely honest relationship—often loving, sometimes stormy, always stimulating. He touched and helped many people in his short and extraordinary life, and will continue to do so through his contributions to this book.

Tom Rusk
Julian, California

CONTENTS

CHANGE:
The Basic Course

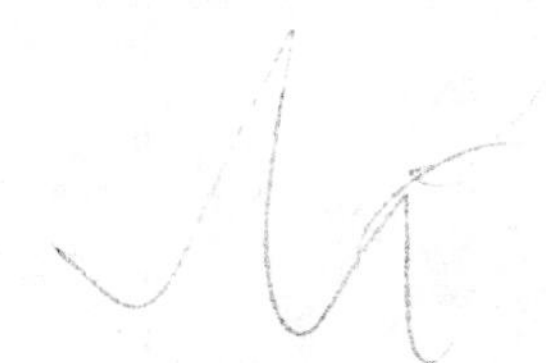

A Life That Changed

"Leave me alone, nobody can help me . . . I'll never change . . . I can't even eat anymore. Look, I only agreed to see you this one time."

Across from me was an emaciated seventeen-year-old girl. Behind her were her concerned parents, whose wealth had enabled them to "doctor shop" from medical center to medical center, from psychiatrist to psychiatrist, seeking "the cure." Now it was to be my turn.

Their daughter (let's call her Ellie) had once been a vivacious girl, with the promise of a glamorous future as a high-fashion model, maybe even an acting career. But as she sat in my office, little hint of that potential was evident. Here was a hollow-eyed, sallow-skinned, very frightened girl.

Ellie was suffering from anorexia nervosa, an illness of unknown cause, characterized by peculiar behavior, lack of appetite, weight loss, and hormonal changes. Some people with this disease eventually die from self-imposed starvation. At best, it is a difficult condition to treat.

So, there was Ellie sitting before me, frightened yet sullen. As her parents ended their litany of all the famous healers they had consulted, she offered her comments.

"I hate psychiatrists," Ellie pouted, talking more to the floor than to me. "The only reason I came was because they made me," she said, nodding towards her parents as though they were her jailers.

"By and large, I am not overly enamored of my fellow psychiatrists myself," I answered truthfully.

But Ellie would have none of it. "Good. Now that we have that straight, may I please leave?"

I could have shrugged my shoulders and let her go, yet I knew that I might have only this one session and she desperately needed help. So, I decided to take a chance.

"You really are stubborn, aren't you? I didn't ask you to come here. If you want to leave, then get the hell out of here right now! . . . But you know, Ellie? Leave and you might lose the best chance you've got!"

Her father stiffened in his seat, and with hurt in his voice protested, "Doctor . . . that's my daughter . . ."

"Mr. Lancefield," I interrupted, "why did you choose me?"

"You were recommended . . . you have a reputation . . ."

"Yes, for getting results by not 'beating around the bush.' That's why you came here. That's why I'm here; not to play the detached, pipe-smoking psychiatrist bit. You've gone that route and your daughter is still a walking zombie. If you want to stop now—fine! Let's stop!"

Her parents were shocked. They had been warned that a first session with me would be hard-hitting. But they didn't expect I'd tell them all to leave after five minutes. Even by our extreme standards this was a bit much.

Yet Ellie hardly seemed surprised at all. She stared into my eyes, defiantly nonchalant, as if to say "I'll leave when I'm damn well ready." By this point her parents were getting up to go. Ellie asked them to wait outside. Confused, they looked at her, then me, then each other. Shrugging and sighing they returned to the waiting room.

"You really upset my parents," she said.

"You should know. You're an expert at it, aren't you?"

This seemed to stun Ellie momentarily. I plunged ahead, anxious to press on, dropping my voice to a whisper. "Ellie, what have you been doing with your life?"

I half expected her to pout, but surprisingly, she opened up. Choking quietly, as though her feelings were too much to bear, Ellie slowly began her story. She stared at the floor, but now and then looked up to catch my glance. She shared some of her experiences, her ordeals and, with some understanding and empathy from me, even showed some of her feelings.

Finally, I interrupted, "You shouldn't change a bit." My tone was matter-of-fact and cool, like an accountant reviewing books—I talked to her not in a tone of a parent or doctor, but rather as a consultant she had hired. "You are clearly better off staying just the way you are, you've got it made."

"Better off the way I am!" she snapped. "*Eighty-nine* pounds . . . vomit at the mere *thought* of food . . . and *you* want me to stay the *way I am!* God, this is a waste of time, I shouldn't have come here at all."

"Absolutely better off," I continued the biting irony. "Aren't you being the way you choose to be? Aren't you getting what you want? Look, Ellie, your dad is a successful businessman, but he's stingy as hell with his time, his attention and his money. Even worse, whatever love your folks are capable of sharing seems to go to your older sister. They always use her as an example of how you should be, right?"

Ellie winced with the pain. "Well . . . yes . . . that's right." Subdued almost to silence, she looked straight into my eyes.

"Of course . . . except for this past year, since you became ill. Aha! That was the difference. Since then your father has had to spend a fortune on you. And, your mother and father both now focus most of their attention on you."

"Are you suggesting that I got sick on purpose?"

"Not at all. But you're sure as hell taking advantage of it. That's why many people who are chronically ill stay that way. Sure, it's not deliberate. You didn't decide 'I'm going to be sick,' but if it's more satisfying to be sick than well . . . any of us can find a way to do it."

Obvious when you think about it. She might have even thought about it before, but while she was listening to me, she seemed amazed and intrigued by the concept.

I continued. "I've never seen anyone who stood to gain more by being sick than you. I've never seen a person so desperately grasping for love. And so ingeniously. You found a way to test your father's love . . . while at the same time punishing him for ignoring you all of those years.

"It's no wonder food won't stay down. Your need to be loved just for who you are, even as a skinny, ugly stick, is so tremendous that it even obliterates your body's need for food."

"Even if that's true," she whined, "what's so wrong about wanting love?"

"Nothing. It's the most natural thing in the world. Some people are in much worse shape than you for want of things far less crucial. But I don't think you could accept tenderness even if it were offered. You're too full of disgust for yourself. I'll bet you're so used to not being held, you can hardly stand to be touched.

"Ellie, everyone predicted you would be an outstand-
ingly beautiful woman with an unlimited future as an 5
actress or anything else you wanted to be. You feared you couldn't live up to those magnificent expectations. Now, at least, you are safe. Just keep being sick and you can cling to the promise of your potential without ever risking the possibility that you can't live up to it. Stay the way you are. You have it made."

"There's *no way* I want to stay the way I am," she protested.

"Yes, there is," I shot back. "Being sick has so many advantages. You're also supposed to be the clever, brilliant one—now you won't have to worry about getting straight A's. You've hit upon the perfect way out—you get concern and attention from everyone, including your parents, without having to be either brilliant or gorgeous.

"It may not be *spontaneous* love, but it beats the hell out of the heavy pressures you were living under just to get any attention at all. At least now you're getting *some*. Just think back to before you got sick. What show of warm love did you get? What hugs, what kisses, what praise? How did anyone show concern about how *you* felt then?"

Ellie, eyes brimming, sank into her chair, burdened by painful memories. I kept pushing. "Best of all, you can *get back at* your dad. You are costing him time and money without having to honestly confront him with how resentful, how starved for love and attention you really are."

"I never said I was! . . ." Ellie stopped in mid-sentence, about to berate me, but fell back to an amazed whisper. "How do you know all this?"

"Here!" I answered, grabbing a mirror off my wall. "Look at yourself! Everything about you says exactly that. You've found an ingenious escape and what's more, *you* are in total control of you . . . not your father, mother, teachers, nor doctors, nobody else—just you . . . nobody can control you anymore.

"You simply can't eat. *Great idea!* And, to top it off, *nobody* can say it's your fault. You are not responsible. You poor, little, sick child. All the psychiatrists and all the king's horses and all the king's men can't put Ellie together again . . ."

Ellie flushed bright red. I knew I was getting closer.

"Ellie, you're powerful. Not only can't I get rid of your condition, I wouldn't even try. Because if *I* succeeded, you might lose a lot more than you'd gain . . . .

"I wouldn't blame you a bit if you chose to keep doing what you're doing. You're outrageously successful. You haven't got the guts to risk living the best life you can, so you'll go on copping out as a poor, fragile, suffering invalid."

The thought that she might be using her illness, channeling her creativity into being sick, seemed to disturb Ellie deeply. I decided to stop at that point and ask her parents to come in, allowing Ellie to stew alone outside my office.

I barely gave them a chance to sit down. "If you want Ellie better, give up your expectations of fame, beauty and academic accomplishments. If you care whether she lives or dies more than how well she performs, then worry less about her eating habits. Don't miss an opportunity to show her with words, hugs and kisses how much you love her. Love her just because she is Ellie, no matter how she performs ever again.

"I realize this change may be difficult at first. Perhaps neither of you were raised with much in the way of open affection. But Ellie's life may depend on it. And I warn you, she may not accept your tenderness readily."

Tears came to Mrs. Lancefield's eyes. Her husband, sitting by her, barely won his struggle to keep his tears back. They had come for magic. All I provided them was the opportunity to realize the sadness Ellie felt, and to consider that doing something differently might help her.

As they left my office, her father reached down to help Ellie from her chair. She shrugged him off, struggled to her feet with her wasted muscles, and haltingly made her own way out the door. As she left, she turned and glared at me. Gone from her eyes was the hopeless, helpless look. In its place was a determined rage.

I have never seen her since. I took a chance. The standard psychiatric procedure for severe anorexia nervosa is emergency hospital admission. In Ellie's case, this had already been tried several times with no lasting change. I wanted to show her that there were better ways to control her life than being sick. When she left I didn't know what would happen.

Not long after, I found out. Several of her college friends came to see me, referred by her for therapy. "Ellie talks about you all the time," they said, "about how you helped change her life in one visit." Miracle stories are so flattering. The only trouble is that her friends also expected one-session "cures." Her friends reported that she was doing well, healthy, more lovely than ever, and excited about her new job with a travel agency in London. Ellie had changed for the better.

***

After such a therapeutic triumph, it would be easy to beat one's chest like a psychiatric Tarzan, proclaiming, "Me big healer!" Books by shrinks are often such struttings of the learned doctor's cleverness. And, typically, the tales of cures by the latest therapy are spiced with titillating sexual fantasies. Well, there aren't any lurid passages in this book.

Neither of us cured Ellie. She changed herself. She was at the outer limits of human experience—desperate, almost dead. And miraculously, she changed. Just like that. She is an *extreme example*, but in a way that's the point—if she did it, anyone can. Small troubles, big troubles, fast changes, slow changes—the power to change is in everyone.

Exercises

Answer the following questions. What do your responses tell you about yourself?

- How closely are you living the life your parent(s) wanted for you? How closely are you living the life your parent(s) expected of you?
- Is your parent(s) satisfied with how you turned out? How much do you care (*honestly*)?
- How do you feel during and after conversations with your parent(s)?
- Were you obedient or rebellious as a child? Have you changed?
- In what ways would you like your parent(s) to change? In what ways would your parent(s) like you to change?
- Does your parent(s) care more about how you feel or how you act?
- Do you care how your parent(s) feels? Do you show it?

Where Should We Begin?

Almost everyone wants to change in some way—become a better lover, parent, golfer, or cook—become less lonely or depressed—become more assertive, make new friends—learn to love and be loved. If you find yourself curious about other people's problems, absorbed in their life stories, it may be a clue that for *you* something is missing. Even idly paging through this book suggests you're probably searching for that something.

Our guess: You want to change, get a new deal, a different script for your life. At off moments you brood about your life, poke at it like an aching tooth. You may not be in agony but then again, you're not *really* getting what you want either. You settle for your life as it is, put up with it, hoping things will somehow improve. But like decaying teeth, lives that ache usually get worse unless something is done.

"I want to change but I don't know how. I'm stuck, I know things aren't quite right, but I just don't know what to do."

We hear variations of this lament several times a day in our practice and so does every other psychiatrist. You've heard it too. It's an honest statement describing a very human dilemma.

And it is widespread. Many people don't really live. They merely exist, passing from one uneventful day to the next, if they are fortunate, or puddle-jumping from one hectic crisis to another if their luck turns bad.

If you only want to get by like that, okay. It is certainly the simplest way. It's easiest because you don't have to do anything differently—don't have to think those complicated thoughts about how and what to change. If that's all you want, then except for its entertainment value, you may as well stop reading this book right now.

On the other hand, if you choose it, there's a whole different way to go. It's up to you. Wouldn't you like the rest of your life to be a lot more exciting and rewarding than it has been up to now? You know what we mean: satisfying, like your daydream fantasies; fulfilling, like the lives of those people you secretly envy.

That's pretty outrageous, isn't it? You've just started this book and already we're intruding into your daydreams. But we're serious. You can probably get much more from life. We've seen people do it. Oh sure, you may think you're unusual, a special case—that your problems are so unique and your life so different from every other human in the history of our species that no book could apply to you, let alone make any impact. Right?

Forget it! No one is that alone, that unusual. Whatever you've got going for or against you is just a variation on the same theme to which everyone dances. Anyway, we don't have your answer. You do. We just want to provoke you into finding it for yourself.

So why are you reading this book? We can't read your mind, but we can make guesses: you're curious, looking, seeking. You've probably read or heard of other "self-help" books and you wondered what this one's like. You may feel bored, confused, frustrated, or guilty. Or you might have that vague, nagging worry that life is passing you by. Or overall, your life is going well, but frustrations pile up and you feel too tired, too old, too lonely, not smart enough, not lucky enough, not good enough. It comes back each time you get stepped on, or feel like you've failed—you've felt it many times. Maybe you hope this book will have THE ANSWER for you.

PLEA: Don't read this book objectively or at a safe distance. Risk losing yourself in it. Allow yourself to be absorbed in it in absolute privacy.

WARNING: Don't read this book if you only want to browse. We are going to try to get inside of you, to coax you from within, to drive and push you to change.

WE WANT YOU TO GET GOOD AT CHANGE, SKILLED AT IT, SO THAT YOU CAN MASTER YOUR LIFE.

The easier path is to tell yourself, "It's impossible, I'll just hang in there, play it safe, act dumb and put up with the crap." Humans have amazing endurance. It's those lies you tell yourself: "I have to . . . What else can I do? . . . I don't have a choice." And with a sigh, or a gritting of teeth, you muddle through. If that's all you want, close this book because you have it already.

Read on only if you dare to hear your feelings. They may be messy, turbulent and hard to understand. Read on only if you're willing to risk taking better care of yourself in a world that gives no real guarantees.

This is, you see, a "gut level" book. A "bite-the-bullet" book. If you'd like to run away now, go ahead. We can't stop you. Nobody will even know. But, if you are willing to take some chances, to embark on the expedition to find your own best path, please join us.

Once you have listened to your feelings, you may decide that you want to change. "But how can I change?" That's what this book is about. How to *listen* to yourself, as well as to others; how to *consider alternatives;* how to *try out changes;* and, most important of all—how to love who you are.

Our purpose is not to offer sympathy, not to get you to "adjust to reality," nor to give you any other excuse to "grin and bear it." We want to show you how to master your life instead of being led around by it. Although our purpose may sound grand and serious, for heaven's sake, bring your sense of humor on this venture with us. Don't take yourself, us, or anyone else too seriously. Use what we say as a tool. We say it as we see it, but it isn't gospel. It's only one way of getting there.

What follows are our ideas about *life-changing,* along with examples of how other people have done it. We hope to encourage you to discover new meaning in your life, to develop your own sense of power and control.

("Oh, no, here it comes! They're going to tell me just-what-it-is-that-I-should-have-been-doing-all-these-years!")

Yes, here it comes: *the* method. Well, *one* method—one we know works. What we are talking about are principles that seem to apply to the kind of life just about everybody wants. It's hard to put into words, but this is how it looks to us.

POINT ONE: DARE TO LOVE YOURSELF IN A WORLD THAT GIVES NO GUARANTEES.

This is the most fundamental rule and in many ways the most difficult to understand. If you've never felt it, love sounds phony. But it's true. Love is the key. It frees you from your fears and gives you the courage to grow. Not that you'll never hurt again. Forget that right now. Life has pain. But through love of yourself and of others, the pain won't matter as much. You'll have an indestructible sanctuary. It begins with self-love. Avoid loving yourself and you will be trapped in a desperate life. It's just you and you; without your cooperation, you're not going to get anywhere at all.

POINT TWO: PAY ATTENTION TO WHAT YOU FEEL. IF YOU DON'T LIKE THE WAY YOU FEEL, IT'S USUALLY A SIGN THAT YOU'RE NOT GETTING WHAT YOU NEED.

Bad feelings are not simply "bad"; they are good and useful, too. They are a way you tell yourself something you might not want to hear. Whenever you have an annoying or painful feeling, it's a message that you're not getting something you need. We're not telling you to seek discomfort, but we are saying when it comes, *listen!* Hurts take many forms: sadness, depression, feeling down, boredom, feeling blah, anxiousness, anger, emptiness. Even bodily symptoms can be signs of hidden hurts: back pain, headaches, tense, tired muscles. When you're missing something, your hurting says "wake up!"

POINT THREE: NOBODY CAN REALLY TELL YOU "THE ANSWER" TO LIFE'S PROBLEMS SO YOU MIGHT AS WELL TRY WHAT FEELS RIGHT TO YOU.

This one provokes quite a response in us. Why? We spend a large portion of our lives working with people who are hurting unnecessarily. People who have "screwed themselves up" in a vain attempt to live up to someone else's expectations. They follow somebody else's rules because they are afraid to listen to themselves. The tragic waste makes us sick. If you saw it every day it would disgust you too.

POINT FOUR: IF WHAT YOU ARE DOING ISN'T GETTING YOU WHAT YOU WANT, TRY SOMETHING DIFFERENT.

Ironclad common sense. Yet this principle is almost universally ignored. For most people, habit rules. Doing the same old thing is always easier than trying something new. It's as though people are terrified that something new might be even worse. If the new thing you try doesn't work better, then *why not try another new thing?* If you're not getting where you want to be, change is the only way to get there. *The best way to change the way you feel is to change the way you act.* Go back and read that last sentence again. It might seem like a simple idea but we have found that single concept to be pivotal to personal freedom.

POINT FIVE: IF YOU'RE GOING TO RISK A CHANGE, TRY SOMETHING LIKELY TO SATISFY YOUR NEEDS WHILE INCREASING YOUR SELF-RESPECT.

Finding your own way is a difficult task. It's hard to ever be sure what is best for you. Your chances for satisfaction will be good if you focus your energies on satisfying your needs and acting in ways you respect. When you're living to please others, it's easy to get confused or stuck. When you give yourself permission to satisfy yourself first, ideas and plans can grow overnight.

POINT SIX: WHEN YOU ARE CONSIDERING A SPECIFIC CHANGE, MAKE A LIST OF ALL THE WORST POSSIBLE THINGS THAT COULD HAPPEN.

Why? Change is risky business. Anytime you do something new, you're taking a chance. Consider the possibilities; look at the pros and cons. Is the change worth it? Sometimes it isn't. But don't let hidden fears decide for you. Get your worries on paper. Weigh the choice of spending the rest of your life feeling the way you do now against the risk of a bad outcome from your attempted change.

POINT SEVEN: BEFORE YOU CHANGE, TAKE A FEW MOMENTS TO PRAISE YOURSELF HONESTLY, COMPLIMENTING YOURSELF FOR SOME SPECIFIC ATTRIBUTE.

Examples? Sensitive, caring, hard working, anything that may apply to you. This might seem frivolous, but berating yourself under the guise of honest criticism is a cowardly but terribly popular habit. Many people actually grow up embarrassed to like themselves. Little wonder they feel disorganized, "untogether." Self-contempt leads to internal mutiny. Treat any person, including yourself, with contempt and he or she is bound to be uncooperative. If you are not giving yourself at least as much praise as you do criticism, you'll never get to use your full power.

POINT EIGHT: IF YOU DECIDE TO TAKE A CHANCE, DON'T JUST THINK ABOUT IT, DO IT!

Thinking has to be one of the biggest wastes of time that humans have invented. Worry is the only thing worse. Insight and understanding change nothing—action does. If you decide to try, go for it! And don't criticize yourself while you're making an effort. Cheer yourself on! Many people are afraid to try anything wholeheartedly. Their efforts are undermined by their own self-criticism, "Aha, you see, it's starting to go badly already!" Avoid that rut; applaud yourself for any honest effort.

POINT NINE: AFTER YOU TRY A CHANGE, EVALUATE THE RESULTS. WHATEVER HAPPENS, CONGRATULATE YOURSELF FOR YOUR COURAGE TO TRY.

Even if the change didn't satisfy your hopes, you will have avoided the trap of self-defeat. Your own support will let you feel better about yourself because you tried, because you risked, because you took the chance rather than pathetically resigning yourself to fate. Ultimately, how you feel about life is how you feel about yourself.

That's our message. No hocus-pocus. No tricks. A restatement of what has been said a million times before in a million other places. Refined common sense. One way to that "better place."

We like to encourage people to experiment with new ways of behaving. We use approaches ranging from getting people in touch with their pain, achieving a heightened awareness of their own personal discomfort, to giving permission, that is, getting people to realize that ultimately they need answer only to themselves.

We often express anger or even scorn when people cling to self-defeating styles of coping with their lives. Our purpose is to wake them up, to get them to try on different ways of living. Difficult though change may be, surely it is far preferable to a life of feeling defective. Searching for halfway solutions simply to obtain a little relief isn't much better.

If we appear to you to be attacking the traditional values such as "don't be too proud," "the experts know best," "work hard, then you'll be good enough," you're right, we are. There have been so many myths about how people should be, we feel it's time to introduce some *counter-myths*. Our current social values pattern the habits that enslave most people. In our view, living *by any habit* is bad. It leads to boredom and dullness. It dehumanizes people and erodes morality. It is a living death.

FREEDOM
MEANS
NOT BEING CONTROLLED
BY SOMETHING
OUTSIDE
OF YOU.

FREEDOM MEANS SELF-CONTROL . . .

NOT
POINTLESS SELF-INDULGENCE,

NOT POINTLESS SELF-DENIAL.

IT MEANS
FOLLOWING
YOUR
OWN PATH AS
YOU
DISCOVER IT.

Exercises

Imagine you died painlessly and quietly while reading this. Visualize yourself standing beside your body and looking at it.

- Are you proud of how you've been living your life?
- What regrets do you have?
- Have you explored your natural talents, your gifts, by enthusiastically trying a variety of activities?
- Have you been resigned to your life, felt that you're getting what you feel you deserve?
- Have you been afraid to try to be different because of awkwardness or what others may think and do in reaction to your changes?
- What would you have changed if you'd been allowed another month, year, decade?
- If you were allowed to live again, how would you change your life?

It All Starts With Love.

Love—the word that's seen more miles of use than a New York taxicab. But what is love? What does the word mean?

Who knows? It probably means just about anything. It can mean affection, friendship, sexual intercourse, or even God—and for that matter, just about anything in between. How you feel about the word depends on a lot of things, but, in a way, can be reduced to a single question—what does love mean to you?

We think love is serious business. Love—if you feel it, immerse yourself in it, live in it—will forever change your life. But if your job, your house, your career, travel, money, prestige, or anything else comes before love, then the whole concept can sound like Pollyannaish self-deception.

The trouble is, in our culture at least, love has had "bad press." It's an easy word. It's got the reputation that anybody can use it for any kind of purpose. A common use is the familiar blackmail, as in "if you love me. . . you won't go to the ball game this weekend." It's also a favorite word of those who try to hide their hypocrisy with religion. For them, love is something in church sermons, a principle easily set aside when the weekday ruthlessness of the real world is resumed.

Of course, love begins with self-love. But in industrialized Western societies, for some peculiar reason, self-love is usually set apart from love as a whole. As though to love everybody else is good and to love yourself is somehow bad. The popular use of the word reflects this bias, as though being in love is primarily a state of obligation and devotion, as though demanding attention and affection is not properly part of love. What happens then is the cycle of tragic waste that marital therapists and other "couple counselors" see so frequently. Two people love each other. They believe that love means giving without any thought of receiving. They never quite say (or even clearly think about) what exactly it is that they want from the other person. These unmet needs on both their parts gradually ripen into resentments. From trivial annoyances, monumental angers grow. All too often, that couple, once sweetly in love, slips into chronic bickering that only hints at the depths of their hatreds.

The escalating divorce statistics reflect, in part, how common this cycle has become. Perhaps in a more quiet time of history, when people moved at a different pace, unspoken resentments were easily buried. But it was also once possible to pile up trash without concern for pollution. Such an approach doesn't work anymore (pile up garbage in one corner and eventually the whole place stinks). Love killed by resentment is so common almost everyone has seen the show or played a part in it. As the love dies it's replaced by clawing, abrading pain. The lovers, without ever planning to be so, become pointlessly cruel. They use their intimate knowledge of the other person, not to get what they want, but rather to wound and hurt in a desperate cry for help.

Although it would be simplistic to blame this "couple breakup cycle" on a single cause, one factor shouts for recognition. Love that keeps conscious of the questions "Am I getting what I want?" and "What does he/she want from me?" is much less likely to slip off to such a sorry end. A person who firmly bases his or her life on self-loving would never let things get so far. That altruistic baloney, "I don't really want anything," is not only a lie—it is an invitation to disaster. Making assumptions without checking as to what the other person thinks, feels and wants is just as dangerous.

Self-love is one of those keys to happiness that people seek but overlook because they expect the answers to be much more exotic. We make a big deal out of self-love. What we see in therapy is a process that looks very much like what happens when one person "falls in love" with another. When somebody wakes up and starts listening to what he or she feels, there's an abrupt change from a life of monotony into an experience of "Wow! I really *can* feel good." Although you still have your job, your everyday tasks, things look somehow different. Your life makes more sense. Everything seems brighter, more hopeful and, in some subtle and profound way, *better.* You walk, talk and move in a way that radiates this new sense of balance. Like loving somebody else, this awakening isn't a very rational process. It can't be explained adequately in words. Rather, it's an experience that can only be grasped by having it.

We know that if you have never allowed yourself passionate self-love, the idea must sound absurd to you. You probably feel angry with us for what you feel is wasting time on this point. Good. Anger is powerful medicine. Soon, we'll ask you to try the preposterous, to center your life on love that is directed towards you. But first, take a look from our vantage point as psychiatrists. Consider the problems we see every day, the human wreckage caused by too little self-love and too much everything else.

Most of what we see in therapy are people who feel unhappy or empty. Of all the social classes, the well-educated and well-to-do are most often torn by that nagging sense of incompleteness. Their "existential depressions" and other related dead ends are side effects of what is euphemistically called "searching for meaning." Searching for meaning through jobs, marriages, careers and children is fair enough. Feeling that one makes a difference is crucial to well-being. But being meaningful isn't enough. Everyone needs to love and be loved too. Searching for meaning through something "out there" without enough love leads to workaholism, loneliness and emotional bankruptcy. It is an attempt to look outside for the real goods that are inside.

The underprivileged and disadvantaged also fall for myths. Poisoned by television's promised land, they often believe that with enough cash they could get it all together. But it is the hungry climber, the striver at the top end of the scale who discovers that possessions, cleverness and entertainment are just last-ditch battles with boredom. You can hunger and hope that *this* will finally be *it*. But all too often when you get in school, or establish your career, or get your house, cars, trips to Europe and glamorous parties, or any of the countless other extra things you think you must have, you find it all feels pointless. Getting can be a let-down. The satisfaction you expect to come naturally with your longed-for objects never materializes. You feel cheated.

Chasing possessions, power, people or intellectual truth is never enough—humans have needs far more basic. The most fundamental is love from within. Some may think the biggest waste of human life occurs with schizophrenics or the mentally retarded. They're wrong. The saddest cases are those whom fate blesses, but who then waste it all by ignoring themselves.

Without a firm foundation of self-love, you will be blind to your own beauty. Condemned to feeling incomplete and inadequate, you will forever search yet never be satisfied.

The well-educated, prone as they are to tripping over their mental shoelaces, can get easily trapped in such circularities: "If I'm having a good time, then I should be able to prove that I'm having a good time." Prove to whom? To somebody else? To some nagging voice within you? "I can't really bring myself to love who I am, but maybe if I can impress everyone else that I'm having a good time, then I *must* be having a good time." What crap! "Prove" to ourselves? If you stand so far outside yourself that you must prove something to *you*, as if you were *somebody else*, you're tying yourself in knots. Lighten up! If you want to be miserable, devote yourself to trying to look happy, successful and satisfied—your only success will be in making some less privileged person salivate with desire—those outside may be impressed by your show but you will become indescribably bored with the monotony, drained by the hypocrisy.

That's where we shrinks come in. Psychiatrists and other lifeguards of sanity are called in most often to rescue the verbal, well-educated, upwardly mobile people—not just because they have money or means, or believe they need such help—but because they hit the dead ends of the status-materialistic dream.

We don't mean that it's inherently bad to look smashing in a tennis outfit, or to drive an elegant sports car, or even to cleverly put someone down at a party. All we mean is that it's stupid to expect such things to ever really do the job, to make your life feel right, to give you that exhilaration that will rescue you from boredom, exhaustion or pain. So what are we selling? You guessed it—love.

Love. Poor word, so often dismissed with a snort. Love—*what the hell can that do?* Well, if you feel it, you find it becomes everything. It's included in the answer to every question and hidden in the secrets of every confusing problem. And if you don't feel it, it's something somebody else is talking about—"There they go again, talking about *love.*"

What we mean by love is a concept, a word for our human perception of some kind of energy or process fundamental to this universe. What it *really* is probably goes far beyond human understanding, but people take one piece of it and act like they know the whole thing. Love is love, and warmth, and compassion, and recognition, and understanding, and approval, and acceptance, and sexual love, and spiritual love, and peace, and action . . . and far, far more.

So it is a very human thing for people to say, "I'm not sure what love is . . . it probably isn't anything." To act like love only means acceptance, as in "if you don't accept everything I do then you don't love me." If you want to you can make love small and restricted, or even pretend it doesn't exist. But if you have the courage, you can let it overwhelm you and consume you.

How do people start feeling love? There are probably an infinite variety of ways. Some first learn through loving another human being and it expands from there. All too often, however, the thread of love gets lost if that relationship fades. Some get love in a blinding flash of light. Love in the form of religious conversions—God is love and love is God. In an instant the connectedness of all things is revealed—it's all love. Profound, real and not at all uncommon. But, if you haven't had a religious or mystical experience lately, the subject can seem like an utter fake. Yet it is there and it does happen.

There are probably lots of ways of getting to that place of peace and tranquility that everyone seems to be after. But one direction is clear to us: love through self-love, self-love through self-understanding, compassion for your personal defects, warmth and caring for yourself. We wish you would *give yourself permission to love you,* to feel tenderly towards all of you; the parts you are proud of *and* the parts you wish weren't there. Love you and you can gradually open your eyes to the face of love. We don't know what love is *really,* but we are sure of one thing—it's bigger than most people take it to be.

What we're saying is to teach yourself about love through self-love. This gate, this path through self-acceptance, self-understanding and self-respect is unusual in Western societies. It is as though people have been trained to be ashamed of their needs and wishes. People seem afraid to look at themselves, as though they fear such a confrontation would blow them to bits.

In a lot of ways, self-love may be too frightening for our society to tolerate. Much of what people do is based on mutual enslavement. Look at what happens in governments, businesses, personal relationships and families. It is perpetuated by parents who raise their children as they themselves were raised, using guilt and punishment for control, rather than being understanding and caring what it feels like to be their child at that moment.

And you can't show love unless you regularly give it to yourself. Self-love is a sort of "bottom line," the final total of how you are towards yourself. True, everybody criticizes themselves and gets impatient with what they are doing. But, if in your average day you insult yourself more than you praise yourself, you're cheating yourself. Thinking nice things to yourself—"I'm really super," or "I really did that elegantly"—seems odd to talk about, much less do. But it's vital to show that you appreciate you.

Self-criticism is so socially expected that it goes unquestioned even when spoken aloud—"I'm really dumb," or "I really messed that one up." Say it, and no one even blinks an eye. You're also certainly safe from outside criticism—destroy yourself and no one can hurt you too badly. That's why we urge such exercises as talking to yourself lovingly in the mirror, acting lovingly towards yourself in the presence of others, being proud of yourself in public. We emphasize these because standing up for yourself seems to be vital to bringing out your creativity. Treat yourself lousy and you'll never get your own cooperation.

Some clichés speak the truth—"If you can't love yourself, you can't love anybody else." Yet so often we see people making half-hearted attempts to give and get love, all the while undermining their efforts with self-contempt. The result? That whole destructive, negative "down trip" that ultimately leads to expecting someone to give you *the answer.* Love yourself thoroughly and deeply enough to accept your own humanity and frailty, and you will open within you that door that connects you to peace and balance.

Loving yourself is simple, once you get the hang of it. Yet it brings with it a heightened awareness of living and acceptance of the inevitable risk and danger that comes with each next breath. It doesn't make the sky turn purple, or everything you touch become gold, but then again such a Disneyland would probably never bring you peace anyway. This grace that begins with self-love doesn't make you immune to the pain and suffering of this world. In fact, quite the contrary; the more you feel the more you might hurt. But it does bring something infinitely more valuable. A sense that life is meaningful and important—that you are not alone and isolated—rather, that you are a part of some larger flow, some larger sense of existence bound to everything else by the energy of love.

In a strange way you *will* feel both pain and pleasure more exquisitely. The pain, though excruciating at times, will never destroy you. An intense vital life is what it's all about. Strange thoughts? Well, that's how it looks to us. A mental health solution with spiritual overtones. Love begins with a turning inward, with *self*ishness, with accepting and loving every part of you, your strengths and weaknesses, loving you just because you exist. Love brings you to a quiet place within you—in the midst of all the turbulence, a haven in which to rest and catch your breath.

Exercises

- Sit alone in quiet, comfortable surroundings—a pleasant garden, a country meadow, your bedroom—and close your eyes, relaxing your body from toes to head. Now begin to visualize and consider yourself as a prospective friend. How do you feel about you? Do you feel a warm glow inside? Do tears of appreciation for who you are and what you've been given come to your eyes? Or, do you merely feel awkward and embarassed? Or, even worse, do you feel irritated, angry or disgusted?
- What is self-love? What differences exist between compassionate self-love and arrogant conceit? Do love and humility go together? Is relentless self-criticism really honest? Can humility and self-love exist together? Here's a thought: Jesus Christ chased money lenders from the temple in a very angry episode, yet he is characterized as being a very loving, gentle being. How do anger and love fit together?

- Count how many times you insult or criticize yourself in one day. Count how many times you talk to yourself lovingly. If there's more criticism than love, the difference is the *love debt* that prevents you from having enough compassion to give yourself and others.
- Now repeat the first exercise.
- Do you see any relationship between either how much tenderness and understanding, or criticism and punishment, you received as a child and how you feel about and treat yourself now? What's the difference between parental love for a child, romantic love between lovers and loving friendship between mature adults?

A Love Story

Gail—strikingly attractive, late thirties, second marriage—was sent to see me by her family doctor. She had been having trouble with her oldest daughter—truancy, running away, shoplifting—the same kind of trouble that Gail's mother had had with her. She was lucky to have a family doctor who wouldn't gloss over what he saw. "You'd better get some professional help," he had told her. "Things are just beginning now, but after a while, the probation officer will become like a member of your family. You'd better all get some counseling now."

Although it was a family problem, the focus fell on Gail and her daughter, Ann. In that first session, I kept coming back to the same observation of much of how Gail and Ann were treating each other was an extension of how they treated themselves. Gail couldn't stand herself. Oh, yes, she had that studied easiness of the modern, sophisticated woman, but her lip service to knowing herself couldn't cover her glaring self-contempt. That self-contempt overflowed to everyone else she cared about—and everyone who would dare care about her.

For a moment, imagine you're there with us now. It's the initial session and, for about the first half hour, the whole family has been in the room. Gail's disgust for herself, however, has become so evident that I choose to send her husband and children out of the room for a while and talk only to her.

"Why did you come here, Gail?" I ask.

She sits, appearing casual and relaxed. "I came here with my daughter because I want to know her better so that we can get along." She talks but her chin begins to tremble.

"Wait a minute, Gail, your chin's trembling. What are you feeling, Gail?"

She moves as if to speak, then her face flushes and she suddenly looks toward the floor.

"Gail . . . you look like you're going to cry," I gently say.

"No, it's nothing. I feel fine . . . really . . ."

"Hey, that's bullshit . . ." My anger flares, provoked by her self-inflicted shame and contempt. "I hear what you're saying, but I'm no more convinced than you are." It would be easy to ignore her nervousness to give her the social slack and change the subject. But to me, it is a vital point. I want her to see what I am seeing. "Come stand over here, I want you to see somebody."

With that I motion to the mirror in the corner of the room. "Tell her . . . you can't fool her because you can see how she feels . . . tell her, Gail."

Gail's face darkens with sadness and anger. She looks at herself with the same reproach she had shown her daughter just moments before. As she sneers at herself, I'm filled with a surge of rage at that human trait of hating oneself, and then hating those who seem most like oneself. How people cripple themselves when they cannot love themselves unless they are perfect! This one habit makes giving or receiving love impossible.

I drag her to her reflection. "Look at yourself in the mirror . . . look at her, Gail . . . *that's you in there!* . . . Look at her! . . . Look how all of these years she has just been waiting . . . waiting for your love, waiting for your acceptance . . . waiting to know that you love her . . . that you care about her . . . believe in her."

Gail, silent as though afraid to move, stands motionless except for her still trembling chin. The tears well up in her eyes and she starts to turn away. I grab her arm and turn her back to the mirror.

"Gail, *look at her!* Look how sad she is . . . how lonely and tired she feels."

Gail bursts into tears. As she sobs, I continue. "She wants your love, Gail . . . just wants you to be proud of her, that's all. Don't deprive her. Show her that you care, show her that you love her and believe in her."

Gail hesitantly looks at herself. "I see what you mean . . ." she says, as if conceding the point in an argument,and tries to quietly slip back to her chair. Insistently, I yank her back up to the mirror: "NO! LOOK AT HER! *Lovingly!* That's *you* in there, Gail." By now I am half supporting her, my fingers clamped to her shoulder. She is freely sobbing and I hand her some tissues, but gently push her still closer to the mirror. She seems almost ready to faint and, by now, my eyes are wet too.

"Gail, tell her you love her . . . it's all right . . . nothing bad will happen. Just tell her you believe in her . . . for just *one moment* don't criticize her, don't tell her how to improve . . . just tell her you love her."

Where Gail had held back before and merely trembled, her tears now flow freely in great convulsive sobs. She is experiencing that unique pain that is felt clearly only when you can't hold it back anymore, like an overwhelming sadness in childhood. You can't think about being sad, or try not to be sad, or analyze being sad, because you are so immersed in the experience of sadness itself.

"Gail, that's it, let yourself feel it, let yourself feel how much you hurt . . . love yourself enough to let you feel the sadness in you . . . it's *all right,* let her cry. Don't try to shut her up to 'be good' . . . give her your love!"

I flow along with her sadness, not interrupting her crying for several moments, just letting her weep. Several minutes pass and, like the calm that follows the rushing waters after a breaking dam, her crying softens to quiet sobs and sniffles.

"Gail, remember how those feelings of love welled up when you had your baby daughter in your arms . . . your beautiful child . . . tell that person in the mirror that you love her with those same feelings . . . that you believe in her . . . that she is a beautiful, fine person."

Gail looks at herself but seems puzzled and surprised as if she suddenly remembers something long forgotten, something essential that was accidentally mislaid.

"I . . . love . . . *I love you*, Gail."

In uttering these words, she seems lost, almost in a trance. She seems unaware of me, as if all of her energy for that moment were focused on her life. But in the moments of silence that follow, she looks first happy and delighted, then slightly anxious, then fearful and then . . . again, again, that look of self-contempt.

She slips back. "But you've got *problems*."

I explode. "**STOP IT!** Look at her! For a moment she thought you'd given her a loving compliment. Look at her . . . look at Gail . . . *you can see it*—she's feeling desperate again . . . and why? . . . because of what you just did—you told her you love her, but in the horrible silence that followed you got scared . . . you panicked and ran away again—*it scares the hell out of you to love you.* Who do you need to tell you that it's all right? What do you want? Would you like God to open up the sky and say, 'It's all right, Gail, you can love yourself.' Is that what you need? Look, Gail, you're afraid, OK, but don't let your fear make you back down from loving yourself. Don't give in so easily, don't let your fears run your life."

Gail, trembling, begins again, "I love you . . . Gail . . . I love you . . . and I *am* proud of you . . . I admire your strength . . . you are beautiful." Now she stays with herself, beaming courage, pride and joy, as though after years of life with crutches she has taken one step on her own. She smiles, touches her reflection like a baby reaching for her mother's face.

Tears of love this time. A reunion of two long apart, finally meeting again. A double image that brought itself back to focus—Gail and herself. She sits down, still crying, but now, with a faint smile. Not an apologetic "good little girl" smile, but rather the look of someone who has just struck it rich. Gail, exhausted and exhilarated, home at last.

As for me, I am weary, I feel as if I have just sprinted a half mile. I feel spent, but well spent. The moment feels right and good.

"Congratulations," I offer. "She was almost resigned to never getting your full attention, but you did it . . . you got through to her."

"Thank you," she replies, squeezing my hand. Then, nodding towards the mirror she makes a promise—"I'll never let her get so far away again."

Either your impulses, fears or habits master you or you run your own show. Mastery of yourself begins by meeting yourself face to face. Embracing all that is within, the good and the bad, the strong and the weak, loving you for you. We don't know why this is, we don't pretend to really understand it. But clearly, love is the most profound mystery in this life. Freedom begins with love. Not lip service, but really reaching out with warmth, understanding, compassion and respect to the *person who is you.* Only through yourself can you deal with the rest of the world.

What happened with Gail is what we both push for in our practices. We thrive on it, because not only does it feel right to us, it gets results. Sure, on one level it may seem like the kind of garbage made for daytime TV soap operas. It's easy to hear the story about Gail and think—"you'll never catch me doing that kind of stuff." It may seem to you undignified or silly. But Gail and her daughter Ann both learned to heal their troubles by learning how to love themselves.

Maybe you think what you *really need* is a "deeper understanding of your relationship with your parents when you were three years old," or a "better comprehension of your bioenergetic flow." Those things are nice but, listen, they aren't vital. Want to get rid of your habits that hang you up? Want to do a better job of taking care of your needs? Then begin by loving yourself right now, loving you for you. Not who you think you are supposed to be, but who you are. You are human, so don't be so stuck up as to think that you're supposed to be any better than everybody else. Everyone has weaknesses and everyone has strengths. Weaknesses aren't flaws, they're just part of a whole person. You may not want to be weak or scared or jealous or greedy or sick, but if you don't love the parts of you that are, you will never get your full strength.

We believe in this kind of thing because we see it work. Even aside from our daily experiences in the private practice of psychiatry, we know people who one day just "woke up" and started loving themselves. It's that personal epiphany that feels like breaking out of a bad dream, "I *am* all right . . . I *can* decide . . . I may not know all of the answers . . . I may not be all I'd like to be . . . but I *am* worth loving."

Using a mirror isn't any special trick. It's just a tool, an implement, a way of focusing your attention on yourself. Use it to break out of the rut of acting as if you don't really exist but everybody else does. Looking at you in there, you're reminded that what's going on in you is about as real as anything will ever be—don't ignore you. It is a simple choice: you can either love yourself or keep yourself waiting. From our viewpoint, it is clear that loving yourself, or self-acceptance, or whatever you want to call it, is the first step to mastery of your life. Otherwise, you are so divided with internal personal wars that your energy is continually dissipated.

And you can't gradually get into loving yourself. Either you do or you don't. It's a leap, a jump. Almost like jumping up into the air and landing on the moon. It would seem impossible to do it, but after you've accomplished it, you can stand there and say to yourself—"Wow, it actually happened. I can really do it." *It's that crazy.* You have a choice. You can either love yourself or keep yourself waiting.

We are at war with slavery. And it is truly war. A battle against that voluntary abdication of responsibility, a surrender to fear. Humans are easily scared and will give up power over their own lives, own souls, in pursuit of peace, security, and approval. "Somebody out there, tell me I'm O.K. and show me *The Way!*" It's so easy to trade self-respect for a pat on the head. Wait for somebody to make sense out of life for you, and baby, you've got a long, long wait.

As we've said before, we'll use anything that might work to get you to consider other ways of living. We try to disturb old habits, agitate systems and stampede people back to meet themselves again. Sound rather dramatic? It is. Try it. Schedule an hour to spend with someone important—you. Or, like too many others, are you afraid to face yourself? Spend some time with you, as though you are really there, as though you are worth being with, *as though you really count!* Rationalize this paragraph away with any excuse, "too busy," "too many responsibilities," "it won't work," or any other bull and you only make your prison more secure. We can't let you out, only you can.

While there isn't anything particularly mysterious about a mirror, the experience can be startling. All kinds of things can happen when *you* confront *you*. You even know what you want to change. It's obvious to you, if you've got the guts to be honest. Look into your eyes. You'll know if you're kidding yourself. Look at yourself in the mirror and tell yourself what you want out of life; what would make you prouder, more satisfied. Not how you have to be, but what your heart wants for you. See if what you are saying feels right; see if it sounds right to *you*. If it doesn't, maybe it is time for some change. Because, in a way, you are like a corporation. You and that person in the mirror are stockholders. If you never let them vote, managing is simpler much of the time, but don't expect their support when you really need it.

You'll probably feel awkward and embarrassed in front of a mirror. Most people do when they try to look within. But love that awkward and embarrassed person, who has found the courage to look you in the eyes. Expect a stilted, unreal feeling at first, especially if this is new to you. You may never have considered doing it seriously before. And don't worry, talking to yourself won't make you crazy or grow hair on your palms. *It's okay to talk to you . . . okay to love you.*

Although Gail had long before grown apart from herself, in that short session she was able to begin recovering her self-love. With practice, she reinforced it, thinking of herself as a worthwhile person and showing those feelings in action. Doing so is extremely difficult and certainly one of the most profound changes anyone can make. She, at least, had the benefit of one of us alternately screaming and encouraging her to face herself in the mirror. All you have is some print and paper exhorting you. But now that you've got the idea, use it.

here is your challenge: Go to a mirror after you read this paragraph. Look yourself in the eyes. (*In the eyes*, please! Don't look down or away.) Talk to yourself out loud. First tell yourself three things you don't like about you. Get the bad stuff out of the way. Now tell yourself three things that you do like—three real compliments. Yes, you *will* feel awkward, but mouthwash, deodorant, and laxative commercials aside, feeling awkward won't kill you. The most important thing is to talk to you and not look away. When you are done, come back to the book. Now is the best time. Please get a mirror and risk it!

Exercises

- Refer to the mirror exercise on page 36. Look in a mirror, full-length if possible. Say nothing at first. Now try to adopt a warm, caring, compassionate or, at the very least, friendly smile. Is your whole face smiling and radiant? Are your eyes soft, warm and tender?

- Switch to a remote, dispassionate, critical stare. Now look coldly and judgmentally. Now glare menacingly. How did each feel? Which came most naturally?
- The eyes are said to be the portal to the human spirit. What do your eyes tell you about how your spirit is doing?
- If you've got the courage, experiment with developing a self-view that includes warm acceptance and tender, tearful pride. With practice, you can learn to see the reflection of the living energy that fills the whole universe in your own eyes. Seeing such "heavy" stuff is much easier if you can first feel loving compassion towards the messy human being you'll be as long as you breathe.

If you didn't do the exercise, please go back and do it. You've got the time. You aren't too busy to stop your habits for a moment and meet yourself. If there is time for TV, for reading magazines, or shopping or breathing, there is time for you to talk to you. Yes, time for yourself. It's okay. Look at yourself. You might find you're not such a bad person after all.

If you won't try the mirror encounter, why not close the book? If you are that much of a coward and refuse even to look at yourself, then what we have to offer won't work. Besides, your cowardice saddens and frustrates us. We have nothing to offer people who are afraid to face themselves. If you couldn't bring yourself to look in the mirror, what does that tell you about yourself? Even if you decide to keep reading, your bias against yourself may be so strong you'll distort everything we say and manage to defeat yourself anyway. You are better off consulting a professional counselor. You may want to refer to "A Few Afterthoughts" to help choose one.

If you did the exercise, that's excellent. You've taken the first step towards listening to you. You were trained as a child to listen to other people. You can train yourself to listen to you, too. A mirror, particularly a full-length mirror, helps you to see yourself as a whole, real person. Talking to you isn't a pointless game; it's an encounter with the pivotal person of your life. *You* looked and talked to *you*. Looking at yourself in the eye and talking could very well be the most difficult action you've taken in a very long time. We know. We do it regularly. Please accept our respect and admiration for your courage.

On Living Your Own Life

You're looking for **trouble** if you try to:

SECRETLY SATISFY needs you're afraid to face . . .
HIDE BEHIND safe habits rather than actively choose . . .
LIVE UP TO someone else's expectations . . .

Trouble? Yes. Pain, boredom, depression, loneliness; however you experience it, whatever you want to call it. For instance, if you're living to please somebody else, trying to show them that you're "all right," you'll probably sense that nagging feeling of never quite "getting there," as though something is always missing.

Why? It's simply that you can never *totally* involve yourself in anything you do *primarily* for someone else's sake—or out of guilt, obligation or fear. If you are doing it for them, it's easy to lose track of who you are. Even more dangerously, you'd be basing your own self-respect on someone else's approval—an awful lot of power to put in anyone else's hands.

Another drawback of living primarily to please others is the danger that you may never satisfy them. Even worse, if you finally do please them, you won't feel fulfilled by their approval. After years of sacrifice, you'll make the horrible discovery that you've become emotionally bankrupt and lonely, despite your Herculean efforts to please. Ellie, from Chapter One, is an example of breaking down in the attempt to please. Ashamed of her needs for love, and unable to live up to the expectations of her parents, she slipped into habits of self-destruction.

Illness and disability—overeating, undereating, alcoholism, paralysis, dizziness, depression (the list is endless)—can provide attention, pity, and a perpetual topic of conversation. Sickness has other advantages too; possible income from disability benefits, an excuse for every other personal shortcoming, and the special privilege of never being openly picked on—for how many people ever dare to get openly angry at an invalid? Despite the obvious drawbacks of any disability, an otherwise temporary problem can become a lifestyle if it offers hidden benefits.

Maybe this is all new to you, or maybe you've thought about it before. We don't know. But it is a good place to start. What we're asking is for you to try some attitudes that might be totally unlike those you've had before. Before you get any further with this book, you can begin changing. And not by trying to be a better person or any other fuzzily optimistic trash that will disintegrate in your next contact with the real world.

What we are talking about is this—if you have problems, they are not some senseless plague that has descended on you from the heavens. Rather, personal hang-ups represent an abortive attempt to get what you need, a half-successful attempt that froze into a habit. Problems are often attempts at solutions. You should learn this from Ellie's story—we think it *is* the moral—*problems have hidden benefits.*

Although life has higher purposes than merely taking care of your own needs, your unsatisfied needs will interfere with more noble and unselfish actions. Frustrated needs—for love, security, meaningfulness or play and relaxation—have sneaky ways of intruding on your attitudes, feelings and actions.

One way frustrated needs can interfere is by making you angry. You get irritable. You begin to blame yourself and others. You become resentful.

It's hard to feel good about someone who is often irritable and angry. The vicious cycle of self-hatred is aggravated by unsatisfied needs. If you don't openly care for yourself, you'll learn, as Ellie did, how to hide in a problem-riddled lifestyle you "just can't help."

You are the only instrument you have to live your life. You can't live a high quality life with a poorly maintained instrument, an instrument you don't respect, you don't appreciate, and you don't love.

LOVE YOURSELF.

MAKE CARING FOR YOU THE HIGHEST PRIORITY IN YOUR LIFE.

TAKE CARE OF YOU. LOOK FOR WHAT *TRULY SATISFIES YOU*.

Maybe you are so wrapped up with self-hatred and/or unthinking commitment to conventional wisdom that these kinds of statements sound like wishful thinking, disgustingly selfish or just too cute. But we urge you to take a chance and let yourself move to the top of all your mental shopping lists. Ellie took a chance. She gave up the security, attention and sweet vengeance that her disability provided. In the same way, we have seen people who have risked changing lives racked with boredom, loneliness, depression, obesity, chronic pain—just about the whole inventory of human ailments—and they have changed beautifully by taking the chance of making the care of themselves the most important part of their lives. Not by following what somebody else thought about them or how they "should" act, but by listening to how they felt. They used their discomfort to give them the courage to *risk living* in more satisfying ways. So how about you? Are there other ways you could act that might get you more love, more control, more fun and more satisfaction?

The usual approach in our society is to see symptoms merely as problems, evidence of diseases to be handled with drugs, hospitals, or long-term therapy. We think that's a waste. Much of the psychological and spiritual suffering people experience is about the same as what you'd feel if you stuck your hand in a fire. It hurts like hell and you want to pull it out. But it is amazing how often people endure emotional fires and stay there, thinking such rubbish as "I'm hurting, that's more proof I'm defective." If you hurt, it's a message that you should be doing something differently.

We think the same goes for just about any psychological symptoms—any thought, feeling or action you have that you don't like. Consider it to be a message to yourself that something needs your attention. Problems don't mean you are crazy or bad, they are the way you tell yourself to take action. Now, sure, some people hurt emotionally because their biochemistry is screwed up. They have allergies, hypersensitivities, metabolic errors, or major psychiatric illnesses, but for the *vast majority* of people, symptoms are messages, arrested attempts at changing, which should be listened to rather than ignored. Your pains, if used correctly, can be your strongest asset, your most powerful tool in changing *you* into the person *you want to be*.

Your life probably isn't as bad as Ellie's, but if you are like most people, you may feel you are missing something—excitement, real joy, satisfaction—something. It starts with you. For although Ellie's pain was used to motivate her, she was the one who chose to change. She picked her way to do it. We didn't. She took her chances at finding love and significance, and discovered self-respect and fun along the way. She made it all right to experiment. She chose to live differently, to prove to herself she was not deliberately creating her illness to escape from (or punish) her parents. *She* changed *her*. *You* can change *you*.

If you came into our office and spent a few hours with us in person, we'd start with the same thing—what you feel, what hurts, what you want, what you can do about it. Only you can change yourself. Nobody can force you or do it for you. (And, in many ways, few others will even really give a damn.) So, we will go through some of those steps with you here. We will jump around a lot, come back and go over these points, but basically that is the format. Start with what you feel, then experiment to see what you can do differently. We will show you some shortcuts, some fancy maneuvers, maybe we'll even motivate you a little, but in the final crunch it's up to you to pick the ways that suit you and to try a few on for size.

In Ellie's case, we saw her pain as an energy source she could harness to give her the courage to risk abandoning her parents' expectations while she learned to live and respect herself. Her parents, much to their credit, changed too. They began to show her love just for existing. They all changed and they all benefited.

Pain, you see, is *power*. Pain can paralyze or it can motivate. It can help you find the courage necessary to overcome *fear* and *habit*. Fear and habit are the two roadblocks that slow people down, the two universal experiences that can keep any of us off our path.

Experiences in brief therapy, such as Ellie's, convince us that such radical approaches—breakthrough techniques to personal growth—are often necessary to help people change. People are creatures of habit. They'll cling to familiar beliefs, attitudes and actions even if they're miserable. Sometimes people have to be blasted out of their ruts. More conventional approaches exist, but much of what goes on in the name of psychotherapy and counseling often seems slow and ineffective. Now, of course, someone is always claiming they've invented a new therapy which will revolutionize the mental health business. We're not about to get into such messianic games by concocting a snappy name for what we do. Rather, we'll offer ideas as simply that, ideas—powerful tools that have been discovered and rediscovered through the centuries. We have merely translated them into a form that emphasizes meaningful change.

The creative use of pain is just one of these many breakthrough approaches that have begun to surface in the field of psychotherapy. Teach yourself how to master these tools and you'll have them to use whenever you need. As we go through this book, we'll share with you stories about other people (names changed and identities hidden, of course, but with the essential facts unaltered) in the hope of showing you ways to master these principles. There is no single route you must follow—the point is to experiment, to find out what works best for you. Ultimately, you must adapt these approaches for your own use. Don't blindly follow us or anyone else. Experiment, explore. Here are tools. Use *them* to change *you*.

Exercises

- What makes you uncomfortable? When were you last bored, sad, irritated, lonely, jealous? Where did it occur? Whom were you with? Where in your body did you feel uncomfortable?
- When you feel badly, when you hurt inside, do you feel alone and isolated from everyone else? Does your discomfort make you feel wrong? Do you believe your unhappiness and loneliness are somehow evidence that there is something fundamentally wrong with you?
- If you knew someone who was feeling what you feel when you're in pain, would you feel compassion and tenderness for that person? Or would you condemn him or her for being unhappy, the way you condemn yourself?
- Try paying attention to your emotional reactions. Treat them as signals, information useful to making decisions as to which experiment to try next, rather than as evidence that you're defective.
- Using your recurrent discomfort in a particular set of circumstances as a guide (e.g., at work, with family, in bed) ask yourself, "What could I do differently that might bring me more satisfaction? What action would make me feel better about myself?"

Taking Inventory: A Look at Needs & Habits

How does a person start to change? There are lots of ways people do it, but we've seen certain patterns that work better than others. The underlying principles are the same—to change, take a look around, see what you have, what you need, then try something new.

But how can you tell where to start?

Hank looked sheepish and ashamed as he sat in my office. "Three months ago if you had told me I'd be in a shrink's office, I wouldn't have believed it. You asked me what brought me here? Heck, it ought to be obvious . . . I've felt fed up and disgusted for the last six months and I keep feeling worse. What should I do?"

Maybe it would have been nice if we had some specific directions for Hank, something like a Chinese fortune cookie with a little message about what to do next. But we don't have that. We're glad we don't. We didn't tell Hank what to do, and we won't tell you either. *We will* show you how to listen to yourself, how to find your own answers. Not the "right answer" but the best answer for you at that moment—whichever feels right, seems best at that time, the one for which you can respect yourself the most.

What this means is living through a sort of refined trial and error, respecting yourself for having the guts to try something new when what you've been doing isn't working.

How do some people manage to find ways to improve their lives in spite of all of the chaos and confusion? How do they know what to try next? They don't have magic answers—no, it's much simpler. *They experiment* to find what takes care of them best. They do what Hank didn't do. They change instead of sticking to habits.

Hank, and people like him, wish someone else would do the choosing. People who hide behind old habits aren't just stuck. They're *devoted* to being stuck. At the slightest mishap they berate themselves, as though they should have known *ahead of time* exactly what to do with life. What arrogance! *Nobody knows exactly what to do with life!* A lot of people sit around hoping that somebody will tell them exactly what to do so that they won't have to make any more mistakes. (That way, if it doesn't come out right, there is somebody else to blame.) If you've got the guts to live your own life, you're going to make mistakes. Only by giving yourself permission to take those real chances in life—trying out new ways of acting—will you ever find out what you could be getting.

If a habit isn't working, try something else.

But what does "working" mean? It all depends on how you look at your life. If you want, you can assume that life is meaningless and there is no purpose to it whatsoever. Whether or not that is true is anybody's guess, but if that is what you believe, if that is what you *want* to believe, where can you go from there? Another extreme is to believe that the purpose of life is to immediately rid yourself of attachments to this world. If that is what you want to believe, you can renounce your present life, give away all of your possessions, and move to a monastery.

What we *choose* to believe is that *part* of what life is about is to do a good job at being you. Part of doing a good job at being you is keeping yourself alive, caring for your biological needs of food, clothing and shelter. Few would quibble with that. But there are other needs too—

psychological and emotional needs. For a variety of reasons, in our culture people often act as though they don't have any psychological needs or that they're not supposed to try to take care of them, as if they should ignore the fact that parts of them are hungry.

By recognizing these needs, each person can do a better job of taking care of them. So, here is one list of

BASIC PSYCHOLOGICAL NEEDS

LOVE . . . feeling like you are genuinely important to someone else. It's also feeling like someone else loves you as much as, or more than, they love anyone else on earth. Feeling like someone really understands you. *Thinking you're* loved or *imagining* you're loved is never enough. *Knowing* that they love you can only come from their showing it regularly and your letting yourself feel that love. It's hard to describe the experience in words. But, for example, when someone is loving you with a look or a hug or a touch, do you ever get dizzy or feel like you're filling up inside, as though you're about to burst? (We are always amazed by people who act as if they don't care whether anyone loves them—and then wonder why their lives are gray and lonely.)

A SENSE OF WORTH . . . feeling like you count, like you really matter. People who feel worthless think that if they died in their sleep tonight no one would really care. A sense of worth means knowing that your being here actually makes the world different, makes it a better place because of you. Once again, *really feeling it* is the important part. Everyone on earth could line up outside your door and tell you how wonderful you are, but unless you *feel it,* it isn't worth a thing.

FUN . . . getting to do what you want to do. Fun is what you wish you were doing when you are daydreaming at *work.*

Pure, joyous, non-productive, goofing around; play, laughter, letting go. Fun is being silly, childlike, uninhibited, carefree, exhilarated and happy.

SECURITY . . . getting all of the above consistently. Feeling like you've got some control over your life, so that what you have now you will probably keep on getting. Part of security includes feeling powerful enough to change things you don't like and courageous enough *to give up control* periodically.

This is only a basic list, one that we evolved partly from what other people—patients, colleagues, friends—have had to say, but mostly from what we hear inside ourselves. It's a list of what many people feel, but there are always more things that could be added. To find out your list, ask yourself what you need emotionally. Don't expect a straight answer because feelings have trouble talking clearly—they mumble and babble and sometimes you have to guess what they are telling you. But please listen to yourself—make a list for yourself. *Write it down.* It won't hurt you. You may feel a little silly doing it but if you don't listen to you, **WHO THE HELL WILL?**

My list of needs:

1.

2.

3.

4.

5.

What do you want out of life? What might it take for you to be happy? (And please spare us the "I don't know what I want" baloney.) Even if you have no idea, start guessing. (If you're stuck, start with what you *don't* want.) Guesses and hunches are where it all begins.

Now, write down what kinds of things would help you get your needs met. Whom you'd like to love you, how you'd like them to show it. What kinds of fun you'd like to have and when you're going to finally let yourself have it. What ways you can start acting more worthwhile, perhaps by encouraging compliments from others or even praising yourself, spoiling yourself! Give yourself some of what you've been waiting for.

In our culture, these psychological needs assume such great importance because people have most of their essential biological needs adequately met. (Although many people in our country do not get enough to eat and lack adequate housing, compared to most of the world we are an obscenely wealthy nation.) Chances are, your psychological needs are not being met as well as your biological needs. Otherwise, you wouldn't be reading this book. Psychological needs are luxuries that become necessities only *after* biological needs are satisfied.

Well, how does all of this apply to you? You've got needs, basic human needs, like us, like everybody else on this planet. Yet, do you often, indeed ever, stop to take stock of what you are getting out of this living? Not this book nor anybody else's can do that for you. The two of us are going on to the next sentence already, but unless you have seriously asked yourself the question: "How much love, importance, fun, and security am I getting?"—*really ask* and *really listen* to the answer—don't be surprised if tomorrow your life is exactly the same as it is today. Unless *you* do something to change it, nothing is going to happen.

So much for our needs. Now, another basic principle about people that's worth considering while you're figuring out what to do with your life.

people are all creatures of habit.

Habitual behavior is the most fundamental aspect of human life. People tend to do whatever they have been doing. The longer a habit has been around and the deeper it is engraved, the more energy it takes to change. Beginning anything new always takes more energy than maintaining the same old thing. This concept forms the basis for such common sayings as "the first step is the hardest" or the more pessimistic "you can't teach an old dog new tricks."

Personality and lifestyle—how a person dresses and eats, stands and speaks, treats others, takes care of his or her needs (both biological and psychological)—are all usually determined by habit. Think about it. If you suddenly acted in a dramatically different way—spoke, dressed, behaved unusually—people around you would most certainly take notice. They might wonder what's going on. They might worry. If the difference were extreme, they might wonder if you were sick, maybe going crazy, or developing a brain tumor. Yet, if you keep acting in the same old way, chances are no one will ever say anything at all. The more predictable you are, the easier it is to ignore you. (But, remember, what is easier for everybody else isn't necessarily better for you.)

Even if your habits were once helpful, *needs can change* and old habits won't work well anymore. Maybe once you liked your job but now you are sick of it. One thing's for sure, it's a lot easier to stick with the old habit of going into the office each day than finding something new. Something new involves risk. You might like your new job even less. Your next boss may be even worse. At least if you stay the same, you know what you've got. It may stink, but at least it's familiar.

It's part of that mass of contradictions and impossible decisions often neatly referred to as "the human condition." And, everyone is in it together. That's the hard choice: "stick with what you've got" or "try something new." In Hamlet's "To be or not to be" soliloquy, Shakespeare underlines the point: ". . . and makes us rather bear those ills we have/Than fly to others that we know not of."

Change is frightening. It stirs things up and, while you are changing, you are unstable, up in the air. Even more scary, change, with its destruction of the old, is akin to death, the giving up of an old life and the going on to something unknown.

Looking at what you are getting out of life is frightening. You might discover you are hurting more than you realized—and then what? To change habits once they have been targeted, once you've decided to get rid of some of the same old ways of doing things, is a lot of effort. If you don't look, you can avoid seeing how poorly your habits serve you.

Habits form the bases of personal styles: passive, assertive, talkative, quiet, energetic, lazy, friendly, lonely—any way a person can be. Is there something about your personal style, your collection of habits that you'd like to change? The way you talk to friends, the way people treat you, what you are doing with your career? Or would you repair those apparently trivial elements of your life? How you deal with clerks, waitresses, or salesmen? (Little habits are a *big deal.* All the little parts make up the whole and the whole is how you feel.)

"I know I want to change some of my habits, but I just don't feel free enough to start."

If you are waiting for an emancipation proclamation, forget it. They never work. Be free or you will be a slave. Freedom may demand a high price, perhaps your life. Only you can decide if it's worth it.

Remember what we said before:

FREEDOM MEANS NOT BEING CONTROLLED BY SOMETHING OUTSIDE OF YOU. FREEDOM MEANS SELF-CONTROL, NOT POINTLESS SELF-INDULGENCE NOR SELF-DENIAL. IT MEANS FOLLOWING YOUR OWN PATH AS YOU DISCOVER IT.

So, if you want to be free, be free. If you wish, take it easy at first with your newfound freedom. Try changing something relatively minor so that you don't lose your balance. If it's hard for you to say "no" to people, try saying "no" five times over the next week, just to see what happens. If you haven't been assassinated by the end of the week, you might want to continue saying "no" when "no" feels right.

Whether or not you give yourself permission to be free depends on what you believe. How you live is your choice. But so many follow the usual rut when they could have the fulfillment of the exceptional.

a. the usual: BE CONTROLLED BY **HABITS** AND ROUTINES • DWELL ON THE **PAST** AND **FUTURE** TO TAKE YOUR MIND OFF THE PRESENT • SEEK **PERFECTION** BY CRITICIZING YOURSELF AT EVERY OPPORTUNITY • STRIVE TO BE **HUMBLE,** BUT QUIETLY **RESENT** OTHERS • DON'T ACCEPT COMPLIMENTS PROUDLY, OR AT LEAST RUIN THEM WHEN THEY ARE GIVEN ("THANKS BUT I STILL HAVE TEN POUNDS TO LOSE . . .") • **SACRIFICE** FOR OTHERS • RESPECT YOURSELF ONLY IF YOU **"SUCCEED"** or **"WIN"** • DEMEAN YOURSELF MERCILESSLY IF YOU **"LOSE"** OR **"FAIL."**

b. the exceptional: LIVE IN THE **NOW** • HAVE **LOVE** AND **COMPASSION** FOR YOURSELF

DESPITE YOUR HUMAN FAULTS • TAKE **RESPONSIBILITY** FOR EVERYTHING YOU THINK, FEEL AND DO • **SELFISHLY** SATISFY YOUR OWN NEEDS BY ASKING YOURSELF "WHAT DO I NEED? WHAT IS RIGHT FOR **ME**?" • GIVE YOURSELF CREDIT FOR YOUR **EFFORTS**, AS WELL AS YOUR "SUCCESSES" OR YOUR "WINS" • REJOICE THAT YOU LIVE WITH **SELF-RESPECT** • TAKE **PRIDE** THAT "FAILURES" DO NOT DESTROY YOU.

It's surprising, but in concept it's really that simple. It's all what you choose to believe. You can live by old habits, or you can wake up to freedom.

Exercises

Using the following "change" worksheet, fill out your problems, scale your needs and satisfactions. Write out some changes in behavior that might better satisfy your needs and reduce or eliminate your problems.

MY MAJOR PROBLEMS ARE:

1. ______________________

2. ______________________

3. ______________________

4. ______________________

5. ______________________

NEEDS

A. I feel genuinely loved by someone other than my parents or my children:

0 ——|——|——|——|——|——|——|—— 10

not at all — very much

B. I feel in control of my life situation:

0 ——|——|——|——|——|——|——|—— 10

not at all — very much

C. I feel worthwhile:

0 ——|——|——|——|——|——|——|—— 10

not at all — very much

D. I have fun:

0 ——|——|——|——|——|——|——|—— 10

not at all — very much

GOALS

I would like to change my life by behaving differently in the following specific ways:

1. ____________________ 4. ____________________

2. ____________________ 5. ____________________

3. ____________________ 6. ____________________

HOPE

I predict I will accomplish *my* goals listed above:

A. Totally C. Partially
B. Mostly D. Not at all

Listening to Yourself: The Noise from Outside

You may disagree with us, but we are sure that you now have, and will forever have, better answers for your life than anyone else can give you. Of course, you can get guidance, ideas, approaches from people, but the ultimate recipe is yours to mix. You have the choice of acting either as a mirror or a lens. Either reflect images from outside, or let the outside come through, creating your own vision from your unique perspective. We could give an endless stream of metaphors on the subject, but what it comes down to is your choice to buy a ready-made role in life or evolve your own view, your own version, so that what you do is *truly yours.*

Some people in this world are distinct, intense, very much themselves. Other people, easily ignored, blend into the gray mass of humanity. This is not a dress rehearsal. Why not risk the intensity? Make your life yours. As a marionette controlled by others, you can move along free of responsibility for your life, if that's what you want. Puppets are everywhere: corporate marionettes, wife marionettes, husband marionettes . . . but consider, real marionettes have an advantage over you—they think no thoughts and feel no feelings. As a follower, you must stifle and crush much of what is you.

It's very human to want to follow somebody. Life is so complicated and frightening that it's reassuring to believe that somebody else can tell you exactly what to do. In our society, children are allowed to make decisions for their dolls and toys, but not for themselves. They are taught to listen to the authorities who tell them what to think, feel and do. "Should" and "ought to" and "have to" become ingrained restraints. No wonder evangelists and gurus develop such large followings. People actually believe someone else can communicate with God, the universe, or anything else better than they themselves can. They retreat into believing experts have all the answers.

It takes a lot of courage to listen to yourself in a world that is never going to make very much sense. Sure, people can make up explanations and rationalizations about what is going on, but the rules for this existence seem to transcend any human system of logic. So, people who can't make sense out of the world turn to some outside system for direction rather than have the guts to rely on their own best judgment and really listen to what they feel.

And look at what happens! Look at how followers handle their own ideas and feelings. They bury them with rigid, humorless lives or booze, pills or other drugs or a host of physical and mental symptoms. Eventually they hide what they feel so deeply that their humanity vanishes and they become efficient (or chaotic), empty robots.

They give up their freedom by following "experts." The magic people who *KNOW!* Leaders, gurus, therapists, the holy and not so holy. It's not that the leaders are necessarily evil or corrupt. It's just that the followers surrender their uniqueness, freedom, and judgment for the sweet relief of having somebody else make their decisions.

Wouldn't it be nice if psychiatrists (or somebody somewhere) really had the magic answers? Really knew all the vital secrets? Or at least could tell you what to do so you would never hurt again . . . could give you some kind of verbal morphine that would protect you against feeling the sharp stings of life . . . ahh . . . Dr. Feelgood! "See all those diplomas on his wall . . . Oh, and look . . . he is smoking a pipe . . . he must be very wise! Maybe he will tell me what to do."

The concept of an expert is tempting. Imagine someone you could trust to handle things while you take it easy, like dropping off an automobile with mechanics for a little tune-up. Come back tomorrow afternoon and it's ready to go; and you never even have to bother looking under the hood. The experts did the whole thing.

It's so easy to believe that there's such a thing as EXPERTS—special humans who are part parent, part guardian angel and part dutiful servant. Get the right expert, the myth goes, and your worries are over. Let yourself slip into believing that and your life will be a sorry mess. It's as bad as waiting for the miracle cure.

If you're in the habit of trusting experts, if you've convinced yourself that somebody else always has a better grip on what's happening than you do, please at least check out what kind of job the experts are doing for you. You might find that you could have directed the project yourself *and* done a better job. Don't automatically accept what the authorities say. Sure, they've probably got some very useful ideas you ought to consider, but *always* check them out for yourself. If you say, "Wake me when it's over," make sure you've done your best to understand what will happen while you're out. That "leave it to the experts" attitude with a car is bad enough; with your life it can be devastating.

But with all these drawbacks, there is one distinct advantage, one reason why humans keep dreaming experts into business. If the car runs lousy, it's not your fault. You didn't have anything to do with it. It's "those jerks at the shop." When people create experts they have somebody to blame when things go wrong. "That shrink screwed me up." If you don't stop to ask yourself, "Is my life going where I want?" don't be surprised if you don't like your destination. It *is* your life, you know; like it or not, you're both the consumer and the complaint department.

As a society people are in love with the notion of experts. They create grand, wise ones who can predict the future, tell them how to live and make pronouncements on any imaginable subject. And, as consumers of this expertise people get such a deal! They listen to what the experts say, then agree, disagree, talk about it, make jokes about it (where would TV talk shows be without a visiting expert?) and then, best of all, smugly sit back relieved of any burden of thinking things out for themselves. Why bother thinking at all when you can get it from the experts? Why bother with the hard work of building your *own way* by trial and error, when you can copy it ready-made from somebody else?

Life is too complex and specialized for stupid consumers to understand, they need to be spoon-fed. That's the lie so many believe. Once again, another generation grows up secretly despising the experts but still letting them run the show. Priests, scientists, politicians—each area has its own "people in the know."

BEWARE OF EXPERTS! Beware of the addiction to believing in what they say. Listen and choose carefully—don't flatly reject, don't swallow whole.

Experts are people too. Just more human noodles floundering around in the same soup. Consider the experts. Listen carefully—the mechanic says you've got engine problems. Use his advice. Try to see how he sees the trouble—but don't ever blindly follow. If you choose to be lazy, whining "I can't understand," you'll never catch on.

The point of this diatribe? "Self-help" books are usually written by self-appointed experts. This one is hardly an exception. We are both psychiatrists and that's a handy excuse for shooting off our mouths about living. But ultimately we're just two more people. Treat us as experts if you must, but at least have the guts to try things out and find what fits you.

It's scary to rely on oneself, to experience passions. It's difficult to sit down and listen to what you really think and feel. It's so much easier to sleep through the alarms you give yourself—the pains and frustrations—to simply doze off again with easy cop-outs. "I don't know what I think or feel" or "Why should I even try, nobody gives a damn anyway" or "My individual life just isn't significant in the larger scheme of things." Or the recently popular and in some ways the worst—"I found *it, so nothing* bothers me anymore." Cop-outs, pure and simple. They let you fall back on the old dead ends: your infantile dream of trying to please your parents or trying to prove something to someone. Your enormous efforts to keep from feeling the explosive intensity of life. Your learned apathy, studied boredom and habits of emptiness.

Self-deception is perpetuated by words—the catch phrases, jargon and double talk on which the "enlightenment" industry thrives. Selling words has always been a part of selling wisdom. People who have gone through therapies, read books or just overheard conversations pick up the jargon. "He's very real." "She's self-actualized." "I really got 'it' from est but still find my insight from TA useful."

All of this weird language can get out of hand. What do these mysterious words mean? To the listener, people using "psych" talk often seem even worse off than most other humans—too glib, too smug. Psych talk is often used like magic spells to chant away the evil spirits of doubt and boredom. Find a name for your troubles and they will magically vanish (oh sure!). And worst of all, you'll come to use the words of other people without ever really listening to what you feel.

Everyone wants to feel on the right track. It's a very human thing to want. Yet, everyone knows people who seem to be keeping up with only the latest fashions in self-help. First it was Gestalt, then "Being One's Own Best Friend," then TM, and maybe a little jogging. They are the seekers, the followers, the true believers. Maybe it's a friend of yours. Maybe it's you.

When we hear someone spouting that stuff, what usually hits us first is how hard they seem to be trying to convince everyone that they have *the answer;* some trick explanation or membership that will make life easy. They talk about the "latest thing" with glowing superficiality, and try to draw more people in, as if getting others to join would make them feel they had it made.

They're such pushers—that book is about it; this famous person raves about it; that study proves it works; this is how it helped me; and on and on and on. What makes us skeptical is not *what* they say—because often it sounds pretty good—it's *how* they say it. The "used car salesman sound" leads us to doubt. It is as if, to convince themselves, they first have to convince everybody else.

A stereotype to be sure, but a pathetically common rut. We live in California, America's mecca of cults. Here the followers and believers are more abundant than our famous smog. What irks us most is not the beliefs themselves, but the believer's passion to follow, the craving to be led. Someone else's words, (often touted as divine truth) when believed too literally, lead to an atrophy of spirit. To say mere words is to say nothing. If you don't feel it in your guts, you aren't there.

When you are trying to fool yourself, you're not fooling anyone. Acting this way isn't the same as trying to learn something; going through that awkward phase before it becomes a part of you. What we are talking about here is a continuing pattern of deception done for the sake of social membership. To believe a doctrine just to be part of an organization; to believe in order to belong. *It's not wrong to want to be liked and appreciated,* but what's stupid is to stop *listening to yourself* just to belong. If someone else's words fit well, then okay, use them. But for God's sake, don't ignore what you feel just so that you can be "in." Don't repeat what someone else says so much that it becomes impossible for you to hear what you feel.

Listen to how you feel, listen to how you sound. If that fake, empty sound is your prevailing manner, if you are not doing a very good job of convincing you, maybe you ought to try something else.

Spend half as much time getting your beliefs to fit as you did the last pair of shoes you bought, and you will be on the right track. You'll never be infallible, but you will be your own ultimate authority. It's frightening work, believing in yourself, and you can't do it without self-respect.

"But aren't you guys telling me to believe what YOU'RE saying?"

Don't believe it, *try* it. We're hoping to get you to think about *your* needs, observe *your* habits, listen to *your* feelings. If you are stuck, we want you to get moving. We don't have any particular destination in mind (it's an endless journey and, trite or not, the path probably does mean much more than the goal). We just wish *you* would steer your life. We want you to drive and navigate.

Stop periodically, relax, and ask yourself, every bit of you right down to the most unused parts of your being, "Is this the direction that seems most right for all of me at this moment?"

You can borrow ideas and beliefs from anyone and everywhere. We certainly have. But make what you've taken yours. Own it. Use it. Take responsibility for it. See if the new ways make you feel better about yourself.

PLEASE WRITE YOUR NAME IN THIS SPACE:

Now, please write **-ISM** after your name. If anyone asks you to label the system of beliefs, the religion, psychology or philosophy that guides your life, give them the name you wrote down. It's *your* way.

Exercises

- Next time you talk to a friend about what's going on, try standing aside mentally and listening to yourself. Even better, start tape recording your side of telephone conversations. Practice will reduce your tendency to perform for the tape recorder.
- Start a journal. Every day sit down for 15 minutes and begin with "What am I feeling about the important things in my life right now?"
- Listen for how much you feel sorry for yourself, insult yourself, blame others or circumstances for your problems, or act helplessly and try to get others to take care of you.

Listening to Yourself: The Message from Within

But what does 'listening to myself' mean? I listen and sometimes all I get is static. Anyway, where would the world be if everybody did just what they felt like doing all the time?"

Okay, last question first. We are not saying "Do whatever you feel like doing, whenever you feel like doing it!" We are saying *listen* to what's in you. For example, you may feel resentment towards someone you love, but have buried your anger so deeply that you believe everything is fine. You might end up going to a therapist two years from now because your relationship is terrible. Why? Because you have been ignoring something very important, something you feel. We're not saying you should go shoot your spouse just because you're angry today. What we are suggesting is this: if you do feel irritation towards someone, ask yourself, "If I could say or do something differently, something that would help me get more of what I need and want out of this relationship, would that satisfy me more? Would that increase my self-respect?"

Once you ask yourself these questions, you've brought the subject into the light. Now it's hard to ignore. You may find that the only way you can respect yourself is to blast the people who upset you with some hot verbal anger the next time they treat you badly. You may find that you can't look at yourself in the mirror unless you stand up for what you're feeling . . . even though it is hard to "hassle about little things." Minor incidents, small hurts, even unintentional slights are really big things. Ignore them and they'll grow.

We're not asking you to do anything in particular, other than to *feel as much as you can of what's in you.* Don't try to systematically exclude part of you by ignoring it. Ignoring a "problem child" doesn't work; ignoring conflicts in you won't work either. Feelings don't just pack up and go away. Like fish, they're best when fresh; left unattended, they spoil and stink. Listen to yourself and then ask yourself, "What action is right for me?"

Notice we said "right for me"—not easiest, not least scary, not guaranteed to work. Right in accordance with your ethical inner sense. Right in accordance with what would give you your own respect and admiration.

And we mean right in the sense of fair to yourself and others. Remember, fairness doesn't mean not hurting another person's feelings.

Failing a student who doesn't make an honest effort and does a poor job may hurt his or her feelings—but it's fair. Similarly, telling the truth to someone you aren't in love with anymore may hurt feelings, but being honest is only fair to both of you.

Now, the first question: "What can I do if I listen to myself, and all I get is static?" There are lots of those "I would but . . ." excuses: "I'm trying really hard, honestly. I am, but I'm just not sure of what I feel" or "I don't know, it's all so confusing." Okay. What do you do if you're not sure of what you feel?

Guess. Don't worry—*nobody* is sure of anything. Oh yeah, a person may look totally convinced on the outside, but inside the mental wheels keep turning.

Who *are* you? Do you know? Not sure? Good. We're not sure who we are either. Nobody is! Part of being human is to be fluid, ever-changing. Look inside you and you won't find a little person sitting there at some master console in your brain. There is not a unitary self inside of you, one well-defined being whom you can get to grow. Inside, humans aren't individuals; they are mobs of partial selves.

Within are countless versions of yourself—different sets of habits, attitudes, experiences—aspects so different it's hard to conceive that they can be contained in the same person. The morning self, the afternoon self, the self at home with your family, the self at work, the self you are when alone. The self who hardly has any feelings at all. The self who loves, the self who hates. The self who wants money and power, the self who strives to be perfect, the self who criticizes, the self who wants love and respect, and the self who just wants to go to sleep. People never have only one voice within. Instead, everyone's head is filled with committees, confederations, constantly shifting alliances, a kaleidoscope of "selves."

Some of these selves are almost whole individuals. One of these versions of self can take over and run things, so that after a while you may assume this is really all there is to you. Later, however, you (and others around you) may be surprised to find that in a different place, at a different time, you are almost a completely different person ("Wouldn't George be shocked if he saw me now!").

Is there a hypocrisy that underlies all of this? Are you somehow inauthentic because you are not consistent? No, you're just human. Everyone has many different ways of being; which ones get expressed depends on where you are and what's going on—and how much you choose to show.

Some of these selves are smaller organizations—urges, fears, childhood fantasies, daydream wishes—they can come and go almost independent of the rest of you. You may be at work with your working self when suddenly a sexual self drifts into the picture for a moment. Or, you may be making love and the working self appears to remind you of your schedule. We don't think this is necessarily bad, it's just part of the good old human condition. But what *is* bad is when people ignore themselves in an attempt to avoid that internal conflict.

Some countries allow only one political party. Some people allow only one self. In either case, anybody who doesn't agree with the party must go underground. As far as we can see, rigid personality styles are like police states and totalitarian regimes. They trade freedom and creativity for security and control. When only one point of view, one attitude, one self prevails, brittleness and sterility are the end result. The more you cut back the brisk flow of possibilities, the more you replace the vigor of life with the stillness of death. Choices can only come from allowing different points of view. There is noise within, to be sure, but there is sweet music too. How much you hear is up to you.

Some people barely notice the difference between their possible selves. They may spend so much of their time in one particular state of mind that they rarely consider their other ways of being. Yet, almost everyone can notice differences between the ways they act on the job and in leisure activities. How you are with intimate friends and lovers is a different version of yourself than who you are with bosses and supervisors. There are unlimited options within you if you only look.

Jeff, once a prominent businessman in our community, now in his late sixties, was struggling with retirement. He came in for help with what he called "my depression." For the previous months he "just sat around the house," sighing, staring at the walls, quite a contrast to his earlier athletic and aggressive lifestyle. His family, amazed by his inactivity, prompted him to seek help. Lines of worry and hopelessness had multiplied on his face. Feelings of uselessness weighed him down. He was convinced that "old" meant "worthless."

During our first hour together, we talked about why he had come. A few months earlier his son had come to see me for help. Jeff felt his son had improved; he wanted the same. He was hoping to "get this depression over with." We talked about what he was looking for: He wanted to enjoy his mobile home and fishing. He wanted to have the energy to play handball and tennis again, he wanted to return to a life of activities that gave him pleasure and satisfaction. He wanted to feel good. Three months of vegetating in his house provoked him to finally seek help because he was "God damn sick of feeling helpless."

There are a lot of different things I could have done with him in the course of our therapy. We could have talked about depressing experiences in his life. We could have talked about his different selves and even made a list of them. But the therapies based on this kind of intellectual chart-making are rarely powerful enough to get through to someone who is hurting. Instead, I wanted Jeff to vividly experience some of the other ways of being, so I tried to push him in that direction. A more difficult goal, to be sure, but one well worth seeking.

Yet he stopped me before I got going. "Heck, I can't sound happy about anything. I haven't felt good for over a year." I asked him to tell me one good thing that had happened in the last few months. But Jeff would have none of it. I was trying to get him to stop his dejected and hopeless role, even for an instant, but he persisted in droning on in the same depressive monotone. Valiantly, I went through a repertoire of approaches I had tried in the past with other people. I even invented a few new ones. All to no avail. He was invincibly depressed and depressing to be with. I felt like a shoe salesman trying to coax a customer who is "just looking" into buying a new pair. I wanted him to take off his depression—if only for an instant—but he wouldn't even loosen the laces.

When you get locked into one self, you have to let go for a moment to try a new one. Some selves are very strong and resist efforts to change. Some are hidden deep within you and almost impossible to see. Indeed, this concept of "selves," these many organizations within you, can be extended from the psychological part of you to your chemical and physical aspects. Just as arms and legs and other body parts are selves, so are proteins, sugars and enzymes. Sometimes these enzymes can have such a strong mind of their own that they can cause you problems. Take, for example, diabetes. Some poorly understood defect in the pancreas reduces one's ability to produce insulin in response to sugar. Whether you like it or not, if you are diabetic, that "sick pancreas" self will let you down.

In the same fashion, some depressions are probably caused by biochemical aberrations. It's as though there is a mood switch inside that makes one feel bad when it is flipped. For most people, that switch only gets flipped during brief periods of sadness or when something extreme happens. Some learn how to flip that switch themselves, as a way of copping out under stress. Other people have a switch that either flips at slight provocations or just goes off on its own. You have a switch that flips itself and it decides to go, you feel badly. Soon that feeling colors everything.

Towards the end of our first session, I was beginning to believe Jeff might have had one of these biological depressions caused by a faulty mood switch. I was even considering prescribing medication for him. He had a family history of depression, that is, his son, his mother and an uncle of his had experienced similar depressions. And he had also been suffering the kinds of sleep and appetite problems that are regarded as classical symptoms of these disorders. Yet, I am reluctant to give out medications. This is such a pill-oriented culture that people rarely adequately explore ways of relying on themselves, ways of flipping their own switches. Rather, they try to find a pill to do it for them. Furthermore, in Jeff's case, I had a hunch that for him a pill was not the answer. His depression lacked the severity and immobility of a biological depression, and he wasn't becoming grossly withdrawn or thinking about suicide. Rather, he was just becoming more *depressing to be with.* He felt bad, but instead of doing things to feel better, he was doing things to bring everyone else down too. His stubbornness was a bigger problem than his depression. His obstinacy was working against him. I could just imagine how awful it would be to live with him. I only put in one hour and it was about all I could stand.

"God damn it, Jeff! It's disgusting watching how you treat yourself! *For one minute, one damn minute,* would you get up out of your chair and laugh, just dance around, scream, anything!"

Jeff slumped back in his chair, looking even more dejected than before. His face had the look of a suffering martyr, as if to say "How can you treat me this way when I feel so badly? . . ." I was repulsed.

"Look, Jeff. If you won't even try, won't even try for one minute to act differently, then I don't want to work with you. Why should *I* try when *you* won't!"

"I just can't understand why I feel so terrible . . . I can't understand why no one can help me . . ."

As Jeff moaned on, I made a crude pantomime as though I were playing a violin, playing sad, sad songs for poor Jeff. A rude provocation to be sure, yet it felt right for that moment. Perhaps, had I been more gentle ("Ohh, *too bad*") with him and spent several weeks of coaxing and prodding, he might finally have made a move. But that just didn't sit right with me. I didn't feel medications were appropriate and I didn't feel any handholding "consolation therapy" would be useful either. I didn't want to risk reinforcing his mood by passively accepting it, even for a single session. I wanted to take the chance. Either he would make a move (one tiny step in the right direction would be fine) or I would quit for now. If he wanted to get off his ass and get his life moving, he could make an effort now. If not, he could come back when he was ready. Until then, I wasn't interested.

I wasn't very happy with this ending, but I chose it nonetheless. As Jeff left my office, I watched him amble down the hallway, wondering to myself why it is we humans often find such obstinate delight in maintaining our ailments. I shook my head with disgust and anger as he slowly opened the door at the end of the hall. He looked like he was climbing into his grave. Then something amazing happened. He stopped to speak to one of my secretaries, a woman with whom he had apparently had conversation before our therapy hour. The difference was absolutely astounding. With her, he was not morose or depressing. He was witty, charming, effervescent—that energetic and lively self he wanted to retrieve. I sprinted to the end of the hall, almost tackling him with the impact, and grabbed him by his shoulder.

"Jeff, come here for a moment," I asked firmly.

As we reentered my office I exploded. "Hey, damn it, Jeff! Look at that! You were beautiful! You weren't depressed, nor depressing to be with, nor in any way the drag you've been for this hour and the last several months. Did you see how you were when you were talking to her? Did you see *her!?* Did you see how her eyes lit up? *And you loved it!* You don't *have* to be so disgusting all the time! You *can* have fun!"

Sometimes I can be so vicious. I suppose there is a part of me that is enraged at those frailties in myself and all other humans, a part that delights in these opportunities to get out my frustration. And, I am sure that one of the selves inside of me was angry that I, the so-called expert, had spent an hour to get him to act differently, while my secretary had succeeded in just five seconds. But the self that felt most right at that moment was the one that wanted to help Jeff change. I wanted to get him in a psychological hammerlock, a grip he couldn't escape, by congratulating him for this new behavior while simultaneously condemning the old habits.

I was, in effect, saying to him "You may have believed that the way you were acting was something over which you had no control . . . you've just proved to yourself that that belief is false. You do have control, but it doesn't come the way you have been trying to get it . . . it comes by letting go, letting yourself act in those other ways. Tune into the feelings you had while talking to her and you may find a way of kicking your depression."

And that's about what I said to him. I encouraged him, rewarded him, congratulated him, and he left, surprised and somewhat shaken.

Much later we had a good laugh about it, he and I. What he did that day blew his cover and made it hard for him to slip back into his helplessness. Even more importantly, it showed him how to gain control of something over which he thought he had no control. One's selves, like any subcommittee, furnish reports to support their arguments. The depressed selves love to say things like "there is nothing that can be done," but little in this world is truly impossible.

Jeff put it well. "It's funny, but I couldn't stop thinking about all the things that had to be done on my kid's house. I really wanted to help him, but everything seemed like an endless job. There was so much to do. I just couldn't get out of that rut. I really thought that when I came into your office something would happen, you'd say something like 'you're cured' and all of a sudden I'd feel different. I didn't realize that I had it in me all along. I just never noticed it before."

You really don't know what you can do until you try. If it's worth it to jog and exercise your body, then it may be worth it to exercise those different potential versions of yourself, to exercise your ability to choose which self you will allow to act. Like any kind of stretching, it's a way of keeping loose. It's a remarkable capacity of the human mind and body: the more you use them the stronger, more flexible and versatile they become.

Exercises

- Keep a diary for a week. Write in it at least once a day. What made you feel good about yourself? What made you feel angry, sad, lonely, etc.?
- Once each day for a week, look in a mirror and ask yourself: "What could I do today to give myself a more satisfying life? What would I respect myself for doing today? What could help make tomorrow even better?"
- Ask yourself: "Am I stubborn? Am I afraid to revise what I believe about myself and others? Do I want to stay exactly the same but somehow feel better?"
- Write a brief description of how you feel about yourself. Write a brief description of what you believe others think about you. Now, are you willing to consider the possibility that you are wrong about one or both of these descriptions?
- Even more ambitious—ask friends for honest feedback as to their observations of you regarding these same issues. Are you willing to consider the possibility that your friends are more accurate than you are about yourself?
- In this chapter, which Jeff was the real Jeff? Who is the real you?

Listening to Yourself: Self-Exercises

Exercising your selves can be tricky to begin. There's no gym to go to, no outfit to buy, nothing outside you. It's all within. Choose a part of you to work on and start there.

But which part decides what to exercise or practice? Who is in charge of your world within? For many people, no one is in charge. They habitually respond to the parts that make the most noise—desires, hates and fears. Often they sell out to some petty tyrant within themselves in the hope of gaining a little order. Or worse, they are blown about without ever gaining a clear sense of personal direction—lives run by mob rule.

It is possible to break loose from slavery to your noisy parts. Your selves are just reflections of the countless conflicts and disputes in each human being. But there is also a quiet place in the center. To exercise yourselves, to exercise your choice over what your life should be, you can begin by centering your being on your clearest aspect. In the very middle of each person there seems to be a silent, observant self who just watches the show. We call this the "compassionate observer" self. It's the self to whom all the other selves talk (or beg, insult or threaten). It is your psychological center of gravity, the focal point of your being.

This compassionate observer self is also the most powerful aspect of you because it is your power to choose and decide. For many, that power is never fully used. People often believe they have no choice or have to do something because some loud part of them insists it's so. In the midst of such racket, quiet intuitive feelings from the center are easily overlooked. But with practice, one can learn to listen to the subtle messages from inside and see possible choices in situations that seemed hopeless.

When you center yourself in that quiet place, you can establish an "internal congress." You can listen in turn to each different self within you—the noisy, the quiet, the brave, the fearful—and you can give each a chance to be heard in open debate. Instead of trying not to think or feel certain things, you can look for your hidden feelings and give yourself permission to think anything at all. Rather than rule yourself by terrorism, you can establish an internal democracy.

Different philosophies and psychologies have chosen different concepts for this focal point of one's being. Some see it as part of ego, the "I" that tries to compromise with the forces inside and out. Others use the religious concept of soul, or see the center of one's being as pure consciousness. Oriental meditation techniques are essentially exercises for strengthening this compassionate observer self. Regardless of what definition you choose, there is a practical fact that you either ignore conflicting selves within you, and let the noisiest rule, or choose to listen to each in turn, with the final decisions always coming from the center.

If you try to excommunicate your unpleasant or ugly selves—the ones who embarrass you or you wish weren't there—you lose much of who you are. You lose energy wasted in burying the unwanted selves. You lose your sense of being whole. You lose the opportunity to caution others against your negative selves and to channel these selves in more positive directions. You lose the secrets of self-respect, fulfillment and peace. Worst of all, you lose the power to choose your own direction, an awful price to pay for temporary comfort. Long-term dissatisfaction is the usual result. Your selves are part of you, and they *can't* just go away.

If you look closely, you'll discover that your ugly selves are really your painful selves, the hurting child within you.

Deny that vulnerable self within you and you lose your chance for joy, carefree play and intimacy.

The usual pattern is never openly to acknowledge the contradictory parts of oneself. Most people talk to themselves, but how many admit it? (The popular attitude: talking to yourself is like masturbation, only worse. Believe that and you'll stay stuck.) When you exile your unpleasant parts, claiming one self as the "legitimate" government, you invite revolution. The examples are endless: denying your anger to deprive someone of the satisfaction of knowing you're mad (the excuse: "What good is getting upset?"); denying the feeling that a transaction you're making is unfair (the excuse: a wise business decision); denying your fears, envy, avarice, vindictiveness or even occasional vicious feelings. Such lies gnaw at your heart. At the least, it's a vague sensation that something's wrong; at the worst, it's lifelong guilt.

When you make decisions that completely ignore some hidden selves, you can pretend to go on as usual, but your feelings will catch up with you. Neglected selves can return to haunt in devious ways (tension headaches, poor concentration, depression, fatigue). You gain a little and the price is high. Refusing to acknowledge your selves saps energy and erodes your self-worth.

What we are recommending is that you regularly explore the different selves within you. Let each be heard in your internal congress; let each have its say. Get to know these conflicting facets of yourself. Get on a first name basis with all that's in you. You'll be rewarded with the strength and flexibility that comes with any exercised system, the suppleness and grace that is gained from using your selves more fully.

Here are some exercises for your inner selves that you can try:

To find your own direction, a good way to start is by focusing on what you feel. Your deep *feelings* are even closer to the truth about you than your *thoughts*—and can be more accessible than you may realize. Inject into your everyday conversation the phrase "I feel . . ." and say whatever it is that you're feeling. Communication theorists call these "I messages" to distinguish them from "you messages." No one knows the truth. But at least what you feel is *your truth.* It may sound silly or terribly artificial but it works.

try: *Openly saying "I feel so damned angry at you for ignoring me!"*

instead of: Silent, sullen withdrawal while thinking "you son of a bitch."

try: *Showing your pain with "I feel so humiliated and angry when you talk to me like I'm an idiot."*

instead of: "You are a rotten selfish bastard and just compensating for anger towards your mother."

Another approach to uncovering feelings is to close your eyes while comfortably seated in a quiet place alone. Turn your thoughts to visual pictures of various people and situations in your life, while saying to yourself "*I feel . . .*" about each one. Use *simple words* for your sadness, anger, happiness, joy, not pop psychology jargon like "*I feel* like he's taking his insecurities out on me." Make it what **you feel**!

The next steps involve periodically *doing* some things that you would "never" do. You don't have to risk your life or do something that would jeopardize everything you've worked for, but do try something unusual, something out of character. Nutty things are good to start with. Talk to yourself out loud (crazy gibberish is all the better—babble, mutter, scream). Unlock the closets in your head. If you don't like to appear foolish or absurd, try *purposefully* looking foolish. Sing a song out loud. If you can't sing, it doesn't matter. Sing exuberantly; make up your own songs.

OR

. . . scream at the top of your lungs
as you drive down the freeway
with the windows up.

OR

. . . open the windows!!

OR

. . . remain silent for one day.

All of these things may seem pretty crazy and may not sound like they have much bearing on what you are doing with your life. But it's so easy to slip into a routine where you do the same things over and over again; novelty and excitement fade, and life becomes boring. What could be worse than knowing everything you are going to do for the rest of your life?

Of course, it is easy to try these exercises and say to yourself while doing them, "Oh, this is silly" or "What the hell am I doing this for?" (You know which selves say that—the ones who want to keep everything the same, the ones who would rather have you in the same old rut than take any chances.) Sure, you can think up lots of excuses and we could probably tell you some you've never thought of. But for a little while, try unlocking your spontaneity, unconstipating the flow of your energy. Try being loose without worrying about how silly you look. Give yourself permission to break out of everyday ruts.

It's the little things that count. Trivial habits and minor events are what most of life is made of. Don't force yourself to look one way all the time. Loosen up. Editing everything before you feel it is a quick way to become a bore. Give yourself a break.

Try doing the opposite of what you usually do.

Try getting passionate with someone you care for. But watch out, passion breeds passion. That person might respond enthusiastically. Then what will you do?

Try kissing someone you care about. Kiss him or her gently behind the ear, or on the forehead, or anywhere else you can think of. Try it. It might be fun. If you're afraid to do this, or worried about it, then by all means try it. This is the kind of thing we hear so often. "We've been together for six years, but I'm afraid to get too passionate with her, especially after all this time. She might think I'm *weird.*" People really believe things like that. Or maybe they just get locked into the selves of old habits and never try anything new.

Rigidly clinging to one self to prove a point is another common game. The unsatisfied, angry selves that never get a chance to really show what they feel (or have to apologize for it when they do) will refuse to change until they are heard. Being afraid to look weird also helps you hide resentments like "I'm still really mad about who ended up doing the dishes last night," and all the other pitiful campaigns we humans run on each other. Don't worry; if you try being affectionate and don't like it, you can always revert to a colder and more distant self. It's easy.

There are dangers in all of this; if you suddenly start acting differently—nonsensical, when you were usually serious, or affectionate, when you were usually aloof—you might raise conflicts you'd avoid in a monotonous life. Many relationships are based on keeping things under control, keeping life predictable and expected—spontaneity and passion can be scary. Changing is dangerous so if you want to be very careful try it only a day a week. How about making Tuesday your weird day?

Try really throwing yourself into what you choose, acting in ways you might have imagined but never dared because they just "weren't you." Try them out. There's probably a self within you that has been waiting for this chance.

If you decide to be different in some way—athletic, passionate, energetic, frivolous, stupid, excited, romantic, sober, etc.—do it as if you really mean it. Don't disclaim authorship for your actions, begging off as though it's not *really* your idea. "Well I just read this book and it tells me to try being passionate. I know it won't do *any good* but I thought I'd try it anyway." Yecch! If you won't take responsibility for your life, who will? Your potentials will wither and die. You can kill your creativity if you wish.

No idea is ever totally new, but when you try one, act like you own it. "The book suggested it but *I decided* to act passionately." Whatever you attempt give it your all. The greatest evil in this world is half-hearted action. Listen! We dare you to hold out your ideas, your actions, your selves to the world as being worthwhile just because they exist. No higher authority than that, not because we told you to, not because God told you to, not because anybody else told you to. Just this: "Today I feel like doing something different . . . this may seem crazy but I'm going to . . ." Even if you don't do it *regularly*, please let yourself try it *once in a while*.

Self-exercises provide the chance to express those internal contradictory versions of yourself that usually don't get any "air time." *Choosing* to let them out gives you more freedom and power than if you continually keep them in. Make it your decision (choice). One of the most common fears in our society is that of looking silly or absurd. Such behavior is reserved for children, and clowns, or people using alcohol. Sober adults should never lose their cool. Well, why not *choose* to lose your cool once in a while, purposefully letting go.

This may seem paradoxical, but the highest level of control, the ultimate mastery of oneself, comes from being able to periodically *give up control.* To be a fluid, flexible being. To just let go. Find a relatively safe place, be careful, do it with people you trust—but have a ball, and invite *all* of your selves.

Exercises

Make a list of ten changes you wish you could make in your behavior. Don't worry about whether or not you'll ever find the courage—it's only a list. Now list them in increasing order of difficulty for you. Look at the least difficult. Can you bring yourself to try it? If so, great! If not, add some easier ones. Keep adding until you find one you can do NOW.

Self-defeating Life-styles

Okay, so you start listening to all the selves inside you. Some are pretty articulate, some just moan and groan. And what's the end result? You have lots of feelings. Confused feelings. Like being angry with someone you love . . . like the urge to strike an insolent child . . . like being unhappy when you "should" feel good.

And life doesn't make it any easier. Just when you get used to one set of rules the whole game can change. Some terrifying things can happen . . . horrible experiences . . . losing a loved one . . . being rejected . . . sickness . . . hospitals . . . car accidents . . . the sickly sweet smell of death from cancer . . .

How much will you dare to feel, dare to see?

IMAGINE: *You've been living with the same person for twenty years. Only recently you started falling in love with that person. Passionately. You're not your partner's slave nor is he or she yours. But you feel devoted and attached in a way you've never experienced before in your life. Every time you see your beloved you get a little dizzy with emotion.*

That person dies. Not tastefully at a safe distance. No, right in front of you . . . a heart attack right at the dinner table . . . blue, bloated, and horrible . . . you try desperately to save your partner but he or she dies anyway.

OR THIS: *You're happy, healthy. You've worked hard and are looking forward to a vacation. Driving to the airport, you're hit by a large truck. After six months in the hospital, you are discharged with permanent back problems. Partially crippled for the rest of your life.*

Life is vulnerability. The more you dare to feel, the more you might get hurt. It's hard to remain open to what you *can* do when things you *can't help* might occur without warning. Life has no guarantees.

Hey, *wake up! Listen.* It's all right. Everyone is in the same boat! We're terrified too. Frightened by age, disease and death. Scared of being lonely, unloved, laughed at or bored.

What we see so often are people who avoid intense feelings, who turn their heads to avoid looking squarely at life. And not by deliberate choice but by *dumb habit.* Through fear of the intensely bad, they block out the intensely good. They miss it—miss the joy, the exhilaration, the peace, the tranquility, the enduring grace.

It's not necessary, possible, or even healthy to feel everything intensely all the time. Too much of anything is bad. But too little is just as bad. Habitual hiding is not a temporary silence, not a day of rest, but a lifelong withdrawal from feeling, an emptiness, a passive suicide, a slow death.

Sure, life is scary and risky, but trying to hide does not help. Those who try to keep it under control by shutting off their feelings lose the ability to find their own way. Their lifestyles become lonely dead ends. And they hurt more in the long run. Some pain in life is unavoidable. If you try to avoid feeling bad at the cost of remaining stuck in habits, you'll still get the lows in life without any chance of the highs.

A FAVORITE SELF-DEFEATING LIFE-STYLE: "IT DOESN'T BOTHER ME."

Know this one? It's easy. Every time you feel something, water it down. For beginners, try acting like what you feel doesn't make any difference. Alcohol or other drugs are often helpful. Advanced practitioners can master the following techniques:

"WHAT'S THE USE?"
"IT'S NOT WORTH THE HASSLE."
"IT DOESN'T BOTHER ME ANYMORE."
"I CAN SHRUG IT OFF."
"I REALLY DON'T CARE."

Soon you can convince yourself that you don't feel anything at all, and after a while, you won't.

Why do people do it? Fear of feeling—"I might get hurt." And without really thinking about their choice, they slip into a habit of partial anaesthesia. "Playing it safe." That's the secret hope. "If I never let myself feel too good, maybe I'll never get hurt too badly." A sort of deal with the universe. "I won't take too much, so please don't hurt me." And feelings get methodically extinguished.

How do people start numbing themselves? Bit by bit. Each pain is used as an excuse to feel less and less. Maybe they were taught as children not to allow feelings. Eventually, what's left is a guarded life where everything is thought twice, worried over, or ignored.

Of course, the benefits are substantial: If you don't feel anything, life—although duller—is much simpler, safer and easier. The less you experience things, the less you get entangled with other people's feelings. And, of course, the less you hurt.

Jean, an attorney in her mid-thirties, divorced, living with her two children, came in "only to quit smoking." Impeccable in her dress and demeanor, she spoke with impressive self-control. But when gently probed about possible sources of pain in her life, she began to slip. Loneliness, gnawing at her for years, broke forth in sobbing sadness.

"I'm afraid . . . Oh God I can't cry, no *damn it* . . . oh *damn* . . ."

"Wait a minute, Jean . . . you're in agony but you just won't let yourself cry . . .," I offered warmly.

"Who'll put back the pieces!" she shrieked, "WHO'LL TAKE CARE OF ME?" Jean burst into a flood of angry tears.

Do you think that because she let herself cry, she would fall apart and spend the rest of her life in a mental hospital? Of course not. Yet that's the fear that had intimidated her into choking back years of sadness. Now Jean wept openly, sobbing for herself for the first time since her teens. In her twenties she cried once after failing a test in law school. At thirty she cried when her favorite aunt died. But today, Jean's tears were for Jean, for all the fear and loneliness she had been trying to hide.

Desperately avoiding the racking inside her heart, she'd tell herself things like "Keep it together, kid." "What's the use?" she'd ask herself, "Who really gives a damn anyway?"

More lies and then back to work . . . oh and yes . . . have another cigarette?

Jean fed her pain with two packs a day. Whenever she felt sad, lonely, scared or worried she had to have a smoke. She had never before discovered the necessity of listening to herself, or of vividly experiencing what goes on inside.

With practice, she learned how to feel upset without pretending, "It doesn't bother me." At first it was difficult, but she did change. She taught herself that it was all right to be human, to be scared and lonely sometimes. In the process she quit smoking. But best of all she learned how to control herself with *love* and *respect* rather than *punishment* and *fear*.

In part, therapy works by teaching people how to experience intense emotions and still maintain control of their lives. It's like learning how to swim in heavy surf. Fighting a big wave invites disaster; better to let an overpowering swell pass by than to vainly try to fight it back.

Typically, people come to therapy complaining "I don't feel good . . ." (lonely, bored, nervous, sick, depressed . . . have marital, health, school, work, or alcohol problems . . . the list is almost endless). In the course of treatment they'll often have an intense emotional experience, usually a mixture of sadness, anger and relief—"I have always been afraid to show my real feelings because I thought I might . . ." (*feel* even worse, scare everyone away, keep on crying, fall apart, go crazy . . .) Only by trying out strong feelings can they face their fears.

Flushed with the adventure of feeling without "losing it" they can risk trying on other new behaviors for size—"I've always wanted to . . ." (be loving, brave, compassionate, sexy, lazy, hard working, fun-loving, spontaneous, silly, assertive, outrageous . . .)

They may not keep the new behavior but now they can change at will. Now their actions are based on choice and feeling, not on habit and fear of the unknown.

You can do it too. It starts with a basic choice . . . what kind of a life do you want—intense or watered down?

People that pick a watered down life often pretend they "can't help it." Their excuses are endless:

I'd let myself feel deeply, take control and responsibility for my life, but I can't because . . .

. . . it's impossible for me.

. . . it won't work.

. . . I'm too busy.

. . . I'm too afraid.

. . . I'm too lazy.

. . . I'm too poor.

. . . I have too many hang-ups.

. . . I have too many people depending on me.

. . . I'm too old.

. . . I'm too young.

. . . I don't have time this week, but I'll be sure to try it out first chance I get.

But you don't really need an excuse. If you're sure that you're getting what you want, that's great. (You don't have to convince *us*.) If you're not—excuses won't change a dissatisfying life. Only action will.

ANOTHER SELF-DEFEATING LIFE-STYLE:

"GOING ALONG WITH THE CROWD"

One of the most common fears is that all-too-human worry of not fitting in. Remember the times you felt embarrassed because you were sure everyone was staring at you? We can both recall times when this happened to us. It hurts! Exclusion is painful. In fact, anytime something terrible happens to a person, one of the first phrases that is uttered is, "Why me?" The feeling of being singled out, picked on, ostracized or excluded, is one of the most painful human experiences.

No wonder people take such measures to avoid rejection; stepping out of line carries such heavy penalties. Neighbors, families, work associates and society at large have expectations that most people seem to accept. The harder a person works, the more others expect him or her to be hard working. Changing a person's established pattern of working—even if that pattern is putting the person's health in jeopardy—would involve opposing the existing social expectations.

Why follow *them*—friends, family, experts, movements, believers? Why not follow *you*? Social membership is a wonderful experience, yet striving for belonging can lead to an atrophy of the spirit. Personal dullness is often the consequence of being one of the crowd, and the downhill slide usually begins with the fear of saying "no."

Marty struggled his way up from the assembly line to middle management. Down-to-earth, dependable, and incredibly hard working, he's a guy who will tackle any problem. He got where he is the hard way—starting at the very bottom. Marty is almost fifty and working on his first heart attack.

"Slow down, Marty," his cardiologist warned him. "Take it easy or you're not going to survive to enjoy it." The company was behind Marty all the way. They wanted him to stay but to slack off a little. His skill and experience made replacing him difficult and expensive. They needed him and were smart enough to realize they shouldn't push a valuable man too hard. But they didn't have to push him. He did it all himself.

Marty came in because he "couldn't slow down." For the first time in his life, he was really scared.

"I tried to cut back on my work load. Even my boss wants me to take it easier. My section has been doing well, even while I was away getting my medical tests . . . but, I just can't relax! I think about problems that they might be overlooking and I worry that if I'm not there things might get worse . . . not only that, but I've got three kids and a wife to think about . . ."

Marty was worried. Sure, who wouldn't be? His whole life had been devoted to a job that might fade away or vanish at any moment! No one had to tell him he was a "sitting duck."

Yet, Marty seemed to be unaware of the two contradictory themes in his fears:

1. If I'm not there everything will fall apart without me. They really need me.

2. If I'm not there everything might go well. Maybe they don't need me at all.

It was time somebody told him, "Hey, Marty, maybe they don't need you at all . . . maybe your section, since you set it up so well, can get along fine without you . . . maybe you're *not* indispensable . . ."

Marty was crestfallen, as though up until now he had been able to avoid the thought. It seemed almost cruel to crush him with the truth of his fears, but he knew it too. Trying to avoid it was literally killing him.

I kept going. "Marty, listen to yourself. You just told me the company will cut back your workload and keep you at the same salary. That's almost too good to believe. They want to give you a vacation, no less, and you're scared *to death* to take it. Last month you had time off, time to have fun, time to spend with family—you *say* you've been beating your brains out for them—but what did you do? You sat around and worried.

"Marty, let me tell you what I think . . . you plan to never retire. You've been hoping you'd just drop dead on the job. You're afraid to back off, afraid to let go even a little bit, because they might find that they don't need you that badly . . . that you're not indispensable after all."

Marty was sick—that greenish, seasick look of a man who wants things to stand still just for a moment: "Stop the world, I want to get off." That cruel world that never really condones vacations, that musical chairs world. That "if I turn my back for a moment, I'll be replaced" world. Marty hid from these fears and his hiding was about to take his life.

With genuine alarm, Marty clutched my arm. "Tell me . . . tell me how I can change."

As if I could answer.

This was a measure of the depths of his desperation, his asking a psychiatrist what he should do with his life. A year ago counseling would have seem ridiculous. Now the crushing pain of angina pectoris, the warning of an impending heart attack, put him against the wall. He was ready to try anything. Pain is indeed powerful.

I wasn't about to give him an answer. I felt his pain, shared it with him, but I wanted him to hurt *even more*, to bleed with his pain, not to hide from it, not to fear it, but to experience it so that he'd never let himself get lost again.

"Okay, Marty, I should tell you what to do? *NO! No*, you tell me. I'll offer some options, but *you* have to decide. You can keep working, and since your cardiologist says you've got a heart attack coming soon, if you won't slow down, you'll probably be dead in a matter of months. Your company got you the best heart man in town, and I don't doubt his prediction. He says surgery is out of the question. That means that working at the rate you've been going will simply kill you.

"Okay, that's choice one. Work hard and die fast with your boots on. Choice number two would be to slow down, give yourself the rest you've been promising yourself for the last twenty years, have fun, spend time with your family and work at a reduced rate."

Then to drive the point home, I gave him a sarcastic jab, "Of course, I wonder if you or anyone else could love or respect you, if you were lazy enough to slow down."

Marty fumed and floundered, so I added a little more, "Let me see, oh yes, there's another one. Choice number three. It's something like starting to drink heavily, or to take drugs so that you can forget about choices one or two! But, that really isn't a new choice, since you've been eating Valium like candy and you still hurt enough to come in to see me.

"Let me add something to choice number two. You could slow down and tell your boss, maybe even your coworkers and subordinates, that you're afraid they might have problems while you're slowing down, but that you won't be available at night or on weekends as you used to be. In fact, if you want to be frighteningly honest, you could tell them you're afraid they might find out that they *won't* have problems, *won't* need you anymore and that's what worries you. Ah, that's a good one . . . the naked truth.

"Marty, it's up to you. What are *you* going to do? Make a choice? Or let your fears and habits decide for you? It's your choice . . . which do you want?" Marty was deep in thought, as if half-hypnotized. "I don't know, I just don't know . . ."

He sat with his head in his hands, staring at the floor, then looked at me. "You know, Doc, I just have to think some more. I don't know what I'm ready for."

I suppose I would have liked him to jump up and exclaim how he was definitely going to take that vacation he had always wanted. Yet, what he said seemed to come directly from his feelings and so was much more real. He was beginning to listen to himself instead of trying to please the crowd. That's what I was after.

But I was still worried. His cardiologist told me that Marty had brought office paperwork to the hospital with him. Eating Rolaids by the pack, he'd look at his watch every few minutes—overall, the picture of a maximum heart attack risk. When Marty left my office, I felt less than optimistic. Change for him would be like a man running full speed at a brick wall, yet miraculously stopping a half-inch from impact.

The next day he called me. "Doc, I want to thank you. I thought about what we talked about a lot after I left. I didn't really want to admit to you how much I was drinking, but I think you knew anyway. I just want to tell you that I finally took the step. I told everyone I was cutting back and even told the guys in my section that I'd be pissed off if they got along too easily without me. Hah! . . . And you know what? Today I'm going fishing with my kids . . . I did it, Doc. Thanks again."

There are no keepers of pure divine truth. The best anyone can muster is a little piece of the whole picture. The two of us want to encourage you to listen to yourself, to learn your own perspective, to live, not for your fears or habits, or to please the crowd. Your own approval counts most and will always be more satisfying than any recognition the world can give you. If you don't give it to yourself, what anyone else does amounts to nothing. If you don't believe in yourself, or at least in your potential, then you won't trust other people's positive opinions about you. If you're not willing to change your mind about yourself, you'll never change. Peace begins within.

But don't reproach yourself for having a weak spot for social approval. Humans have been worrying about each other's opinions since prehistoric times. In those days a person alone was usually helpless and defenseless. Primitive man hunted, slept and ate in groups. Anything that opposed the group's opinion could be truly life-threatening to the welfare of all. The family or the tribe provided for everyone. Not fitting in could be deadly.

Today, people continue to long for membership. Clothing fashions and consumer fads are living signs of how much we desire to be "in." Ethnic groups, social clubs, nations, political ideologies, psychological and spiritual movements have willing supporters. Even in the intimacy of one's personal relationships the fear of rejection and exclusion is a potent force.

Consider this: When was the last time you gave in to your fears of rejection and didn't tell someone what you felt, because you didn't want to hurt their feelings or didn't want to start a fight?

We challenge you to show who you really are.

Here's one place to start:

Choose someone you know and try telling him or her exactly what you feel for a period of one week. Don't tell them what you think, or your ideas of what's wrong with them. Rather, tell them how *you feel*: happy, angry, sad, lonely or whatever is in your guts. Choose someone who you care about. It might make it easier to let the person you choose know how difficult it is to expose yourself. After awhile you will realize that when you deliberately reveal your feelings you become less vulnerable because you are in the position of control.

Even if you end up admitting to love which is not reciprocated, do not feel badly about yourself. Unrequited love is painful and lonely, but the ability to love at all is a wonderful gift. To be loving (and therefore vulnerable) says: "I can love openly and deeply. I am not so afraid of hurt that I close myself to love."

Paying attention to what you feel and taking the chance of letting others know is the best way to begin listening to yourself, and not exclusively to "them" out there. Listen to all those noisy selves inside and act like what *you feel it is important to act like.* If you don't prize yourself, it makes little difference what others may think of you.

Exercises

- List your five major excuses for maintaining the status quo in your life. What would be the cost of ignoring each? Other than fear and cowardice, what stops you from risking change? Where can you buy the courage to overcome fear?
- List four experiments with your life that you would consider risky. Consider one in each of these categories: physical risk, psychological risk, financial risk, social risk.

- List five of the most risky things you have ever tried. What were the consequences of each attempt?
- List five times when you did not do something because it seemed too risky, and later you regretted not trying.
- List five times you took risks and the results came out worse than you had anticipated.
- List five risks you would take now if the odds were better or the stakes worth gambling for.
- Look over your lists. Do you see any patterns? If you are not pleased with what you see, what changes do you want to make?
- Ask the two people who know you best whether or not they think you are rationalizing away something you haven't the courage to do.

The Process of Change: On Your Mark . . . Get Set . . .

I want to change but I don't know how."

Life sweeps along. Opportunities may last but an instant. The fundamental problem is how to put it together—how to change, how to grow, how to find your own way. You may want to, but how to is often hard to discover.

In Chapter Two we offered some basic principles of life-changing. Simple and brief, they barely filled four pages. But putting them to work can be tricky. In fact, mastering change consists mostly of learning how to avoid excuses, self-deceptions, cop-outs and dead end habits. You must get in shape, by practicing love and self-reliance before you can hope to master the process of change. Without that training, you'll collapse when the pressure is on.

The principles we offer aren't new by any means; they're the same ideas that have been around for centuries. What we have done is put them in a new perspective, another way of seeing, so that the apparent contradictions make sense.

But remember these principles are ultimately just words. They are utterly useless by themselves. For it is only your personal experience of making changes that can set you free. Little or big changes, the effect is the same. You foster the self-reliance that becomes freedom by listening to and respecting yourself, by taking responsibility for everything you do. Freedom can be had. You can make it.

This process of growing can be painful. If while reading any of the stories in this book you think things like "Oh no, that's me. I do that all the time," don't feel too badly. It doesn't mean that you've been wrong or stupid. It only means that, like most people, you're human. It's okay, you still have the rest of your life to adjust your course.

Let's review the basic principles again:

- **POINT ONE: DARE TO LOVE YOURSELF IN A WORLD THAT GIVES NO GUARANTEES.**
- **POINT TWO: PAY ATTENTION TO WHAT YOU FEEL. IF YOU DON'T LIKE THE WAY YOU FEEL, IT'S USUALLY A SIGN THAT YOU'RE NOT GETTING WHAT YOU NEED.**
- **POINT THREE; NOBODY CAN REALLY TELL YOU THE ANSWER TO LIFE'S PROBLEMS SO YOU MIGHT AS WELL TRY WHAT FEELS RIGHT TO YOU.**
- **POINT FOUR: IF YOU'RE GOING TO RISK A CHANGE, TRY SOMETHING LIKELY TO SATISFY YOUR NEEDS WHILE INCREASING YOUR SELF-RESPECT.**
- **POINT FIVE: WHEN YOU ARE CONSIDERING A SPECIFIC CHANGE, MAKE A LIST OF ALL THE WORST POSSIBLE THINGS THAT COULD HAPPEN.**
- **POINT SIX: BEFORE YOU CHANGE, TAKE A FEW MOMENTS TO PRAISE YOURSELF HONESTLY, COMPLIMENTING YOURSELF FOR SOME SPECIFIC ATTRIBUTE.**
- **POINT SEVEN: IF WHAT YOU ARE DOING ISN'T GETTING YOU WHAT YOU WANT, TRY SOMETHING DIFFERENT.**
- **POINT EIGHT: IF YOU DECIDE TO TAKE A CHANCE, DON'T JUST THINK ABOUT IT, DO IT!**

POINT NINE: AFTER YOU TRY A CHANGE, EVALUATE THE RESULTS. NO MATTER WHAT HAPPENS, CONGRATULATE YOURSELF FOR YOUR COURAGE TO TRY.

What do these principles add up to? Love yourself, listen to yourself, respect yourself, trust yourself, experiment with yourself. Everything in the universe, yourself included, is in a constant state of flux. Many changes are out of your control, but you do have some influence. You can enhance your degree of freedom and increase your chance at fulfillment by deliberately applying yourself to these nine points. Like anything else, unless you've had a lot of practice, putting these principles into action can be difficult at first. But for a freer, fuller, more satisfying life they are *vital*. At the very least, you'll get to know yourself better and increase your self-respect.

The more you love yourself and the more you listen to yourself, the easier it becomes to formulate the changes you'd like to make. As you become more sensitive to your own feelings you can learn to anticipate changes rather than wait until the last minute. With enough practice, you don't even have to go through the steps of thinking, planning and doing. Instead you just flow into changing. But, if you don't practice very often, you may feel clumsy at it. So here's our guide to mastering the awkward moves.

ON YOUR MARK: *Pick Something to Try*

If you don't like something about the way you feel, listen to all the selves inside you, then pick something new. At first pick a small, safe change, a lightweight risk that won't destroy your life if it doesn't work out the way you had hoped. Try being more like that person you secretly want to be.

"Okay, so I'm not satisfied with my life. That's bad enough; what's worse is I don't have any idea what I'd like better!"

Stop kidding yourself. We've never met anyone who didn't wish he or she were different in a variety of ways, in a variety of situations. Aren't there times you wished you had acted differently with your spouse, kids, family, boss or strangers? We're talking about hopes and wishes, the dreams that give life direction. Everyone has a sense of ways in which he or she would like to be different, would like to grow. Try a little dream, indulge yourself. Periodically trying out new approaches in your life is a good way to exercise your ability to change.

Ask yourself: "What way could I act differently that might give me more self-respect or take care of my needs better?" Think about it. Concoct something totally new. Even something outrageous. Take a stab at it, invent it, pull it out of the air. You can even think about something you'd "never" do. Let yourself have the fantasy. Don't choke off ideas before they begin to breathe. The only way to be creative is to give yourself permission to have many ideas, the "bad" ones along with the "good."

If you want, you can short-circuit the process right here. Scare yourself into submission. You can tell yourself that you "just can't," or that you might "look foolish," or that your "luck's too bad" or "what's the use anyway?" or "why am I even bothering to read this book by these two crazy shrinks?" or anything else to keep you in place. It's with such myths that people are kept trapped, kept helpless and hopeless by their convictions about the "impossible." Believe them and you might spend the rest of your life looking for magic in self-help books. But, if you have the guts, start with some crazy daydreams about how you'd like to be: more assertive, less serious, more affectionate, less fearful, more honest, less hard-working. You pick the direction.

GET SET: Weigh the Pros

What are the advantages of a change? What are the costs? First start with the pros about what you've got right now, the benefits from your present way of acting. Sure, there may be some obvious cons, some costs that hurt so much that you may overlook the hidden benefits. But consider the benefits. Stay the same and if nothing else, you'll have at least one thing going for you: You'll know exactly what to expect. You may be unhappy, but at least you know the routine. You're in control. And, whatever your problem is, it provides you with a built-in cop-out anytime something doesn't work out.

Take being overweight, for example. If you are fat, you are probably less attractive, have more trouble finding clothes that fit, stay home more, have fewer friends, and are physically ill more frequently than most people. But, on the other hand, the fatter you get, the more you are guaranteed immunity from demanding relationships. A thick layer of lard is enough to repulse almost anybody. Get fat enough and no one will even try to get close to you. That way you never get hurt. Safe and lonely . . . but safe to be sure. And you can get *pity!* Although people may find your weight problem funny, sad, or disgusting, few will ever openly say anything. Most people will feel sorry for you. You can spare yourself with the dream that *if* someone loves you in spite of your pounds, they must *really* love you . . . perhaps enough to never leave you (a tragic and poisonous myth).

Another hidden benefit in staying fat is the enormously satisfying and rewarding fantasy life you can have. Sit back, dream about how beautiful, successful and happy you could easily be if only you weren't so fat . . . and while you dream, why not have a little something to eat? It will help you deaden your feelings.

Look carefully at the hidden benefits whenever you have a problem you'd like to change. Unless you recognize the benefits and replace them with some other gains, you will be defeated in your attempt to change. (Remember Ellie in Chapter One?) In our practices, we constantly see people who have "careers of failure," who devote their lifetimes to having problems. That way they are safe, get pity, can feel sorry for themselves, blame others and always have something to talk about. Even if you aren't hurting that much, don't take your bad habits lightly. Problems take care of *some* needs. Part of changing is finding other ways to take care of you, all of you, even the selves that hide behind your problems.

If the change does a better job taking care of your needs and your hidden selves, it may be well worth the effort. Best of all, you might find that you really *can* make your dreams come true.

CONSIDER THE WORST Start with the worst possible consequence when you consider changing. Think of the most horrible outcome that could possibly be produced by your new change. Go to the absolute extreme. Think of some nightmares come true. Face them squarely instead of hiding from them. Look right at your fears and, if they don't melt in the light of day, they will at least shrink in size.

We told you about Hank in Chapter Six. He wanted some answers, some guarantees. Very human things to want. Part of his trouble was his fear of failure—also very human. Another part he talked about was his "problems relating to people."

"I want to ask Karen out to lunch with me, I mean, I really want to go out with her, but I don't know how to approach her, I don't know how she feels at all."

Hank was talking, but not really to me. He was looking off into space, asking the ceiling, as though waiting for some encouragement or reassurance from above, some guarantee that everything would be taken care of. I sat there for a moment, speechless at such idiocy, even though every day I hear almost the same thing from someone.

"You should know ahead of time?" I asked sarcastically. "What makes you think you're so special?"

Hank looked a little hurt but more annoyed, as though he had been just about to get through to whomever is running the universe and I had somehow unplugged his connection. "What! What do you mean?" he whined in protest. "What are you talking about?"

"Well, this *is* what you are saying, isn't it? That you should know how she is going to respond before you ask her? That you should have some guarantees about the future, huh?"

Hank shrugged his shoulders and grumbled. "Well, I do think it's *pitiful* that I don't even know what she thinks about me at all . . . I mean, I should at least know that!"

"Great, *now* you can put yourself down for that! You should be able to read her mind, to know what to say in every situation, be at ease with everyone in the world and jump tall buildings in a single bound!"

He looked at me with a flash of anger; then, as if realizing the futility of his self-imposed trap, burst out laughing. "Well . . . I guess that is pretty stupid."

My anger exploded. Not only did he put himself down, now he put himself down for *putting himself down!* "Hey, Hank, would you stop insulting yourself? I mean, it really makes me sick. I want to *vomit* when you do it. I'm not interested in hearing you call yourself names! I've got better things to do today than listen to this harangue. Look, what I want to know is this—what are you afraid of? You are never going to have any guarantees about how she is going to act when you ask her. Sure, you might have a rough idea, but you are never going to know exactly. So what's the worst thing that could happen?"

"Well . . . I don't know . . . I guess she could say 'no' . . . she might look at me like even if I were the last person on earth she wouldn't go out with me." A half-formed tear glinted in his eye.

Pay dirt. Feelings always get through to me. (Most good therapists grew up with a lot of pain and are easily hurt. No one chooses careers by a roll of the dice. Why shouldn't some of us parlay our vulnerability into making a living and help others in the process?) "That would really hurt . . . wouldn't it?" I said, almost whispering. Hank's face reflected the confusion of feelings that rushed through him, but at least he was listening, listening to his fears, listening to his hopes, listening to himself.

"I guess it would hurt . . . I'd feel pretty bad . . . in fact, I'd feel terrible."

"Yeah, Hank, I can understand that. You might even feel as much pain as some of those times you described before, those times when you've been really hurt by other people."

Hank's voice had changed from his detached philosophical tone to the sound of a man whose heart was in pain. "Yes, I'm hurt! It hurts to feel like a piece of crap!" Every word rang with emotion. Anger and desperate sadness burned through his tears.

"It sure does, Hank." I was delighted he was listening to himself. "It's that way for everyone. It's a tough pain to endure." We sat in silence for a moment. Then I continued. "But you know, there's something much worse than feeling like a piece of crap."

Hank looked up, brushing away a tear. "What's that?"

"Letting the fear of having someone confirm it run your life."

Hank isn't that different from anyone else. Fears are part of everyone. Let them have full voice when thinking of a change. Consider what they have to say, because if the attempted change doesn't produce the results you wanted, your fears will say "I told you so." That's why people give into them. Fear of being wrong, fear of losing.

This is how fear stops people. Fear is a bully. If you let your fears intimidate your, they will push their roots deeper. If you confront them, you can cut them down to size. They may never go away entirely, but at least you will be able to manage them. Why be a slave to fear? Why not run your own life?

The Secret to Managing Your Fears

Stand back and look at the fears that stop you from trying out a change, a change that might increase your self-respect and satisfaction in life. Chances are it's fear of rejection, failure or some other outcome that you would interpret as evidence you aren't good enough, evidence that would transform your worst fears about yourself into a hopeless certainty. You'd rather be afraid you're defective than convinced of it. So you're afraid to try a change or maybe even consider one.

This is the usual reasoning that keeps people stuck. In simple form it says: "If what I do has a bad outcome, that's evidence I'm not a good enough person." Baloney!

No one is intrinsically bad. No one. Everyone is capable of either superb or horrible actions and everything in between. You can use yourself well or use yourself badly. The challenge in life is to make the best use of what you have within you.

Try this reasoning: "If I try to do what would increase my self-respect despite my fears, then I'm courageous, I'm doing the best I can right now."

CHANGE THE FEAR OF THE UNKNOWN INTO THE FEAR OF SOMETHING SPECIFIC

That's a big change to make, but once you name the fear, once you put your finger on it, it's not nearly as frightening. It's when you are afraid to even look that fear takes over your life.

Consider the worst possible outcome of change you might make. Remember, the outcome says *nothing* about your worth. Though good outcomes may be more satisfying than bad ones, both can be used to refine your efforts. Now weigh the pros and cons of your change. If it looks like it's worth risking something new, why not take a chance?

Or, you can stall. Wait around in the hope that maybe you will get lucky or something will pop up and take care of you. So, sit tight and wish, worry or pray. Maybe God will do it for you. Take it easy. If you want to wait, there's plenty of room and lots of time . . . maybe.

FOCUS ON YOUR STRENGTHS Mastering change requires you to use your strengths to act, to choose, to overcome weakness and pessimism. Changing is basically a question of whether you want to focus on your weaknesses or your strengths. Franklin Roosevelt, though paralyzed from the waist down, managed well as President of the United States. Others, with disabilities far less severe, choose careers of chronic invalidism. Exercise your strengths and not only will others view and treat you differently, your own outlook and prospects will change.

Focusing on weaknesses is the very thing that blocks so many people. But at least it's familiar. A negative self-image is a lifelong partner—give it up and you may find the emptiness and uncertainty terrifying. If you secretly believe that you are a failure, at least you have a tradition within yourself, a self-concept you can always return to. Letting go of your fears is like leaving home. You become vulnerable, naked, almost devoid of roots or tradition. Many people worship their own self-torment and study the ways they make themselves miserable, as if their problems were their own private religion. Bemoaning your weaknesses won't change them. No one can be strong at everything. Everyone has weaknesses. Don't be fooled; some people hide their vulnerabilities behind masks of apparent perfection. Why not use what you've got instead of crying about what you wish you had?

Focusing on strengths may sound like a self-deceiving pep talk or "power of positive thinking" hoopla, but it is true—you are who you believe yourself to be. Or, more accurately, you have many different selves, different possibilities of you. Focus on one and it will grow. But don't get stuck on any one self—give all of them a chance.

Focus on your ability to choose, to decide. Focus on loving yourself. Choose, risk, experiment and you will become stronger. Remain secretly convinced that you are a failure and you will remain trapped in the struggle to "just get by." Don't merely think positive thoughts; put them into action.

Exercises

- In writing, or into a tape recorder, go through the nine steps covered in this chapter with a specific set of changes designed to deal with your dissatisfaction. What qualities do you have going for you? What help can you get from others around you?
- Make an "I can" list. Fill in "I can . . ." with ten statements of things you are capable of doing.
- Propose an experiment to improve your current life situation. What are the risks? What are the benefits? Who will decide whether it's worth it to try and experiment?
- Is fear the major thing that blocks you from changing? Are you waiting for something to decrease or eliminate your fears before doing what you'd respect yourself for doing?

The Process of Change: Go!

Now that you have picked something to try, weighed the pros and cons, considered the worst and focused on your strengths, you're ready to change.

GO: ACTING AS IF Human beings can learn new things in a short period of time. We refer to this basic process as learning by acting "as if." Instead of waiting to be ignited by some kind of spontaneous combustion (a hopeless vigil), you start by changing yourself right now, this very minute.

You can do this by *acting as if* you are already the person you want to be. Take that one particular aspect, trait or habit you would like to modify and try acting as if it has already changed. It sounds almost silly to say, but that's how it starts; by acting as you wish that "you" to be, by behaving *as if* you already are that "you," *by doing just what that person you want to be would do.* This isn't faking or naive self-deception. It is a positive act of strength. It is the self-assertion that you *can* learn something new.

Slowly, almost imperceptibly, your acting becomes real. Before you consciously realize the difference, change will set in. Others may notice the transformation first, but in time, you'll see it too. Gradually it will dawn on you that you are that person you wanted to be. You have taught yourself how to change.

When we make these kinds of statements, we often encounter a lot of opposition. People say things like "well, it's not that easy" or "you just can't act differently to change." But, if we were talking about some other form of learning—because that's really what it's all about—and we said "here is how people learn," there'd be few arguments.

For example, take the learning of a physical skill like riding a bicycle.

Before
you
know
how
to
ride
a
bicycle,
you
don't
know
how
to
ride
a
bicycle.

Obvious, huh?
You get on the awkward contraption, then act *as if* you know how to ride by fumbling at the pedals, clutching the handlebars and trying to get a feel of it. You may use mental images you have of what other people look like on bicycles and how you would like to look. As the learning theorists say, you use "modeling" and "imitation." Now, at first, of course, you will be pretty awkward. You will feel anxious—stepping off into the void of the unknown in anything is intimidating. And you're right to have some apprehensions. If you do muster up the courage to try, you will find yourself falling over a few times and looking less than graceful. In general, you'll make it apparent that you don't *really* know how to ride a bicycle. But, if you keep at it, keep acting *as if* you know how to ride, you'll learn. Through a process of trial and error, you'll learn how to do it.

Now, if you wanted to, you could avoid learning to ride a bicycle. You could let fears dominate you—the fear you might fall over, the fear you'd look silly, the fear you'd never be able to do it anyway because you have a weak heart, or any other excuse to keep you from trying. Or you might start to try and then, after a couple of days of practice, take a bad spill and decide to give it up because it just isn't worth the risk of falling again. But if you really want to learn, you keep at it. By acting *as if* long enough, you catch on. As you get good at teaching yourself new skills, your ability to learn from yourself increases. You become more free. And it all starts by acting *as if* you can already do it.

That's what life-changing is—learning. When something isn't going well in your life, you can learn something new. You can *teach yourself* what you need. Instead of waiting for some expert to tell you what to do, some authority to give you the answer, you try to find your own way. Now, if you'd rather, you could spend your time trying to understand your dim past, or realigning your biochemistry, but even if you do those things, you ultimately come back to the same problem—what are *you* going to do?

Another way to describe this approach is learning by trial and error—or even better, trial and success. It's learning through experimentation, trying a new way on for size. What we are urging you to do is to give yourself permission to take a stab at some small way of making your life different. To throw yourself into it so that you can experience the feeling of learning from yourself. But it takes a *passionate* attempt, using all your energies, spontaneity and intensity. Not "Well, I'll try this new thing because these two shrinks told me . . ." Yecch. That will kill it for sure.

There are endless options for ways to try it on for size. For example, if it's hard for you to openly tell people when you are angry at them, you could pick one person and clearly let them know the next time you feel angry. Even if it is over something trivial, *let them know* loud and clear. In other words, take the chance and say something like, "Hey,

I'm mad at you. I don't like what you just did," rather than lying with a smile, rather than trying to ignore it, rather than sullen pouting, rather than waiting . . . waiting . . . waiting . . .

Now, expressing anger openly may be something that is difficult for you (by "openly" we don't mean just bitchiness or irritability, but instead, coming out and saying exactly what it is that is bothering you). If so, try showing that feeling directly. You can rehearse it ahead of time by closing your eyes and imagining the scene. Try losing yourself in a daydream (or nightmare as the case may be), as though it is actually happening right now! First, fantasize that your friend is grossly offended and rejects you because of what you said. If this upsets you, keep rehearsing the scene with the worst of all possible endings, over and over again. After a while, it won't intimidate you nearly as much.

Now, imagine some really positive endings. Like a warm, accepting response. Feel how good it would be to have that person actually listen, to accept your feelings and recognize your right to exist. Your right to feel. How good it would be to say what's on your mind instead of dropping hints and hoping that somebody will get it.

After mastering the imaginary battle, you can increase the stakes by rehearsing your lines out loud. Perhaps you could act them out with a close friend. But sooner or later the time comes to "bring it to Broadway"—to try on your new way of acting in the real world. Try your new role before the most terrifying audience of all—those who could hurt you the most. Those you love, hate, respect, or fear: friends, family, bosses, lovers, the important people in your life.

Changing yourself is frightening at first, but, fortunately, the worst possible result very rarely occurs. Your own self-respect for having the guts to try something new will increase regardless of the consequences. Even more, you'll be amazed how often life rewards courageousness, how other people's respect will match the increased self-respect that comes from your bravery.

Remember, if it's worth doing, it's worth doing well. When you try it on for size do it with enthusiasm, passion and your full concentration—the total involvement of your being. Commit yourself to the effort. Ignore how you look, how you sound, "how foolish this seems," or anything else that would distract you during your attempt. After you try, you can review what you have done, but during your attempt don't try to be a critic. And don't worry—you *will* feel and look awkward, stilted and artificial. After all, how elegantly did you swim, type, ride a bicycle or even walk with your first effort? Praise yourself for your courage to make mistakes. Risking something new is the essence of learning.

COMPARE THE RESULTS When trying something new, periodically take stock of where you're headed. What did your new way accomplish for you? Does it take care of your needs better? Regularly stand off, take some distance and evaluate the results. Get feedback. Critically review your performance. Collect views from other people. Once again, weigh the pros and cons. Are you satisfied with your new direction? Can you look yourself in the eyes with greater respect? Are you doing a better job of taking care of your needs? With each assessment, you can correct your next movement. You'll never be perfect, so don't even try. Instead, concentrate on getting the knack of steering yourself, finding your own direction from your heart. What is most important is that *you are doing it*, not waiting for someone to tell you how, not mechanically following old habits. You will have gained the confidence that you can indeed be who you want to be. Through this experimentation you get three treasures more precious than fame, fortune, or power—*self-worth*, *self-respect*, and *self-reliance*.

When you change you may find some people resent your efforts. They will want the "old you." What right have you to change? Now *they* must adjust. You didn't even ask their permission. They were used to who you were and now you have complicated their lives. That's *their* problem. If all you want is encouragement and reassurance, then go back to living for their approval. Sure you can consult them, ask their opinions, consider their feelings, but ultimately keep the final decisions for yourself. Whatever you do, *someone* won't approve. *Someone* will resist your changes. Don't let that stop you. Your life is *yours*.

You change because of your dissatisfaction. Your changes may produce dissatisfaction in those closest to you. But then again they may like the "new you" even better. As you benefit, so may they. Where compromises are useful, make them, but don't ever give up your self-respect.

Hard choices are hard because they're *not easy*. You may never know which choice was right but you can always tell which you'll respect yourself for making. And that's the best any of us can do.

By the way, excellent results are often the scariest of all. Then you will hope for more and be expected to produce. People will act like you are a winner. The better things get, the more bad results will shock you. (Just like the more intensely you feel, the more intensely you can get hurt. Failure is indeed safer.) Daring to get good results can scare the hell out of you. It teaches the shocking truth: What you do *really is* largely up to you. The best way to learn how to change is by changing.

Exercises

- Visit someone who has a young child. Spend an hour or two watching the child play. Watch him or her imitate, experiment, try and fail, try and succeed. You once learned by this method of trial and error. You can do so again.
- Write out a brief script including all stage directions with you as the hero or heroine behaving in a difficult situation in the way you'd like to handle it. First, play it out in your mind. Second, act it out alone or in front of a mirror. Third, with someone in the real world.

Some Objections

Acting like I'm somebody I'm not sounds hypocritical. Trying to impress people that I'm somebody worthwhile, while knowing I'm insecure, can't work!"

Exactly! Trying to be a good student or learning to swim, or acting more assertively primarily to please others (parents, spouse, therapist) never works. You exhaust yourself despite your hypocrisy and feel the hollowness of an empty life. To pursue those same activities in the hope of greater self-satisfaction, to please yourself, takes the utmost courage. It involves hearing but not obeying all the screaming selves within you and overcoming the ones that continually mutter, "It'll never work." Within everyone there is a self that feels like a total failure. That's part of what it is to be human. But that's not all of you. Don't overlook your strengths. Try anyway. Don't disregard the part that knows you can do almost anything.

Doing it for the approval of others doesn't work. We have frequently seen students with so-called "study blocks." Invariably, they seek grades rather than education, not for themselves but to impress parents and peers. Many of them are aware of their desire to please but far less conscious of their resentments, their hatred of having to perform to get approval. They'd love to be loved for just being who they are. Accepted for themselves. Loved simply because they exist!

Instead, these underachieving students develop a habit. They spend hours trying to study but just can't concentrate.

Failure to study well means poor grades. Poor grades hurt their parents and are not even the student's fault. After all, they have a "study block."

If that same student decides to learn and do well because of an interest in the subject, the study block disappears. If the student decides to drop out of school entirely, the study block disappears. But either way, to get rid of the symptom, the student must do what is right for him or herself. And that may mean disappointing both parents and peers!

"But isn't trying to be different just faking you are something you're not? That's not a very authentic way to act."

Maybe. Anytime you try to learn something new, in a sense you're pretending you're someone you're not. Authenticity is often just another cliché that misses the point. Humans are fluid. They are never *one* thing. It's a far bigger self-deception to tell yourself that something is impossible when you haven't even given it a passionate try.

Bill wants to feel good about himself, but he just doesn't know how. He thinks that somehow, one day, he'll just suddenly wake up loving himself and he'll live happily ever after. But it doesn't work that way. People who take pride in themselves avoid the addiction of self-insults. They are not afraid of having their fine qualities recognized by others. Bill decides to stop waiting for magic and, instead, to try acting like he's worthwhile. He chooses to try this new attitude on for size—not tentatively and apologetically, but enthusiastically, as if it's already a part of his life. He practices praising himself to his reflection in the mirror, speaks well of himself before his friends, accepts compliments on his good qualities with agreement, "Yeah, I think that's really fine about me too." Soon, Bill no longer feels insecure. He has changed himself.

It does happen that way. Yes, just like learning to walk or drive a car, you can change yourself. Of course, you can make up a million excuses for yourself as to how life isn't that simple, that it's easy for us to say, that learning doesn't change the human condition, or any other lie to convince yourself that you shouldn't even make an attempt. If you want to believe it's hopeless or you want to wait for magic, go ahead. But you will always have that nagging doubt that somehow you are missing something. Maybe missing the kind of life that you wish you'd have. Maybe missing the fact that we humans can mold ourselves and grow. Maybe missing the point of life itself.

Bill learned how. He had always been told that he was bright, talented, and sensitive, but he used to squirm when complimented. He learned that habit in childhood. It had to do with his relationship with his parents. No matter what he achieved, they never *really* seemed happy with him. He was afraid to feel too good. He preferred the comforting familiarity of worry, the cheap protection of expecting the worst. But after a while, he got fed up. He wanted to get out of his rut.

He wasn't really sure where to start; he wasn't seeing a therapist and didn't have anyone to help him brainstorm new possibilities. But he had attended one of our lectures and picked up an idea we offered. "Before you change, look at the pros and cons. Check what you are doing now for hidden benefits." So he did that. He made a list for himself.

Bill didn't like how depressed and lonely he had been. He worried that he was beginning to feel nothing at all, that his life would become cold and empty. He came to another lecture and told us of his progress.

"I was really surprised how easy it was," Bill beamed, as though he had just won a prize. "I started standing up for myself. Where I used to say things like 'I don't think I'm really that smart,' I started saying things like 'Thanks. It feels good to be appreciated.' People were shocked at first, particularly my partner. I think he believed I was going nuts. Now letting myself feel good about who I am is easy.

Whenever I think about how fortunate I am to be me, it kind of gives me a little lift. And you know, it's funny, I've suddenly found that I'm a really creative guy."

Life contains mini-plays and daily micro-episodes—it's up to you what your script will be. If you don't like the way it's been going, change it. If you're in no hurry, a little bit of change is the safest. If you want to be more assertive or proud, or loving, or angry try doing it one day a week at first. Slow change is far better than doing nothing. Move at your own pace, slow, medium or fast. But whatever you do, don't stand still.

"Won't some people feel Bill is conceited if he appreciates himself that much, if he brags about himself that way?"

Yes, but so what? He's not putting anyone else down. Bill didn't like the way he felt before. He decided to risk the resentment of those who can't stand a happy, confident person. If you are afraid of offending someone, then by all means make yourself miserable. At least somebody will always feel sorry for you.

Other people, whose own self-respect immunizes them against resenting Bill for his self-love, will prefer him and seek him out. Why? Because people that accept themselves, are usually a pleasure to be with. The falsely humble are but pits of seething resentment.

Self-love is needed to overcome the social myth that it's all right for children to learn . . . all right for children to look awkward or foolish . . . but grown-ups should never falter or fumble. That myth is pure bunk. It takes guts to let yourself learn something you did not already know well. If you are good at being afraid, for example, try on the awkwardness of being courageous. Cowards and heroes are afraid. The quality that differentiates them is how they deal with it—cowards run away from their fears, heroes confront them. Every fear is an opportunity for personal heroism. If you want something different to happen to your life, allow yourself the awkwardness of exploring an alternative. Try some heroics.

And when you try, try with passion. The military discovered some time ago that the most efficient way to learn a new language is by total immersion. Americans could learn Chinese rapidly by living, eating, sleeping, breathing, thinking, hearing and speaking only Chinese. When you try something new, immerse yourself in it. Give it your all!

Let's look at the process of learning to ride a bicycle again. What we are saying is that you go from "not being something" to "being something" by practicing until you get good at it. The principles are pretty simple:

What learning is for—The purpose of learning is to develop a personal feel for what you are doing. Knowing what to do may be part of it, but can't ever substitute for the actual experience of doing it. Naming every part of the bicycle and analyzing every physical movement involved in riding still doesn't mean that you can get on it and go. Getting the hang of it takes practice, and that is what it's all about. This is a common sense point and is probably why so many people are suspicious of "intellectuals." Book learning is nice, but in the real world, experience counts.

How learning works—Learning is, at best, refined trial and error. With bicycling you start with a rough idea of how to do it, an image of what people on bicycles look like, and a few instructions of where your arms and legs should be. Then you make a trial, take a stab at riding, crudely imitating, maybe even thrashing about. But by correcting your body movements, and eliminating mistakes that lead to falls, you refine your riding. By and large, all this means is keeping what works for you and discarding what doesn't. Learning is a crude process to say the least, but, since you weren't born on a bicycle, it's the only way to ride.

When learning should take place—Learning is a lifelong process. Like other growth phenomena, it occurs in spurts. You may practice your bicycling, make some progress, then get stuck for a while; you keep falling every time you make a left turn. Then one day, mysteriously, you don't fall anymore. Why? Who knows? You fooled around enough, you got a hint from somebody, you finally got the knack. Maybe that day you just didn't try so hard and it suddenly came easier. If there's a secret to learning, it's "find your own rate." Push yourself a little but not too much. The more you fight against your own individual rate, the more you slow yourself down. There will always be difficulties, but give yourself permission to experiment to find what's right for you.

These basic principles should be self-evident, but consider (just for the shocking contrast) these disgustingly widespread and self-defeating myths regarding learning:

What learning is for—The purpose of learning is to find out the "right way to do it." The right way is determined by society in the form of parents, experts or authorities. Your way, or a personal feeling, for what you are doing is nice, but unnecessary. All that counts is doing it right, or—even worse—doing it perfectly.

How learning works—Learning is a process of collecting right answers so that you never have to lose or be wrong. Winning and being right are what it's all about. By age twenty-one, a person should have enough of a grip on him or herself to know what to do in every situation or at least know which experts to ask for the right answer.

When learning should take place—Learning should be accomplished in childhood or adolescence. Any learning in adult life should occur smoothly and without upset.

Not everybody believes these myths, but enough people do to keep the world's experts in business. Learning how to ride a bicycle and learning how to change your life are more alike than different. Learning is learning is learning is learning. It's not always simple and it's not usually smooth, but learning is vital to that process of the controlled chaos called growth.

Uncertainty is part of learning. People who live with self-enforced rigidity learn poorly. Flexibility helps since learning something new is a feat as improbable as swimming on water. If you relax, take a chance, and throw yourself into it, you can swim along while cowards sink to the bottom. It takes practice and confidence. Convince yourself you can't and you never will.

"Isn't there an easier way to change?"

No. But there are lots of phony alternatives; escapes you can use to fool yourself. You can stay in therapy for years to understand why you are dissatisfied with your life. You'll fail to change, but you will be able to rationalize why you are stuck. You can make half-assed efforts to show others that you are at least trying. You can blame your spouse, parents, children, age, sex, wealth, poverty, job, brother, sister, physical or mental disability, socio-economic background, minority group, or astrological sign. You can hide your dissatisfaction in alcohol or other drugs. You can pretend you are doing fine while secretly you are miserable. You can pretend you really don't care about anything at all. In brief, you can lie to yourself in ten thousand ways rather than risk the tremendous effort it takes to teach yourself to change.

Heed an additional warning: The more you are in control of your life, the more you will feel. The more you feel, the more self-respect becomes important to you. The more important your self-respect becomes, the more you will want to act by choice rather than habit. Not detached rational choice, but by the passionate direction of your heart. The way that you find for you.

The rewards are high: self-respect, love, self-control. But the pain can be intense too. A full life can bring sharp hurts. Your reward will be the experience of being as alive, as aware, as involved as you possibly can be. It's up to you. Retreat to your habits if you wish, or move ahead if you dare. But never again say, "*I want to change but I don't know how.*"

Exercises

- List six skills you have. They can be recreational, avocational or vocational. Think back to your awkwardness, your hesitation, your fears while you were learning each one. Imagine yourself in your mind as you were while learning each one. Recall your feelings. Can you remember how you acted *as if* at first, probably imitating others you'd observed who were more accomplished?
- Now imagine yourself trying out a change you're considering. Keeping this change in mind, list your three major objections to the change process described in this book so far. Do your objections have more to do with weaknesses in our approach, or your fears? To double check your opinion, why not discuss your objections with your best friend or therapist, or both?

It's Too Hard!

Self-help books seem to fall into two general categories: the "recipe" book or the "nice friend" book.

The recipe book contains foolproof directions by an "expert": *The Doctor's Step-By-Step Plan To Health And Happiness.* Follow the book and if things don't work out, at least it's not your fault.

The "nice friend" book is vague, platitudinous, and inspirational, a pleasant diversion that makes you feel really good for the moment, but afterwards it's back to the same old grind.

There's a cynical "snake oil remedy" quality about much of the self-help industry. Readers are often treated as though they were simpletons who deserve little and will settle for less. Many good ideas are watered down in the effort to sell something. It's a pathetic routine of packaging and promotion—worthwhile approaches become oversimplified into rigid commands or are inflated into grand-sounding peptalks that are little more than philosophical masturbation.

Obviously, we're in a poor position to categorically condemn all self-help books. Some are excellent tools. What bothers us is the tendency of so many to approach life along a single dimension. "Just do *this* and everything will be fine." Sure, it's good to say "no" without feeling guilty, and good to be your own best friend. But living is just too complex, too paradoxical for one-answer solutions. In fact, that's the core of our message. Grow. Stop looking for simple answers. Be whole. Learn to see all sides of life's subtle paradoxes. Take a chance.

We wrote this book because the other ones we saw seemed to sidestep the confusing parts of life by implying that if only one would get "fixed" (actualized, analyzed, primal screamed, est-ed), life would be smooth sailing. And that's the cheat—suggesting that the central useful idea from such books could ever be a permanent solution.

Life just isn't that simple. No one idea is THE TRUTH. Nothing works forever.

Self-help books often play into the human desire for "the final answer." They imply, if not actually state, "THIS IS IT!" But "this" is never all of "it." Each new idea is just one more step. We think the closest one gets to the big "it" is in learning how to find useful ideas, grow with them, and then gracefully release them when they're worn out.

The written word's too poor a tool for THE TRUTH. The best that can be shared are glimpses. Even the best solution, in time, can create new problems. We've offered our guidelines only in the hope of introducing you to the process of finding your own: self-love combined with careful experimentation, a balance between a critical mind and a feeling heart, seem to work the best.

Life, if you really face it, demands your inventive best. Formulas, in a sense, are always retrospective. It's easy to see what worked, but experimenting to find out what will work is a high art. Directions may seem clear, but later vanish. It's okay, keep going.

Ideally, self-help books should self-destruct after use. Like crutches after an ankle sprain, they are useful when one begins to make some healing changes. Prolonged use creates crippling dependency. Rely on yourself. Experiment. Awaken the parts of you that are asleep. Allow your weaknesses, but dwell on your strengths. Have compassion. Have courage.

Do you have the guts to be as alive as you can each moment? If so, we applaud your efforts to push forward in a world that has so much pain; where even successes can lead to problems. And remember, no matter how well things might go, pain can come again: "I thought I wasn't supposed to hurt anymore." Just feel and learn. Changes *will* always come. And so it will always be, as sure as the rising and falling of the tides. No free lunch. No free ride.

If you allow and expect the chaos inherent in human existence, you can bring an order based on what you find in your own heart. You will find magnificent highs along with the pain. Life's ecstasies can outweigh all its agonies.

Publishers and other "people in the know" have warned us, "You're asking too much of readers. Who wants such crazy visions? Most people are only looking for a little peace and quiet." Maybe so. But we just can't believe that everyone who reads a self-help book is cowardly and lazy.

We are talking about *peace*. It's just a rather noisy kind. "There are no permanent solutions . . . experiment carefully. Be tender towards yourself . . . listen to what you feel . . . assess where you're going. The reward for a courageous life is magnificent freedom!" We think many people know these ways already, but may be hoping that somehow, somebody will bring the magic, pain-free world for which they secretly wait. "Someday . . ."

This book is intended to work like medicine, and at times it may be as difficult to swallow. You may be getting a lot of satisfying insights—"Aha!" or "Oh, no!" experiences. "I never realized before" revelations. Excellent. But, if you're not putting your understanding *into practice*, using what you teach yourself as a tool to get more mastery over your life, then you're wasting your time. By next year at this time the only thing that will be different about you will be your age.

Change is hard. It's difficult to begin and it never ends. Yet, somehow, the joy that comes from continuing growth surpasses all the petty satisfactions humans usually seek.

Most people have established uneasy truces based on lifetimes of capitulating to their fears. They drift along, trying to avoid hassles—until they trip over the psychological dirt they've swept under the carpet. Of course, in time, you can learn to bury feelings to a point where all that remains are insatiable appetites and bitter aftertastes. At that point, nothing can fulfill you. Boredom, emptiness and longing are all that's left.

If you've got the guts to change, we respect your courage. Just sticking with us this far is an accomplishment. We're purposely giving you glimpses and flashes instead of ready-made plans. Anything you extract from us will be your own mixture.

For at least a month, keep a weekly diary of what you're trying. Put your ideas into action! Write down where you've been and where you want to be. Write down ten ideas (even crazy ones) on how to get there. Pick the best five. Experiment. Find out what works. It doesn't even matter where you're going, as much as how you get there. For a month, try using all of yourself to experiment and find your own way. Try living your life to the fullest.

Yeah, life is hard! But its difficulties provide a delicious challenge for those who face it squarely—and incessant discomfort for those who try to sneak away.

When we work with people in therapy, we have the advantage of seeing what they do. If they push to master their lives and work hard to change, we can see their progress. But you, dear reader, are invisible to us. Only *you* know if you are using this book as a source of cute quotations, a pretense at working on changing or a tool to actually change your life. If you have been brave enough to truly listen to yourself and try some changes, we applaud your efforts. Bravo! Please don't take the preachy sections as criticism. Delight in your efforts. Delight in your growth.

But . . . if you are goofing off . . . get moving! This book is almost half over! Use it to change you, before you go back to chasing magic.

Exercises

- Have you begun to make some changes yet? If so, have you taken some satisfaction in your courage to try despite your fears and awkwardness?
- If you haven't begun, can you list your reasons? Do they feel like good ones?
- Do you want to feel the same way about yourself tomorrow as you do today? How could you increase your self-respect today?

GROWTH:
The Advanced Course

Compassion: The Need for Selfishness

Life can be a magnificent kaleidoscope. In this book, we're trying to share a vision of the world—a way to see from so many different angles at once that even the paradoxes become clear. Cult movements, formulas, pat answers and religious dogmas provide internal peace by substituting obedience for individual struggle with the contradictions that seem to fill life. The exorbitant price of self-deception is that it robs you of your endless potential for growth. The very complexity of life that boggles the mind also gives infinite freedom. Ideas, books, and teachers can help, but they are only little parts of an endless puzzle. Please don't follow anything or anyone like a slave.

Learn from this book and then discard it as you find your own path. Feel the ecstasy of guiding yourself with your heart and mind. You've got everything you need inside, if you've got the guts to try.

What we have covered so far are some approaches to breaking out of common ruts. Some ways to listen to yourself and to learn. Now we'll try to bring these complex and confusing ideas into another focus by dealing with three general principles. Such lists can readily become vintage baloney, so we recommend them only as temporary guides. Like binoculars, they can offer a clearer view, a way of seeing the scene in sharper detail.

COMPASSION—Love (or if the word "love" is too embarrassing, "tender regard")—first for yourself, despite your human faults and, yes, even because of them. Then, as you feel more worthy, love for everyone and everything else. But start with love and compassion for yourself, or you'll never have any to give away.

COURAGE—This is a crazy world. There are no guarantees about anything. No one can tell you what is truly going on now let alone in the future. At the moment, anything—the worst or the best—could happen. Your choice: Will you accept responsibility for all you think, feel and do? Will you accept the burden of searching for and making good use of your gifts? If you give yourself permission to live fully in a world where nothing is ever permanent, where each solution must be tried and shaped to fit, where experimentation and risk are vital to forward motion—if you have the courage for all these things—you will find the peace that cowards never see.

FREEDOM—Have the humility and grace to accept your place as a human being with your share of limitations, instead of beating yourself up for not having everything you'd like. At the same time, beware of worshipping anyone else. Balance is the key. Be neither glib nor morose. Although you can't buy or beg your way out of this existence, you can still grow.

There may be some big TRUTH that underlies everything. If there is, no human can ever tell you what it is. No words can ever completely say it. Don't ever think you've got the final answer. Make beliefs and ideas your tools. Don't be their slave.

Use our temporary signposts if you wish, but learn to make your own. Compassion for the self and the courage to experiment will lead you to freedom, freedom from you and your habitual, enslaving beliefs. It is a task that will take all of your effort, but then again, what the hell are you doing that's more important than your own life?

"Selfishness is just one of the qualities apt to inspire love. This might be thought out at great length." NATHANIEL HAWTHORNE

According to Roy Harvey Pearce, an eminent American literary scholar, Hawthorne made this pithy observation and then never wrote further on the subject. As far as we can see, Hawthorne was on the right track.

In an earlier chapter, we emphasized the importance of love. Here we are talking about putting love into practice in the way you act. We are pushing for a quality of compassion—compassion towards yourself, despite your human defects. We are pushing for selfishness—caring for and looking after yourself. Unless you do it and get good at it, self-reproach will trap you into staying with old habits. Love and compassion towards yourself—if you're not tender and understanding towards you, you'll be afraid to learn anything new.

Natural selfishness is a mental attitude that is difficult to describe. It is easier to say what it is not. It's *not* trying to hurt everybody else. It's *not* avoiding intimacy under the guise of "looking out for number one." It's *not* hoarding meaningless material goods while your heart longs for what you really need.

Being cruel or obnoxious alienates people. It makes you lonely and isn't what we mean by selfishness. Natural selfishness is paying attention to taking care of yourself.

Natural *self-ishness* is stopping the lies. It's centering your life in you, mastering the art of looking after the person who is you. And not unless you excel at selfishness can you truly give. Till then there's always the subtle "when do I get mine" that creeps into every action. Be honest about who you are and what you need. Lying gets you nowhere.

Hugh, a minister, wanted marital therapy for himself and his wife, Ann. In the past they had tried both individual and marital counseling but felt their problems remained unsolved. During his individual session with me, Hugh recited documentation of eight years of his tireless, unselfish, "Christian sacrifices" in the marriage, including seeking out and paying for extensive individual therapy for "poor" Ann. He regularly bought gifts for her and the children. He worked on their house during his well-deserved vacations, while the rest of the family visited relatives all over the country. He never even contemplated infidelity.

His reward for his dedication—cold rejection, indeed, insolent scorn from Ann.

Ann, in her individual session, stated emphatically that she had had it! She too could document her case with a litany of stoically endured abuses.

"I'm tired of being chief cook and bottle washer, maid and prostitute with no respect or love from Hugh. He acts as if he's our commanding officer, uttering divine truths, forcing everyone into line. He alternates between giving orders and screaming over trivia . . . and he's worse when he drinks . . . which has become more and more frequently."

Both clearly felt no understanding, warmth, love or respect from the other. Both were painfully lonely and tremendously resentful of the other for the rejection each felt despite *trying so hard to please*. After all, if you sacrifice for somebody, that person should sacrifice for you. Right? *No way!*

Consider Hugh and Ann, both afraid to reach out, afraid of being crushed by another brutal rejection. Hugh and Ann both dug in. They hid in their separate psychological trenches. They could live together as long as they maintained a distant, cold relationship—engaging each other only in brief, vicious, verbal artillery strikes across the "no man's land."

Each knew the cause of the problems—the *other!* The marriage could become tolerable only if the other partner could be helped (made?) to change.

I challenged them: "What do you want? Do you want to separate and divorce? If you feel you've tried everything and can honestly say with self-respect, "I've done what I can and it's hopeless," then divorce may be the best solution.

"If you decide to break up, I'll help you begin that painful course. Or, if you're too cowardly, then continue to be lonely, angry, and dissatisfied, but safe in your distant, barricaded positions. You don't need my help at that—you're experts already.

"But if you want to improve your life within the marriage, you're going to have to take risks and experiment with different ways of behaving."

Ann jumped at the chance. "I'm willing to try anything but I don't think Hugh could change. He's just not capable of love. I think he hates women and if you knew his mother, you'd understand why." Once again, Ann was telling Hugh what was wrong with him.

Hugh squirmed in the chair. He cleared his throat and began in a remote, emotionless voice. For an instant, his sadness and pain broke through as tears filled his eyes. "That's unfair."

Apparently Ann underestimated him. He felt, and felt deeply. I asked them to risk their first experience—I suggested they simply hug each other as if they meant it while I left the room for a few minutes.

When I returned, they were sitting far apart. Hugh caught my eye first. He looked as if he had swallowed the proverbial canary. Ann appeared confused, embarrassed and uncomfortable. Ann summarized the result of the experiment—much to her surprise, Hugh had hugged openly, warmly and enthusiastically. But Ann could manage only a brief perfunctory squeeze despite her concentrated efforts. She was beginning to see how much easier and safer it was to give up rather than to risk, hope or try. If it was "all Hugh's fault," she could give up. But, if she were involved, if she had to change, that would be a real struggle.

The easiest path would have been for both of them to stay in their corners and point at each other, "It's your fault." I wanted them to try a different tack.

"What could each of you do to get the other person to treat you the way *you* want? Imagine you're so selfish that you want to be listened to, looked at and touched exactly the way you want. Bargain, negotiate, deal in some way, so you both can selfishly take care of what you need. Take care of yourselves instead of playing martyr. Nothing is more naturally selfish and satisfying than to find out what pleases your partner most and offer that very thing. It immeasurably enhances the likelihood of getting what you want in return. Besides, giving your partner what he or she wants is loving. And being loving makes you feel warm and good (another harmlessly selfish payoff).

Although Hugh scoffed at the idea that he was a problem drinker, he agreed to stop alcohol for several months because he knew it wasn't helping their problems. He decided to make efforts to court and romance Ann. He would begin to solicit and consider her opinions. He would display open, verbal and physical warmth to Ann and the children.

Ann would stop demeaning Hugh, as a man and as a pastor. She would not side with the children against him. If she were angry, she would tell him but would stop sniping at him. She would reciprocate if he risked being loving, rather than hold off until some vague future time when he had "redeemed himself."

Neither would expect anything: both would explicitly appreciate anything the other did, taking nothing for granted—his working, her cooking, everything was to be warmly acknowledged.

Both would practice being empathic without being parental. That is, they would actively work to get the other to communicate, especially if they could see the other was feeling something out of the ordinary, pain, sadness, excitement or joy. They would try to show each other they were interested and understanding, without having to solve each other's problems.

They bought the suggestion; to feel understood is to feel loved.

Three weeks later they returned proudly arm in arm, pleased with their courageous efforts. The changes were awkward and a bit frightening for them. They credited the inspiration to their personal religious faith. Why not? Love by any name is love. They now felt a love and respect for themselves and each other never present in their entire sixteen years of marriage. Even sex had been a triumph.

This kind of transformation is rare. Few couples can so readily give up their habits. Great desperation helps.

We had one more session a month later to insure that wasn't simply a temporary truce in their marathon struggle. They made the change work.

Moral One

Love yourself
enough to
take care of your needs.

Clearly express what you want. Don't nag, bitch, moan or wait for others to change if you're after more satisfaction in your life. Be willing to negotiate but never give up your self-respect. Use your leverage, from giving favors to refusing sex, all in order to demonstrate that you are serious. But make clear what you want—sulking is useless. Experiment, use what works. If all else fails, leave. If you'd "never leave no matter what," you are simply a slave. Free people use leverage.

Ann was able to say explicitly and tenderly to Hugh: "I want your love, I need it, and I won't sleep with you unless you start showing me warmth and tenderness. I want at least one hug and kiss each day. Once a day tell me something you *like* about *me*. If you won't or can't give me that, I'm going to leave." Hugh, under this duress, agreed to try. Ann took a tremendous risk; he might have replied, "Forget it, I'm leaving."

We see so many people who stay in miserable situations, sacrificing their self-respect, their needs unsatisfied for fear of losing what semblance of a relationship or security they have—housewives who feel used like Ann, husbands who feel suffocated like Hugh, executives who suffer silently for fear of making waves, people overwhelmed by responsibilities with few rewards—humans who put up with something bad out of fear of something worse. In effect, what all these people are saying is: "I'm afraid to take the chance; my self-respect isn't worth the trouble."

What a price to pay!

If your life
leaves something
to be desired,
change it.
Have compassion
for yourself. You have you
to look after your needs.

Moral Two

Don't ever
deceive yourself that you're
sacrificing for someone else!
Most martyrs secretly
wait for a payoff that never comes.
(At least in "this life.")

Both Hugh and Ann felt that they had sacrificed for each other and the children. They would do things they didn't like to do and not do things they dearly wanted to do. They both took a heavy loss on their investment of time, energy and emotion.

They claimed that in sacrificing, they expected nothing in return. Baloney! They expected rewards for their sacrifices. Sure, it feels good to see someone you love feel good. But don't forget, you also want something in return, if nothing else, love and respect. It's only natural to want the same thing you give.

What went wrong for Ann and Hugh?

A. They denied their natural selfishness, and instead sacrificed to keep the marriage going.

B. They avoided direct, honest communication especially about what they each wanted.

C. They lacked compassion for themselves.

Let's look at these points one by one.

NATURAL SELFISHNESS AND SACRIFICE

Since Ann and Hugh, like the rest of us, have needs for love, security, worthwhileness, and fun, why not admit it? Everyone does what they do on the basis of making thousands of choices, second by second, minute by minute. Not all of these choices seem conscious or deliberate, yet, at some level we choose. Sometimes we choose the lesser of two evils. For example, given the choice of boiling to death or dying quietly in my sleep tonight, obviously I'd choose the latter. Even if you pick the least offensive of several bad options, you still choose.

Parents don't really sacrifice for children, wives for husbands, or vice versa. People do what they do out of habit, because they think it is best or because they wouldn't respect themselves otherwise. But they almost never choose for selfless motives. (A very disquieting idea for the self-righteous.)

"But sometimes I have no choice," we're told. Take an extreme example. A prisoner is led from his concentration camp compound toward the "showers" by two burly, armed soldiers. He knows death, not cleanliness, awaits him one hundred meters away. He has no options. Or so it appears.

In fact, his alternatives are either to kid himself by denying the reality and hoping that indeed only a shower awaits him, to plead for his life, to offer to trade information about fellow prisoners in exchange for his own survival, to go to his death stoically and proudly while making peace with the Lord, to confront his guards with their role in the carnage or to resist them and require them to kill him in front of his fellow prisoners. His choice, like that of any of us, ideally would be based on which alternative would allow him the greatest self-respect. Surely, he detests all the options, but will choose one over the others. Even pretending not to choose is a choice.

****

Peter, a very successful young financier, recounted a story from his own life. He wanted to play tennis with his favorite partner. Instead he played with his eleven-year-old son, not because he wanted to, he argued, but because he would feel guilty if he didn't.

Scores of similar examples flooded into my consciousness as I listened—unmarried children in their thirties still nursing a widowed, ailing parent, the parents of a disturbed 25-year-old "child," unable to live their own lives because they "must" take care of him, the spouse of an alcoholic who nags, bitches, complains, but persists in her martyrdom, the perennial patient who uses psychotherapy to hide from ever making real changes.

Like Peter, they don't *want* to, but they feel *obligated* to sacrifice their own desire. They insist there's no choice, but even like the tragic figure about to die in a concentration camp, they had choices and they choose. You *always have choices*, whether you see them or not. You can pretend not to choose and let events simply sweep you along, but in that case you have effectively chosen to take no conscious, definite action. Or you can claim you are a passive victim of circumstances; that way, whatever happens, you are not responsible.

Peter wanted to play tennis with his adult partner. Playing with this friend would be more challenging than playing with his son. Despite that desire, he played with his son. He didn't decide to play with his son because it would meet his needs or add to his self-respect. He chose his son because he was afraid of feeling guilty. We think his rationale stinks. Wouldn't it be better to act out of free choice for the sake of self-respect rather than out of a sense of guilt?

Sacrifice is a sham. All martyrs choose their fate. Others may choose to worship or respect them for the choice they make. But none of them really sacrifices. All do what they prefer under the unenviable circumstances.

A parent can do without, in order to provide something for a child, not as a sacrifice but as a free choice. Then both child and parent are free of obligation and guilt. The child lives without unpayable debts, the parents without smoldering resentment.

So with Peter. If he adopts the attitude we suggest, plays tennis with his son out of *free choice*, then he can proudly say to himself, "I wanted to do it and my son owes me nothing. Nor has he deprived me, for I like myself better if I play with him than if I play with my friend." Best of all, flushed with a sense of well-being and proud of his decision, Peter can immerse himself in the experience of being with his son and truly enjoy the time they spend together.

Or he can say, "I'd rather play with my friend today. Today I choose not to play with my son."

Either way he avoids the traps of guilt and resentment. Guilt so often is used as the price people pay to continue their addictions. In a similar way, resentment is used as the alternative to taking difficult action. These last two sentences are the key to 95% of psychological suffering.

Peter can continue to play with his friend and avoid his son as long as he is guilty. The alcoholic can continue to drink; the obese can overeat, the letter can remain unwritten, the house uncleaned . . . it's all right, as long as you feel guilty.

Guilt, the attempt to appease some higher power, is an obscenity. Guilt is founded on the myth that you become better if you keep putting yourself down. It's a lie. Self-torment makes you afraid to risk changes. Guilt traps you into staying stuck.

Guilt can be unlearned. An easy way to start is to avoid "should," "ought to" or "have to." Openly admit you choose to do everything you do. Even if you don't like what you're doing, you like the alternatives even less. Have the courage and the honesty to enjoy and take responsibility for what you do rather than feel guilty about it. And, if what you're doing is not right for you, just try something else.

Okay, let's review for a moment. First you place guilt to the side. You decide what would best satisfy your needs; otherwise you'll eventually feel deprived and become bitter and resentful. You responsibly accept that you must choose a course of action to satisfy your needs and self-respect. You decide to do what you want from the alternatives you recognize. You don't pretend to sacrifice. You either do something because it makes you feel good or you contract for something in return.

HONEST DIRECT COMMUNICATION

One morning I took my two boys to play racquetball. I enjoy taking them. They love it. I took advantage of my leverage. "I like to take you, but in addition I want something in return."

"What?" they asked warily, knowing me and my contracts.

"Wash my car."

"It's a deal," they concurred.

If I had taken them without negotiating beforehand, and then later asked them to wash my car, I'd have felt used and resentful by their refusal. "Look at all the thanks I get after spending my Sunday morning with them and I didn't even get a good workout!"

"But does everything have to be negotiated explicitly? You make every relationship or interaction sound like a business deal, so cold and calculating."

The coldest, most calculated interactions we see involve those very people (like Ann and Hugh) who don't clearly, explicitly, and honestly state their wishes. It's far kinder to openly demand to refuse to cater to another unless you receive something in return. Love relationships are partnerships. Partnerships work better when the demands and negotiations are up front, in the open. When you're honest with that other person you're taking a chance—you can't be sure how they will respond to the truth. But telling them is the best way to make your needs clear. Hiding what you want behind "if you really loved me, you'd know without my asking," is absolute rot! Even the best lovers can't read minds.

the ultimate risk is explicit honesty, with self and others.

COMPASSION FOR SELF

Most people are programmed early in life: Be perfect. Should, shouldn't. Do, don't. Hugh and Ann learned their lessons all too well. They did not feel like fine, lovable people because they had not yet lived up to the standards drummed into them.

They were programmed to sacrifice for others first, rather than to be naturally selfish and seek satisfaction for their own needs.

They were programmed to be obedient to parents, authorities, country, God, their church, their spouse, the kids, rather than to put responsibility for their own thoughts, feelings and behavior first. They were taught that respect for others was more important than self-respect. Parental feelings, ideas, and attitudes were to be listened to above all. One's inner voice, the sensitive, needy child inside, was better ignored "out of respect for others."

If Hugh achieved enough, he would be a good person and be loved. If Ann served well enough, caring for house, children and Hugh's needs, she would be good and appreciated.

Both applied themselves according to their long-established programs and waited ever more impatiently for return on their investments. With each new failure, they reapplied old habits. They waited, hoping for some magic while trying not to think about tomorrow. And, of course, resentment grew.

Righteous indignation also grew. Depression increased. Needs unsatisfied, their hungers became ravenous. Despair replaced hope.

Worst of all, they began to hate themselves for their "un-Christian" bitterness. They had learned to measure their self-worth according to *results* rather than efforts. They looked to rigid rules of conduct and excluded their selves and inner voices. No wonder they felt like failures. They felt unloving and unlovable.

Surely you must have compassion for your own vulnerabilities if you are to love others. But it's difficult to give up the fantasy that someday you'll be the perfect person they want you to be.

"Are you suggesting I give up the values I was raised to cherish? Give up my life goals?"

Not necessarily. But have you the guts to review them critically?

Would you mind loving and respecting yourself for who you are right now? Would you reconsider your goals from time to time to be certain they're still yours rather than theirs?

Do you feel you haven't been living with enough passion and enthusiasm to justify your own love and respect for the efforts you've been making? Who's stopping you? Self-love and self-respect come with your first enthusiastic try, when you lose yourself in the effort and say to hell with the results; results aren't in your control anyway. Have the compassion to let yourself selfishly enjoy this life.

Exercises

Answer the following questions. What do your responses tell you about yourself?

- Were you an obedient child, a "good" boy or girl? If you answered "yes," are you still trying to please?
- Do you pay attention to your feelings to see if your needs are being fulfilled?
- Do you often feel envious, jealous, resentful or guilty?
- Do you try to find out what you could do to please the people you're close to?
- Do you ask for what you want from others?
- Do you accept responsibility for what you do, or do you pretend to have no choice?

Compassion: Moments of Weakness

"Faith in a holy cause is to a considerable extent a substitute for the lost faith in ourselves." ERIC HOFFER

Inside, all people are changeable creatures. You are really never anything in a permanent way. You only pretend to be. That's part of what makes existence so hard. Life doesn't stop a moment to let you catch your breath. It just keeps moving. You can be dragged along or flow with it. What we are talking about here is cultivating suppleness, a flexible self-control, rather than lip-biting and teeth-clenching rigidity. Riding the turbulence of life, like steering a canoe through rocky rapids, takes more timing than muscle. Life isn't so much a contest of brute strength as it is a feat of nimble endurance.

We are giving you terribly vague advice, aren't we? *If it feels right, try it*; then afterwards, ask yourself whether it is right for you to continue in that direction or whether you should try something else. Hah! Try it indeed! If we've got the answers we ought to be able to tell you exactly what to do, right? No way! *You've* got some answers even if you can't see them clearly now. Have some faith, some trust in yourself, and you will have the courage to take a chance.

Remember that what you are working for doesn't really mean anything compared to *how you feel about yourself every step of the way.* Will I have compassion for myself even if the results are terrible?

Make it all right to fail, all right to totally blow it. Allow at least a few moments of weakness. You're human, remember? The idea that people have to be perfect before they can be happy causes so much self-inflicted misery. Make the rules of your life such that even if the worst imaginable results come from your efforts, you will still love yourself. And we say *make* because it is an action of choice. Without compassion, you never get to use your full strength. You will be too torn up and worried inside to ever *really* try something new.

Testing your self-compassion is actually pretty easy. After doing something you wish you had never done, after taking some action that had unhappy consequences, grab a mirror, look into it and tell yourself these words (or anything with the same meaning)—"I wish things didn't turn out the way they did. In some ways I am angry at you for your part in it, but I want you to know something. No matter how angry I get, I love you and believe in you. I am proud that you put your best effort into it and, my friend, that's all that counts."

Only with that kind of love, compassion, and assurance towards yourself will you ever have the guts to really feel. Of course, if you love yourself, you *are* going to offend somebody. But then again, if you want to kiss everybody's feet, you don't need to read a book to find out how. Feeling love and compassion for yourself may bring you into conflict with others, but you will always have a place where you'll feel at home. **YOU.**

The realization that you are largely in control of the rules of your life is a sudden and radical experience, almost as surprising as if by flapping your arms you would suddenly fly off into space. Like flying, it's a scary experience. After raising yourself above the ground you worry "what if this stops working?" The indispensable root of it all is confidence. But confidence requires some successes. Successes are impossible without enthusiastic attempts. Attempts mean acting *as if*. You may not be totally in control of your life; for that matter, all of your perceptions and thoughts may be in some sense illusions, but it doesn't seem to really matter. After all, the safety of dull habits is just as much an illusion.

To a surprising extent, you can get away with acting *as if* you are totally in control of your life. Grasp what control is available and try on a new system of rules for size. A system that says you are beautiful and worth loving; that the only actions you will perform are *not* solely to please others or to fulfill their expectations, but rather ones you respect, have put your heart into and that show promise of fulfilling your needs. One of the most radical steps you can take is this leap into loving yourself, no matter what kind of mess you make. Once you give yourself permission to run your life, no one can take it away.

Will was a guy who always wanted to be more self-reliant. A friend of his had benefited from therapy so Will tried it too, and dramatically changed from his previous whimpering style. Where he used to be indecisive, he began to create his own solutions.

"I'd always felt like a fool," he said, recalling how he used to be. "But I changed and I sure am glad. Before I *had* to ask somebody else—my wife, my brother, you, anybody. I was afraid to make decisions on my own. It was disgusting to live that way."

Will had changed himself in a few weeks of therapy. Now, six months later, he returned for a session as if on a visit to an old high school teacher to say, "Hi! Look how well I'm doing."

"When I finished here I was really pleased with myself. I wasn't a crybaby anymore. I really felt in control. I couldn't believe the difference, but I think underneath it all I was afraid I would eventually slip back.

"For a couple of months afterwards, I felt really good. Things were surprisingly easy. But one day something happened that changed me as much as anything I did here in therapy. I was playing touch football with some of the guys and I broke my wrist. It hurt badly. I started screaming and crying; you know . . . just like I used to before when I'd get scared and couldn't make up my mind. It hurt so much I panicked and was blubbering like an idiot. My friend, Gil, took me to the hospital, but I don't know how he put up with all that crap. I was really coming apart. I can laugh about it now, but I was scared to death then. I really went to pieces.

"But you know what? I've decided that it is all right to go to pieces sometimes. If I did it every day, that would really be too much. But once in a while, why not? I guess it is part of me and, you know . . . I'm not ashamed of it any more."

Will was beaming, delighted with himself, as though he had found out that he was better than he had ever hoped to be. As though he could cherish himself more because of his unique imperfections, because his defects made him all the more perfectly human.

"What I came back to tell you is that I have learned something new. It suddenly hit me the day after I broke my wrist. I realized I was bringing on those panics before because I was afraid I was going to panic! It's like the other part of allowing myself to act weak sometimes, and to know that I am never strong or weak, but can be both at various times. After all, I'm only human."

Truly a paradox, somehow all of this doesn't seem to make sense on the surface. But then again, where does anyone get off expecting life to be logical? If there is any basic lesson life's trying to get across, it's that life isn't logical; or at least not according to the everyday logic most people use. So, if you want to be worthy of your own respect, go ahead—even if at first you don't believe you're worthy. To change, you've got to *change*. You can't be the old you and the new you simultaneously. And, remember, only the practiced you can be smooth. The new you *will be* awkward at first.

Strengthen your position by doing things you respect yourself for. Will realized that he is a person who displays his emotions very readily. He chose to love this part of himself. Self-love was something he could choose to have or hide from. It's okay to change how you act and who you are.

Your ability to change will be maximized if you have compassion for your weaknesses in this human struggle.

Cliché though it be, lack of love and compassion toward yourself does make it hard for you to love anybody else—and nearly impossible to love anyone whose weaknesses remind you of your own. In fact, this may be how self-contempt is transmitted from one generation to the next. Parents, unable to love something about themselves, see the same trait in one of their children. Instead of giving the child a message like "Hey, that's not a very good thing to do, it will just cause you problems later on," the message usually passed on is "If you act that way, it means you're bad." This negative communication takes place with a minimum of words, often just with a disapproving look, an emotional slap in the face. After countless subtle put-downs, the child learns the same self-doubt, self-recrimination and buried self-hate that the parent harbors. The misery continues. Another generation of neurotics keeps another generation of psychiatrists in business.

Joe, a man whose financial success was matched in greatness only by the misery in his twenty-year marriage, finally moved out of his home. He was in his late forties and felt so confused and unhappy that he took a friend's suggestion to see a psychiatrist. One of the things that bothered him most was his inability to explain his reasons for the separation to his children honestly and directly. He "couldn't," it just wasn't "right." How could he tell his son and daughter how much he detested living with their mother? How much her constant self-deprecation sickened him? Years of her whining, her slovenly appearance and housekeeping, her coldness and prudishness had worn away his love for her. Sure, he realized he had contributed to the decay, even if he had done nothing openly destructive. By quietly tolerating their worsening relationship for the past ten years, staying away from the house and hiding in his work, he had also helped destroy the marriage.

Now his sharpest pain was wanting his children to understand, but feeling unable to tell them his view of the truth. How could he describe his suffocation, his feelings of imprisonment? How could he explain his panic in realizing that the "someday" he had been waiting for wasn't coming? Because he was convinced he had no right to burden his children with his feelings, he had left without any explanation other than "Your mother and I can't live with each other."

"John's only ten and Betty is eight. They just wouldn't understand. It would upset them too much. I'll let their mother tell them whatever the hell she wants. I can't do anything else."

"Come on, Joe," I starting pushing. "Just stop and think for a minute. Is that how you deal with your customers, employees or colleagues in business? Do you equivocate, beat around the bush, tell flimsy stories, make excuses?"

"That's different. They are not my children and I don't care as much about them anyway. And I am not responsible for them either."

"You are extremely successful as a clear, direct, honest businessman; but, with your children, you feel like a failure. In business you tell the truth as you see it. At home you are lying with your silence. What's the worst that could happen if you told your kids what you felt? They'd hate you? They'd never again be able to have a satisfying relationship? They'd be depressed for the rest of their lives? Come on, Joe, you just aren't that powerful. You've got a lot better chance of hurting them permanently by unexplained rejection than by confessing your honest feelings. They'll probably cry and be very sad, but what you'll be telling them won't be all that shocking. Kids know when something's going on."

Apparently that little push was all he needed. Soon thereafter, during one marathon weekend, he privately confronted his wife with the depths of his feelings about her—something he had never really done before—and shared his decision to stay away even though she was threatening to destroy him financially. Then he talked with each of his children, risking and weathering his own pain at their tears, even risking the possibility of permanent rejection by them.

The results were far from uniformly positive. His wife refused to believe him and, instead, mocked and insulted him. His daughter was sad and frightened; she ran to her room before he even started talking. His son listened carefully, seemed to be understanding it all, but then, when Joe had finished, asked him when he would be coming back home again. In many ways, that weekend was the most difficult two days of his life.

"But I felt relieved afterwards. Unburdened. Before, I'd look at Betty and John and I'd feel so much that I couldn't talk about anything at all. I wish I hadn't let things get this far, but right now, for me, the only thing I want to do is get out. It's been like living a lie, pretending, and now I've finally broken out."

"Looking back, was it worth doing, Joe? Was it worth the chances you took? Did you get the results you were after?"

"Hell . . . I don't know . . . I realize part of the reason I was coming here was just for any chance to escape. I believe perhaps you might tell me something that would make it all easy. I was afraid. I love my kids and I didn't want to hurt them. But you know, like I told my son, I hope maybe he and Betty will learn how to prevent a marriage from being killed by pretending everything is all right, when it really isn't. I hope they will learn something it took me a long time to understand. I am still not sure what I really feel, but I am beginning to know now when I am holding something back. I was just so afraid of making a mistake . . . afraid of being weak or wrong . . . so I didn't do anything. It feels good to have finally made a move.

"I'm going to try to keep letting my wife and children know what I feel and think. I'm going to stop controlling the news. If they're going to hate me, they may as well hate me for who I really am."

I can't tell when somebody makes the "right" decision, but when they rely on their own inner sense, it shows. Joe had been living a lie and when he broke out of it, the change in his self-respect was a shock. When tensions are stored for many years and then released in a devastating spasm, the result can bring great pain and suffering. The trick is not to let things get so out of hand that the eventual change causes mayhem. But sometimes things do get that far and only self-compassion can let you say, "I've made mistakes . . . it's time to change."

I felt sad appreciating how hard it is to maintain a mutually satisfying relationship, how easy it is to slip off into disruption and divorce. Some have used the overwhelming rates of marital dissolution to suggest that the traditional marriage and family group are becoming obsolete. Maybe so, but even prolonged affairs seem hard these days. It's as though the world is heating up, and humans, like gas molecules, bounce around so quickly that sticking together gets harder all the time. But in any crisis, when you're hurt or when you're lost, only compassion can rescue you. When you wake up too late, when you miss the boat, it's tenderness towards yourself that can let you say, warmly and lovingly, "Okay. I didn't make it. It's all right. I'm still beautiful. One of the best things about me is how I can love myself even when I hurt so badly. Pain is painful, but it doesn't mean I'm bad."

"Maybe other people hurt like I do. Maybe they need love and comforting as much as I do. Maybe we're all in this struggle together."

Exercises

- List the six most important people in your life. Write down how you feel about your relationship with each of them as of today. Be honest—it's your own private list.

- If each of the people you wrote about could read what you've written, how would each feel? How would each react?
- Based on the above, do you have an honest relationship with each of the most important people in your life? What would you need to do or say to make it honest? Wouldn't honesty make the relationship more intimate and fulfilling?

Compassion: Some Objections

"There is luxury in self-contempt. When we demean ourselves we feel others have no right to criticize us." OSCAR WILDE

At the risk of beating it to death, we want to talk about compassion a little more, this time at those inevitable objections, the "Yes, but . . ." excuses:

"I feel good about myself . . . most of the time . . . I think."

"How can I like myself considering what I've done?"

"When I graduate (lose thirty pounds, get divorced, married, finish my therapy, make a million), then I'll have more respect for myself."

"I can't just love myself and give up on my high standards."

Can you imagine the sadness we feel on hearing such poison? "No matter how hard I try, I'll never be good enough." "Once I feel good about who I am, just the way I am, I'll stop growing, I'll never become a better person." "God will like you better in the long run, if you are dissatisfied with yourself and miserable."

What junk! But it's what many people secretly believe. Why? It's safer to keep yourself mildly unhappy. That way painful experiences can't catch you off guard: "Naahnaah! I was feeling bad anyway!" Make yourself numb and no one can hurt you anymore. Not God, the devil, your parents, your spouse, your neighbor, nor your boss. You showed them.

Great! Safe and sorry. But if you've got self-compassion, a tenderness towards the frail child within you, then you can let yourself feel deeply, even though "they" might hurt you.

Imagine yourself
touching
someone you love . . .

Don't just read this, damn it, have the guts to IMAGINE AND FEEL this situation.

You're touching someone you love—will they feel a rush of warmth from your touch? Are you enough to bring them joy? Not simply sexual pleasure, but a deep satisfaction with *your presence*. Does the thought anger or embarrass you? Why?

You won't feel good about yourself if you touch someone while feeling maybe someday you'll be a finer person. If you don't love yourself and let yourself feel SPECIAL, you'll always hold back a little, never giving enough or getting enough. Lukewarm life.

But to touch someone lovingly, while feeling good about yourself, to experience the beauty you see in another, is one of life's exquisite experiences. But to have exquisitely beautiful experiences, you also have to be willing to have exquisitely painful ones. The pain is bearable once you realize feeling hurt doesn't make you a bad person. The pain is bearable, if you recognize that life is often painful and if you accept your need for comforting.

So it is with everything you do, every waking minute. You have a choice. Either try to earn that impossible dream—"someday I'll be good enough"—wasting your life in one project after another with little real satisfaction,

OR . . .

KNOW . . . BELIEVE . . . you are fine, yes, even
MAGNIFICENT,

despite your obvious human defects,
BECAUSE *you are so aware of your humanness . . .*
or just
BECAUSE *you are alive . . .*
BECAUSE *you are unique . . .*
BECAUSE *you can choose . . .*
BECAUSE *you are sensitive enough to feel life's inevitable conflicts . . .*
BECAUSE *you try . . .*
BECAUSE *you are willing to take a chance . . .*
BECAUSE *you are willing fail and learn from each mistake . . .*
BECAUSE *you feel pain . . . jealousy . . . anger . . . loneliness . . .*
BECAUSE *you have the potential to help someone else appreciate their uniqueness and beauty . . .*
BECAUSE *you may see something no one else has noticed . . .*
BECAUSE *you are you, with all your strengths, weaknesses, fears, hopes, and limitless potential.*

Life is not something to be lived "someday." Life is NOW! (Wham! . . . Another instant just went by. No "time outs" in the big game.) Although you can change who you *will* be, who you are right now is *who you are.* Take it or leave it . . . No, *take it!* Please! Love you. Love you *right now!*

There is a paradox in all of this: who you are right at this exact instant is a different creature from who you can be. Even the next moment in time is a different world—the possible, the potential. This moment *is*. Who you are right this second is *totally impossible* to change; it's already happened. But who you are one second from now has not happened yet. You still have some choices.

For you to be able to change flexibly, you must love who you are at any instant. Otherwise you get lost in the "no man's land" between "now" and "someday." You can change in any direction you want, but at each moment you must love yourself if you want to stay free enough to change.

And you can change by living every next moment more the way you'd like. You become free to change in whatever direction you seek with self-compassion. It's so much easier to get there if you allow yourself to know and accept truly where "here" is. Self-worth comes from how you think and feel, what you do, every choice you make, every second you live.

To feel fulfilled is so simple . . . yet so difficult. Behave more in ways you respect, as opposed to ways you have acted up to now, and you will please the most crucial critic of all . . . you.

Remember the children's story in which the grandfather looks in vain for the glasses propped on his forehead? Grandpa cannot find what he wants. Why?

In the first place, he looks away rather than at himself. Secondly, his search is blurred by the lack of the very thing he seeks, his glasses. It is so for anyone. If you hope to find yourself through others, in the past or the future, you, too, will look in vain. To find yourself you must look to yourself, now.

Oriental traditions have long directed people to find their "center." Western heritage offers the same wisdom. "To thine own self be true . . . and . . . thou cannot then be false to any man."

Grandpa can't see clearly because his vision is blurred. If you experience your life feeling inadequate and defective, then you, too, will see everything that happens in a distorted way. If you feel inadequate, you may attempt to fool others with a facade or try to buy the respect you won't give yourself from them. The worst consequence is that you then believe others love your act rather than the real you. You hate yourself even more for your pretense and end up preventing yourself from accepting whatever love or respect others may offer you.

- *"But they wouldn't care for me if they knew who I really am."*
- *"But I don't feel good about me, my life or what I'm getting."*
- *"I think I'm okay, but others haven't got the message."*

Sure you'll think such thoughts, but self-compassion will save you and lead you out. If you berate yourself with such thoughts, then worries will fill your mind. That's the choice—self-pity, or saturation with love. Which will it be?

Self-pity is addicting, and so handy in times of stress: first, feel bad, then get angry at the others who caused it all. Next, take out the anger on yourself. It's like beating your kid after he gets beaten by the class bully and then feeling guilty for being so mean to him.

Self-pity is deliciously private. It feels so righteously correct. "Why is the world the way it is?" In our psychiatric practices, whenever we hear that liturgy of "poor me," we attack. I keep a stringless violin in my office. It's the perfect prop for an unsuspecting self-pity addict.

I offer it to them and say, "Ah, you're so sad. Play yourself a sad, sad song."

"But, there are no strings!" they scream.

"You can play your whiny lament, but I'll be damned if I'll listen to it!"

And that's how it is. The world keeps turning. You got hurt? Too bad. "Ohh, poor baby . . . poor, poor baby, mean world that won't play fair." Self-pity is begging for a break. It's asking for a handout of love—which our pity addict, of course, then refuses. "I didn't want a *pat on the back.*"

No, the pity addict wants to refuse any offer as if to say "The world's bad, you're bad, I'm bad, it's all bad." Great. The Depression Express. The miserable construct a secure haven of hopelessness. At the root of self-pity is an endless well of self-contempt.

Just compare:

Self-pity: "It's all hopeless, I'm sick of being used, and you make it even worse."

Self-compassion: "I hurt so much right now. I feel like things are hopeless. But please listen to me, please help me by sharing my pain."

People who *know* they deserve the best go about the business of getting it. And not with hostility but with self-assurance. They attract the respect, the admiration, love, yes, and of course, sometimes the jealousy of others. But never are they ignored!

"I go out of my way to please people. I often do without in order to help others. I try not to be mean or malicious. All I ask is a bit of the same in return . . . but what do I get!"

Please spare us the details. Choosing to sacrifice in the hope of buying some sort of pallid approval never works.

WAKE UP!!

We recommend strongly that you avoid the temptation of viewing everything you do as a sacrifice for others; they'll more than likely resent rather than appreciate the sacrifice. No one wants to be in another's debt. Sacrifice, as we noted earlier, is but a devious way to get what you want.

What a waste to spend a lifetime apologizing for the past, or making promises for the future. Zip, there goes your life. Used up in a flash. Old before you know it.

To put it succinctly: You must feel that you are at the center of *your* world, not *the* world, *your* world!

You must take responsibility to ensure satisfaction of your needs for love, security, fun and significance. You must compassionately love yourself despite, and paradoxically, because of your imperfections. *Must?* Ah, wait a minute, not really. No, it's a *must* only if you want the courage to be free.

Exercises

- List all your worst faults and weaknesses. Review them. Do you view them as evidence you may be inherently inadequate or flawed? If you knew someone else had exactly those beliefs and feelings about him or herself, would you doubt his or her worthiness as much as you doubt your own?
- Reread the "BECAUSE" list on page 166. Do most or all of those statements apply to you?
- Ask yourself: "Since I only have myself to work with, how can I improve if I won't accept how I am now?"

Courage: What Kind of Life Do You Want?

"You will never know how much you can do until you extend yourself to your limit, and you don't know that until you fall trying." ROYAL ROBBINS

Humans are naked and vulnerable creatures, babies in a swirling universe. Little wonder that much of our species' early history was made in caves. Dark, safe crevices, caves gave early humans a place to hide, a place to make myths. Today people still use caves—mental caverns of familiar beliefs and habits. You may take risks, you may try to venture into the big world, but even small hurts can often send you scampering back to the safety of your old ways.

Although the two of us may write like bearded prophets, we certainly don't have it all figured out. The whole mess called life is pretty cloudy to us too. Over the years, however, it gradually became clear to us that courage, like self-compassion, is a pivotal issue. But why "courage?" Why that word? Courage seems so out of fashion, a leftover from the stiff upper lip crowd of Victorian England, or a scrap of rusting armor from medieval Europe . . . why bring up such an outdated concept, a relic from the heroic ages?

In stumbling along, looking for what we're trying to say, we often write notes to each other. From shared thoughts grow new ideas. Courage became a central concept for us around the time I wrote this note:

COURAGE AS THE CHOICE TO BE VULNERABLE

"I'm coming back down out of the mountains, traveling toward the Pacific, and I smell the faint traces of ocean still far away. This has been a strange trip for me, for I have tried not to have any particular plan of what I am doing or where

I am going, but rather to flow with its direction. At times this has meant sitting around the same place for three or four days and, at other times, frantically trying to cover as much highway as I can.

"And, in giving up preconceptions and destinations, a flood of thoughts have come to me. The first is the issue of *courage*.

"I had a fascinating experience while driving. I stopped at a cafe in a small town for some orange juice. Perhaps it's my urban arrogance, but I was bored as I entered the cafe, only dimly aware of the other people inside. Cross-country travel fosters impatience and cynicism. I was tired and wanted only to get something to drink and go.

"But the woman at the counter suddenly caught my attention. I studied her as I waited for my order. She was in her sixties, incongruously dressed like a teenage soda fountain waitress of forty years ago. I was struck by the simplicity of her face, beaming ingenuously as though she were fifteen and at work for the first day.

"While emptying the contents of my pockets in search of some loose change, I dumped out a few pieces of Canadian currency. She picked up one of the coins and looked at it with a mixture of amazement, delight and reverence, wordlessly saying, 'Isn't this amazing? Aren't there some wonderful things in this world?' I, too, became amazed, but not by her Pollyannaish naiveté. No, I was moved by her softness, her vulnerability, her readiness to be touched by the intensity of experience. It's not sophisticated or hip to be so soft. But she radiated an innocence that most lose at childhood's end . . . that same grace we 'complicated' adults forever long to regain.

"I had for so many years tried to become invulnerable, to be Superman himself and have the bullets of pain bounce harmlessly off my chest. I thought that 'strength' meant 'hard.' And I believed that I could think or do something that would protect me from ever getting hurt. Some magic, some formula, some trick that would make me immune.

"But here was this old woman, who didn't worry about losing her balance, or how she looked—she joyfully gave her heart to the moment. Ah, what a gift . . . to jump courageously into the void of the instant. I am sure her life had its tragedies, but she let herself fly into that moment anyway. Bliss with a Canadian quarter.

"It takes courage to be vulnerable. Courage to feel. Courage to love yourself. Courage to let go and be blown around, be moved. Courage to face life's whirlwind of contradictions. Courage just to be.

"People get incredibly hung up trying to protect themselves from every risk. They buy so much insurance against every exigency that they can't afford to live. In the end, carefulness is futile. You can't protect yourself against every form of danger. There's just too much.

"On the other hand, courage isn't blindly jumping off a cliff or anything so melodramatic. People tend to worry about what courage looks like (would it be courageous to . . .?), instead of what it feels like. What it looks like when someone else does it, is never as important as what *you* feel like when *you* do it.

"Just as any force is defined by the resistance it overcomes, we could define valor by the fear it surmounts. And again this goes back to what's inside. Ultimately, you have a sense of when you're being cowardly or over-careful or any other cop-out. Courage isn't for somebody else, for medals, applause or moral debts—courage is what, at that moment, feels most right for you. Not just "situational ethics," but what feels right in your heart. The word 'courage' originated from the French word 'coeur'—the 'heart'. Courage truly is 'of the heart.'

COURAGE AS REFUSING TO BE FEAR'S SLAVE

" 'Cowards die many times before their deaths; The valiant never taste of death but once.' What does that mean? The valiant are never afraid? I doubt it. No, I think it just describes a different relationship with fears, hopes and experiences.

"Instead of frantic and desperate moves, courage feels like squarely facing who you are. Being vulnerable to your own humanity. Sure the valiant get scared (courage is meaningless in the absence of fear and danger), but they don't say to themselves, 'Oh, no! I'm afraid! I give up!' Instead, the courageous say, 'Okay, I'm scared to death. Now which do I choose? In my heart, which looks best to me?'

"That's the courageous choice. Will I decline because the risk is more than I want to handle right now, or would I be untrue to myself if I gave up? The valiant at least pause, agonize over the alternatives, then choose. It's not an easy choice. And, no matter what you pick, you might later wish you had gone another way. Hard decisions are just that—hard decisions. But courageously facing the choices brings freedom from the tyranny of fears. Taking on your fears brings the light and peace you seek.

"Facing fears relieves the burden of worrying about what you should be doing. Or at least it allows you to relate worries in a different manner. Through the willingness to stand off and observe yourself, you become free to think new thoughts, to flow into new ways. The lady with the quarter didn't immerse herself in worrying 'Will they think I'm an old fool if I get too excited?' No, even if she had that worry, she let it simply be present in her mind, neither panicking nor overcompensating. It is as if she said to herself 'Yes, I am human and I fear rejection, but I choose to take the chance of immersing myself in this joy.' She let herself feel and, by the courage of that act, strengthened herself.

"Humans fear being humiliated and overwhelmed with feeling more than they fear death. They fear feeling anything too intensely, as if by pretending to be half asleep you can protect yourself against harm. Carried to the extreme it yields a lifetime cowardice. That's the coward's hope: If I am half-dead, half-gone already, maybe I'll have less to lose. Being fully awake does raise the stakes. The more conscious you are, the more hurt you'll feel.

"Yet if you give yourself to the intensity of an experience you can rise to a higher level, a place where nothing can crush you. You prevail by resiliency rather than rigidity—a profound paradox to be sure. By dismantling your defenses against fears, by removing your self-imposed blinders, your spirit gains the strength to become indestructible.

"There is no objective standard for courage. The ultimate judgment can only be made within one's self. 'Is this really right for me? Am I really standing up for what I need?' The right answer is never clear—it's far easier to tell when you lie than when you finally speak the truth. And life doesn't seem to hold many decisive battles. If anything, each one is only an inch gained or lost, progress is slow. Winning or losing isn't the point, though. What's important is *how* you fight the battle.

"Courage is daring to ask hard questions, to look at the void and emptiness in the face and feel the imponderables. Not to have to reduce things to pat answers. To strive for a balance between head and heart. Courage is daring to feel the incredible vulnerability of being human.

"Cowardice is shutting off half of what you see in order to make life simple. Such lying to yourself is like cheating at solitaire—what good is there in winning? For the petty satisfaction of having things work out neatly, you have to be willing to ignore the fact that cheating robs you of peace. Courage means to see and feel eternal questioning and agonizing uncertainty. It means being open, ready and willing to discard all that one believes rather than to be a slave to our habitual beliefs.

"This leads to purity and self-reliance. Courage is required because you can never completely count on anyone else or anything else. A fulfilling life is largely a self-help, do-it-yourself exercise. No cop-out philosophy will ever take the weight of existence off you. Since you are here, you might as well be here in your totality."

COURAGE AS FINALLY GETTING FED UP

After that note, we began thinking about courage more and more. It surprised us, for character, choice and the psychology of will fell out of fashion a hundred years ago. But as we looked closer, this relic, courage, seemed to have a fresh message for people of today.

People don't change when they feel good. They change when they're fed up. When things are going all right, you tend to do what you've been doing all along. Pain pushes you to those crucial turning points: finally to stand up for yourself, finally to allow intimacy, finally to feel love for yourself, finally to throw away the bottle and mean it. You hurt, hurt, hurt. Then, finally, you choose. It's that adverb *finally*. Enough is enough! Anger can be a loving and encouraging force.

If "coeur" or "of the heart," is part of courage, then perhaps the other part is rage. Some obstacles are so high, or so thick, that you can't surmount them by calm choice. It takes determination, dedication or perhaps an internal war of morals.

It's as though a vital part of courage is the act of "drawing the line." If you give in and give in and give in and never say, "No, that's enough!" then you are a slave. Free people draw the line. There has to be some limit somewhere, some point of no return. If you capitulate forever, you ultimately lose everything that's important in life.

The American Revolution is an excellent example of people getting fed up. If only a disgruntled few are fed up, it is impossible to push a country to rebellion. But if substantial numbers are dissatisfied, one more insult will trigger the explosion. People will do the same within themselves. If small parts of you are fed up, no revolution ensues. But if enough of you is bothered, you can lead yourself to change.

By developing self-compassion, you are in essence learning how to take public opinion polls within yourself. You can check the consensus to determine when action is needed. To be sure, there are times where slow, peaceful change works the best. But at other times, movement can only be accomplished by revolt.

Tom was fat as a boy—a miserable and lonely fat. He was ridiculed for his roundness and, through the strict cruel rules of adolescent society, found it impossible to find a girlfriend.

One day, after a shower, he caught a glimpse of himself in a full-length mirror. Rather than hatred or contempt, he felt an overwhelming flood of anger. "Look at that disgusting fat. You're not going to spend the rest of your life like that!"

People are always tempted to beat and humiliate themselves whenever they suffer. Self-deprecation is socially acceptable. But what Tom did was to say to himself, in effect, "I respect, love and cherish you, and I'm not going to let this happen." He became a general for his own revolutionary army. He finally had had enough and led the fight to change.

COURAGE AS RESPONSIBILITY

Your life is your responsibility. *You* belong to *you*.

For many people, the concept of owning oneself is an alien thought. American culture seems to teach obligation to others, rather than responsibility to oneself. The lessons begin early. Children are usually treated as though they are property, "my kids." Order and commandments come next: "You have to! You better not! You must!" Such commands teach habits of guilt. Natural self-reliance is unlearned, and in its place grow rationalizations, excuses and pathetic cop-outs.

Children are stormy clouds of impulses. It's hardly surprising that parents often train by containment. Teaching responsibility from the start is much more complicated. "How would you deal with this situation, Johnny?" takes time to ask. "Do it my way," is so much easier. The fallout from child-rearing practices is part of why adolescents can be so hard to deal with. They are asked to make the sudden transition from being parental possessions to becoming people in their own right. Some can't quite make the jump. Often the result is more humans who are to live with nagging doubts, feeling "wrong" or "not good enough."

Learning responsibility is not learning how to get a pat on the head—that's learning servility. For many, the habit of looking outside for guidance combines with the natural human desire for attention. They become obedience junkies. Rather than take responsibility for everything they think, feel and do, people often look for something else to run their lives. Patterns may seem varied, but are actually equivalent. Adherence to a cult, passive dependence on a spouse, reflexive adherence to social fads, or even surrender to the guaranteed routine of drug addiction are some examples. In each of these ways, people give up self-ownership. They get cheated.

Ed, an accountant, had been raising his three kids since his wife, Jean, died of cancer ten years before. He had several relationships over those years, but never remarried for the fear things would not work out. He felt somehow responsible for his wife's death. He believed that if he hadn't worked so much or had only earned more, or if they had moved, or if something—she might still be alive. Since a new wife would ultimately be someone else to worry about, he played it safe and stayed single.

On his fifty-sixth birthday his two oldest boys gave him a present—a rafting trip with them on the Colorado River. Ed liked the outdoors, used to camp and fish years ago, but had never considered something as far-fetched as white water rafting. But he went anyway and had a wonderful time.

"I went half expecting to be cold or bored, but I loved it. And something happened to me while I was there. At one point we hit some really rough water and I was hanging on for dear life. I looked over at my eighteen-year-old, Eddie, and he was yelling and laughing with joy. I started shouting with him, both of us whooping and screaming, and I suddenly realized I don't *have* to worry. It's not up to *me* to fix the world. It's not my fault when things beyond my control go wrong. I'm just here along with everyone else.

"Before that moment I'd always assumed that I *had* to take care of things—that I would be held responsible when things went wrong. That may have made me a good accountant, but as a person I was miserable. Now I only accept responsibility for my own actions. I care what happens, but I'll be damned if I'll waste my life just being afraid. And you know what? The woman I've been seeing over the last year, well . . . I think I'm getting up the guts to ask her the big question. Nothing's worth staying afraid and lonely for."

Imagine you're about to drop dead right now. Did you get the kind of life you wanted? No? Who will you complain to? If you demand a refund on your life, do you think you'll ever get it?

If you're not getting what you want nobody's going to get it for you. Life's a car you've been given. Where you drive it is largely up to you.

But listen to how people hide. Listen to those all too common complaints:

"I have everything; why do I feel empty?"

"I feel used, not respected, not loved."

"Why do I drink so much?" (or often)

"Why does she/he?"

"I feel depressed. Nothing seems to make any difference."

"I can't seem to make a decision as to what to do."

"Why do I become upset so easily, even at trivial things?"

"I did everything to please him, now he's sleeping with another woman. It's humiliating!"

Note that every one of these protests implies that some thing has happened to the person. Each one has been possessed by outside forces. A demon perhaps? ("The devil made me do it!") For although these complaints sound reasonable, they smell of cop-outs and self-deception. The ultimate question remains the same—"What are *you* going to *do* about it?"

Couples almost always come in to marital therapy pointing at their partners. "If only they would treat me better, everything would change." But change begins within. To change "them" requires that you first change your habits toward them. The common complainers miss this point. They take no risks. They no longer try new thoughts, new dreams, new experiences. They live in caves. It's hardly surprising that for them, life just doesn't "make it." They feel no enthusiasm, certainly no passion. Life without strong feeling can be pretty empty. Even hate is more invigorating than petulant resentment.

Sam, an executive in a large aircraft firm, decided to try giving up his self-imposed anesthesia. Booze kept him numb and he agreed to try "going dry," even though he insisted he wasn't an alcoholic.

"Okay, Doc, I won't drink for at least three months. You say that I might feel reborn. You say that my three drinks a day means I'm always either partially intoxicated or coming down from last night's drinking. You say I no longer know what it's like to be just me, Sam, rather than Sam drinking, or withdrawing, or hiding behind his booze, okay, we'll see!"

Three months later he reported the second of two recent temper outbursts. The first was at his stepson, the second was at his wife. For a change they were only verbal tirades, with no physical violence. "I was furious at Mary and said so, I told off Jimmy too! I was wrong by the way—foolishly jealous on one hand and overprotective of our boy on the other.

"But it was *my* stupid anger. It was *my* jealousy and *my* overprotection. Not the booze talking but ME! All my life I was afraid to get angry at people I love and need, so I would wait till I was loaded. Then no one blamed me. It was the booze talking. What baloney! I've lived my life like I was dancing in a room lined with mirrors. No more! I'm not just the person reflected off my wife, my boss or anyone else. I'll risk being me, thinking what I think, even though half the time I'm just a narrow-minded hypocritical bigot. But feeling what I feel, even my stupid jealousy . . . and doing what I do. Even growing this ridiculous beard for the first time in my life is worth it. I DID IT! ME!

"Doc, I feel liberated. If it weren't for you, I might have died never living my life."

A very generous compliment, but Sam deserves the cheers for how beautifully courageous he became. He went from being a typical executive drunk to becoming part of that valiant minority willing to live a life of change and responsibility. He learned to wake himself to his own courage and beauty. The risk, responsibility, credit and rewards are his, not ours. We can take credit only if we do as Sam did and does.

A good step is to rid your vocabulary of "should," "ought to," "must," and "have to" for one month. Instead, use words that admit you do what you choose. "I will," "I want to," "I'm going to." You can take each action out of choice and commitment, or you can hide behind the presence of ineptitude and helplessness. Remember, even not choosing is a choice. As long as you remain conscious, choice and responsibility will confront you.

You begin dying from the moment you are born. Yet you can choose to be reborn at any and every moment before death. Each change is a "little birth"—an end to the old and a chance at the new. What survives is your spirit, your willingness to grow. You can live far beyond mortality, through your creative efforts, children, students, art, your good works, and the relationships you establish. If you define yourself narrowly, you waste your life fighting to defend a small garrison. Courage looks toward the bigger picture, the struggle to transcend mere existence. As Jean Cocteau observed, the most sublime creation of all is making one's life an art.

COURAGE AS RISKING

All too often humans indulge in the cowardice of being too careful, selling out for a promise of security. And they get cheated. You've seen it. The futility of using one's job as a way to hide. "I am a lawyer" (doctor, manager, etc.) as if to say, "I am a lawyer and nothing else." Or the futility of seeking meaning through a spouse's accomplishments—the "doctor's wife syndrome." (Also seen in the spouses of politicians, business executives, ministers, lawyers, entertainers; indeed in any wife or husband who believes that vicariously enjoying a spouse's success is enough to make their life more meaningful. Pathetic!)

It's futile to live for some future time when things will be different, believing that as soon as "I'm older," "richer," "more educated," (or in a more sophisticated vein, "when I finish my therapy") then all will be well; dream on, for these are but futile delusions.

It's also futile to live in some past phase of your life when "I was younger," "stronger," "my spouse was living," or before "my marriage," "my divorce," "my surgery," "my heart attack," "I lost my job," "the children were born." These are just more hopeless dead ends.

Charles Dickens depicts the tragic figure of Lady Havisham, sitting in her bedroom in full bridal regalia decades after rejection by her would-be groom. Her monumental cowardice keeps her afraid to face her life as it is. If you want, you too can have dreams and cobwebs, fantasies about what was or might be. Thomas Wolfe made the same point in *You Can't Go Home Again.* An old vaudeville joke says the same thing in yet another way: "Your money or your life," the robber demands. "Take my life, I'm saving my money for my old age," the over-cautious hero replies.

Incredibly, many people continue their old life-styles and habits even if they feel miserable, lonely, bored, inadequate, or abused. Why? Because habit is an easy place to hide.

A woman marries several alcoholics sequentially, insisting she never suspected.

A man spends his whole life working 60 to 100 hours a week, trying to get rich. Why? Because he watched his father slave his life away, never enjoying himself, dying while working, and he doesn't want this to happen to himself!

Others attempt to live cautiously in the safety of established patterns. They do not feel fulfilled, but they have found a formula for avoiding failure. This is the living death—when security becomes the overwhelming consideration. People do not live by security alone.

Life has inevitable risks. Heart attacks, auto accidents, tax assessment, business problems—every conceivable kind of bad news waits to spring upon you without warning. You can't count on your next breath. So it's hard to play the gamble of life. It's a difficult balance. At times you might put too much on the next spin of the wheel, and at other times you might feel so hurt and cheated that you want to stop playing forever. But the goal, in a sense, is to find a style of playing the game of life that keeps your hand in without keeping yourself out.

When you reach beyond the safety and familiarity of habits and behave in any way different from routine, you experience some tension. It may be mild, a slight tightness in the chest; or more pronounced, a rigid heart rate, nausea, diarrhea, fainting, or even panic. If you think about the possible consequences of a new change too long, fear may overwhelm you. The risk-taking in life is very much like investing money—the potential returns reflect in part the degree of risk. The higher the stakes, the more frightening the game.

And the clock keeps on ticking. Time accelerates with age, of course; nothing can be done about that. Yet, two minutes in a roller coaster are far more intense than eight hours of boring meetings. Variety prolongs time. Change wakes you. Share time with different people, in different places, doing different things, and you can experience a week in just one day. Times of high emotional intensity, as in passionate lovemaking, can last far longer and fulfill far more than the same physical acts without passion. Perceived time is an elastic commodity that depends on your age (uncontrollable) and on how you consume it (controllable). The intensity dial is in your grasp. You are given time—how much you make of it is up to you.

Human beings need some stress. They were designed by evolution to survive in the stress of food chain competition. A certain amount of pressure is necessary for health. Of course, too much stress, like too much sound, is bad. But no stress, like total silence, makes for imbalance.

Many people try to insure themselves against every possible danger. They want never to hurt, never to be scared, never to be lonely. So they adopt a formula of life whereby they live for material goods, feel as little as possible and hide behind old habits. Yet that hunger for natural stresses remains. Gradually they fill the gap with internally manufactured stress—worries and fears.

Of course they don't consciously say to themselves, "I'm going to adopt a life-style which will minimize my chance-taking, even though I'm aware it will give me an empty and boring life." They just grow up that way. But you can say to yourself, "How much chance-taking is right for me? What kinds of stresses and risks will help me on my path?" Some may find physical stress helpful—sports, exercise, or even fasting. For others, the answer may be skydiving, motorcycle racing or passionate interpersonal relationships. For still others, it will be retreat to a monastery and a courageous journey through the turbulence within. Life is a full time job: to fill one's needs, to find what stresses and risks fit best, and to relax and play once in a while.

BOREDOM IS THE LEGACY OF FEAR.

Risk-taking is a major part of the cure, so don't hope that somehow you'll be able to avoid it. Chronic capitulation to fear only insures mediocrity. The life-style we are advocating is one where you ask yourself for each new thing you try, "What's the risk and what's the possible payoff?" It's an attitude whereby you accept taking chances as part of what you're doing on this planet. Not necessarily crazy risks—if people get too extreme they don't hang around long enough to learn anything new. Careful, measured increases in risk seem to be the best way to enhance your life. For example, when you're learning how to ride a bicycle, you don't start out in heavy automobile traffic. Instead, you pick a street where, if you do fall down, at least you won't get run over.

So explore and experiment. Look for that balance between taking suicidal chances on one hand and running away from risk on the other. Some days will feel right for risks, others will feel better if you play it safe. Experiment to find out what's best for that moment. Since anything new will always be stressful, judge yourself by your efforts. No matter what you try, there's probably somebody else who does it better. The point is to find those things that let you feel exhilarated and alive. The point is to learn to season life's banquet with those redolent spices of stress and risk.

COURAGE AS LOSING YOURSELF

Courage is *not* a feeling. Courage is jumping off into the void, risking the unknown and untried. Courage doesn't develop. Courage is *letting yourself go for it*, despite your fears. Desperation and inspiration from others help. But there's no sense in waiting for it to happen. Courage doesn't come to you. You must do something despite your fears. Only then do you become courageous.

The ultimate experiences in any life are those that transcend day-to-day existence. The sweet, rare times when involvement in an activity leads to a fulfillment beyond one's wildest dreams. Artists and the devoutly religious base their lives on this high, but anybody can get it. You can have it with someone you love or even someone you hate. It can come from cooking or woodworking or just walking.

It's an experience that's like being lifted up and swept away, forgetting worries and self-consciousness. It's been called "merging," "flowing," "satori" and countless other names. Like love, however, it's one of those things that has to be experienced to be believed. Any human endeavor, from checking out groceries to tuning an engine, can be either performed in this creative state or reduced to a perfunctory routine.

One of the things we've often seen are people sitting around waiting for "it" to happen, as though they'll suddenly get a membership badge they can show other people to say, "See, I rate. I've got 'it' too." But, like anything else done primarily for the benefit of the audience, it's a performance destined to flop. If you are standing on a hilltop looking out over the countryside and suddenly have an experience of flowing and being part of nature, but then try to condense that experience into a tourist snapshot for the folks back home, you'll lose it in an instant. It can't be canned. You can experience it, but you can't sell it.

And, in a sense, that's the greatest risk of all. You can't possess it. You can't prove it. You can only be it. You can let yourself go in what you do, or you can hold back. You can strive to immerse yourself and take the risk of losing your identity in what you're doing. Or, you can stiffly straight-arm your life to keep it at a safe distance. You can try to reduce everything into explainable experiences. You can label and classify all that you see in a desperate attempt to stay in control. Or you can stop strutting and fretting and let go.

Fundamental to this process of gaining courage is the issue of losing control. There is a paradox in it: "The highest form of control is when one surrenders all control." It's similar to the idea that you never really own anything unless you can give it away. When trying to learn something, if you struggle to stay in control, you learn slowly, if at all. You'll fall down more frequently when learning to ride a bicycle, if you keep struggling for control, stiffly directing your arms and legs with commandments on how to behave. Instead, you can surrender the myth of being in charge, surrender your separateness and let the bicycle become part of you.

People learn best by losing themselves. If you can be strong enough to just forget about who you are for a moment instead of taking yourself so seriously; if you can forget about what you think, believe and want; if you can take the risk of forgetting yourself—you can learn with the grace of a blossoming flower. It takes the highest courage to use this self-surrender in any activity. But the rewards are equally high. You can realize a sense of rightness, peace and, most importantly, your full powers to create and grow.

This is the advanced course of acting *as if.* Instead of pretending that one can ride a bicycle, one gives oneself to the activity. Rather than trying, one just lets go. Technical mastery is a means, not an end. It requires a tremendous amount of dedication. The reward is then being able to let yourself go. Unless you have this experience of letting go, unless there is some area in your life where you have struggled through the technical mastery enough to give you that ability to flow, you'll never believe that such things happen.

If you want to play handball, for example, there are some technical skills that are useful to learn. But ultimately your game is the creative way in which you string the basic elements together. If you see them only as separate and isolated elements, you'll never have an exciting game. You'll just be another robot trying to imitate somebody else.

What kind of life do you want? How courageous will you be? The choice is yours.

Creativity is a fascinating topic. Throughout recorded history people have studied the very creative to find out their secrets. The gifted people themselves have reflected at times upon their own experiences and attempted to find some sort of formula. But there is none. Creativity isn't a step-by-step process.

More than any other group in present-day American society, athletes seem to be conscious of how creativity is learned. "Concentration" is the word most often used to describe that state, which is the essential prerequisite for peak performance. A good game can often be differentiated from a bad game by the degree of concentration. This state of concentration seems to be a suspension of doubt and self-consciousness, a way of clearing the mind of all distracting rubble and trash.

Some Eastern philosophies have made this state of mind their primary focus. Indeed, the concept of acting without self-conscious thought was probably first crystallized by the samurai swordsmen of medieval Japan. Using some of the philosophical concepts of their time, they determined that the best way to beat one's adversary in a duel was to fight without the delay of thinking. Polished technical skill was a prerequisite, but the actual moves were dictated by feeling rather than thought. They were able to develop a state of mind that minimized the clutter of such thoughts as "Oh, no, is he going to try to attack me from the left or the right?" by refining their intuitive sense through the constant discipline of practice duels. Instead, poised and balanced, the samurai could respond as if he were at one with his opponent, as if he knew each moment what would happen next.

The body learns instead of the mind. In other words, when you are learning something, it's worthwhile to turn off, unplug, or tune out the mind for a little while. You can't tell the mind to shut up because it will just talk back to you. You can quietly note what it's telling you, then concentrate on another level. Like the samurai, Zen archers of the Far East gained their discipline by striving for the feeling of rightness in the shot and by focusing on the target. If the shot was right, hitting the target came naturally. Hitting the bull's-eyes on tiny targets in darkened rooms is part of what Zen archers did, but not for the sake of hitting targets. Their purpose was a form of meditation, a quest for that experience of rightness.

If you want to learn something new, why not concentrate on getting that right feeling that is true to yourself? Take the risk of letting go of the precious little control you've struggled to gain, of letting go enough to immerse yourself in what you're doing. Then do it.

Sure, natural or genetic endowment, study and practice and even luck all play important parts in creativity, but ultimately what is necessary is giving oneself over to what one does. We like to think of it as a two-phase process—

first, you immerse yourself in *creative action*, you let go and do it. Second, *critical review.* You mentally stand back a little, take some distance and weigh the results. "Did it get me closer to where I want to be?" Like a painter before the canvas, first there is a brush stroke that occurs in the trance-like state, then a step back to gain a new perspective and gaze on the outcome. These two phases flow into each other, but in a sense represent separate states of mind—creative action and critical review.

The point is that many people become preoccupied with achieving a particular result, such as fame, fortune, approval from others or even something as evanescent as happiness. But if you get locked into outcomes, you'll never be able to let yourself go long enough to experience intensely. First give it a good try, then think and review. Don't try to review while you're trying to create. Edit after you invent. If your awareness is focused on the outcome, you won't be able to let yourself go.

Ultimately it comes down to what kind of value system you want. You must choose between "All that counts is winning" or "To try is to succeed." The creative state requires forgetting about winning and focusing on trying. Anyway, playing just to win is a dead end. In the big scheme of existence, what game ever matters that much in and of itself? What could be worth the brutal cutthroat craziness of forcing yourself to play only to win? All humans really want is to feel good, to feel right, to find peace; they just get tricked by the myth that winning brings all those things automatically.

One of the most common reasons why people try to control everything else but don't take control of themselves and don't accept responsibility for everything they do is fear of failure, fear of being a loser. Only by giving yourself credit for *every effort* can you even find the courage to immerse yourself in creative action.

If you live by the principle that to try is to succeed, that to give your best effort is what it's all about, you can gain this mastery and peace. With this attitude you can slip more easily into cycles of creating and reviewing. Good results are only a fringe benefit which may come and go, but what you do with yourself is always in your control.

A farmer for fifteen years has always managed to produce a good living for himself and his family. He has never asked for a handout or special treatment. To him, welfare is an obscenity. Independence, hard work, "As ye sow, so shall ye reap" are his guiding principles.

One year, despite his fine efforts, a freak storm wipes out his entire crop. His reserves are inadequate to meet his financial obligations. Reluctantly he goes on welfare and accepts disaster aid. Both are "handouts." He feels he is a failure. Do you agree?

We hope not. If you agree, then we understand why you fear change, risk and experimentation. Fear of failure must paralyze you. Letting your self-respect depend on results makes you a slave to every whim of chance. Break free. If you're going to love yourself, love yourself no matter what. Actually what we are saying is not all that new: "It's not whether you win or lose; it's how you play the game." But that noble tradition has been dying a slow death. Coach Vince Lombardi often said: "Winning isn't everything but trying is." Yet didn't you think he said "Winning is everything"? This common misquote shows a tragic truth about our social values. People hear what they want to hear.

Be a strong coach for yourself. Encourage your own efforts. If you set a goal but don't reach it, you have a choice.

You could put yourself down:

"I *knew* I couldn't. Maybe some people can change but I can't. My childhood screwed me up so badly, I just *keep* making the same mistakes over and over again. I'll *never* get it together."

Or you can cheer yourself on: "I tried magnificently. I'm proud of me. I was truly immersed in the effort. I failed in my attempt, I accept that, I accept the pain. I remain proud and love myself for my courage."

What is success? Who measures your value, you or your audience? Whom are you trying to impress? Your parents, living or dead, your spouse, your neighbors or that mythical, vague "they" out there you learned to dress up for on Sundays and holidays so as not to embarrass your family?

The myth, the cruel hoax perpetrated by schools, the media and some churches defines success as a place, a status, a thing, a level to be attained. Choose a career, work at it until you achieve "success." Then others will respect you and you will be happy . . . ridiculous!

Few experiences are more resonantly hollow than being hailed as successful, only to feel undeserving of the admiring horde. You need only look at the catalog of superstar entertainers whose lives prematurely ended in an agony of self-destruction. You play first and ultimately to an audience of *one*. Disappoint that one and you are bankrupt.

Cowardice stems from grasping desperately for a success you feel you don't deserve. Learn to lose yourself in your efforts. Learn to let go and you will have gained true courage.

"What else can I do?"

Strive for as much courage as you can. But don't work yourself to the bone. Play is a vital need too. Don't wait for neat formulas, tricks guaranteed to solve your problems. Some days will be hard and some easy no matter how clever you are. Let go with love and energy will fill you. Success is courageously living each moment as fully as possible. Success means the courage to flow, struggle, change and grow. Success means being true to you, being the person you admire.

Exercises

- Have you ever done something despite being afraid to? Think back to all the things you've learned to do, all the risks you've taken, physical and emotional. List eight of them. Every time you took a chance despite your fears you were courageous, you changed. Everyone has the capacity for change, because everyone experiences fear yet still takes chances.
- Sometimes it's easier to take risks with the support of others. Sometimes it's easier to do alone. Which is usually better for you?
- List three things that would increase your self-respect this week if you had the courage to try them. Is your major concern for not doing them based on your fear of other people's opinions? Are you worried about the result of taking such risks?

Courage: Dealing With Others

Once committed to courageously loving yourself you still face several choices. "Should I live in isolation, like a hermit in the wilderness, or involve myself with other people?" "How much of my thoughts, feelings, hopes and dreams will I share?" "How much of my day-to-day life will I share?" "How much should I negotiate and compromise?" For that's the rub; how can you maintain personal integrity and your self-respect while fulfilling your needs for love and security?

This is only one way we know of—finding the courage to risk the trial and error of relationships. And it is a risk; no matter how loving, reasonable or pure you are, you can't govern exactly how the people you care about will act toward you. Once again, you're only in control of your efforts, not the results. And the essential, unadvisable risk is that once you have a fine and beautiful love, once you have a relationship you cherish, you suddenly have something to lose. There is no way out of that vulnerability—you can kid yourself all you want, but the person you love may get fed up with you, run away with somebody else, drop dead, or just disappear. Remember, there are no guarantees. Even if everything goes fine, one of the two of you, unfortunately, will eventually die.

How you handle your love relationships determines how good you feel. Humans need love and attention from other humans as much as they need food. If they don't get it, they get irritable and desperate.

So we've decided to devote a couple of chapters to tasks that require great courage: dealing with the people who are closest to you: close friends, lovers, spouses, children, and families in general. We share these observations with the hope it will provoke you to consider how much you've been getting from the people in your life.

What we are really proposing is a sort of power politics for love, some guidelines on how to get intimate relationships to work. Some of these ideas may seem a bit radical, but we base them on what works.

We offer guidelines for those who feel little or no intimacy in their relationships . . . for those who want to live together and share more than expenses . . . for those who feel ignored or oppressed by their partners . . . for those who are never sure of anyone's love . . . for anyone willing to look beyond fairy tales.

First, let's debunk a few destructive myths:

"If she (he) really loved me, she'd (he'd) understand without my having to explain."

"If he (she) really loved me, he (she) would do it for me without my asking."

"If we really love each other, we shouldn't have to argue or hassle."

"She (he) should know I love her (him) without my having to show or tell her (him) all the time."

"Real love is when you know that he'll (she'll) be there no matter what!"

"We know each other so well that we know what the other is thinking and feeling without having to make sure."

"Real love is forever."

"Love is never having to say you're sorry."

GARBAGE!

ALL GARBAGE!

As with all myths, the tiny grain of truth has been buried by appealing lies. These notions of automatic love are a pathetic hoax. "But I thought if you loved me, you were supposed to . . ." Each part of a relationship takes doing, nothing is automatic. Love makes some aspects easier, but the more honest people are and the more they change and grow, the more effort is needed to sustain the relationship. Mutual support is the reward brought by a growing relationship. Ignoring anything and taking anything for granted can kill the deepest love.

People often have such a hard time getting a grip on themselves that they tend to tighten their grip too severely on those they love. They believe if they hold on to others tightly enough, they will suddenly become more secure. The paradox is that it works just the other way around. If you force love to mean there must be no disagreement or anger between you and those you love, you strangle them, yourself and the love you have. Only by allowing the inevitable flow of harmonious struggle, of opposition and balance, can you make growth possible.

Everyone wants to feel appreciated and respected. But the price is the courage to risk confronting the inevitable pain that comes in any relationship. If you focus on your weaknesses, your pessimism will become boundless. You may hope someone's love will save you, but if you won't love yourself, how can you ever have the courage to risk letting anyone get close to you? ("What if they ever found that I . . .?") But if you have the courage to be who you are, to take the risk of intimacy, you may find that freedom from nagging loneliness is a rich life indeed!

All people sense their own inadequacy, their own deficiencies. Some, of course, feel the weight far more than others. Some freely admit shortcomings. Some deny their flaws even to themselves . . . except on lonely, sleepless nights. Some expand concerns about themselves into an entire self-denigrating self-concept: hopeless, helpless, worthless, unlovable. This miserable (but safe) identity is free of the risk of failing.

What has this to do with love and courage? Ultimately the fear of intimacy is based on fear of two kinds of losses. The first is loss of another person just when one has risked the vulnerability of loving and needing her or him intensely. The second kind of loss is loss of one's self, one's separateness, one's familiar habitual identity. There's no way around it—to be in an intimate partnership, you have to be willing to change and be changed. You can't blend with someone else and remain as you are.

If your early family life was not in a caring and understanding home, then you probably had little experience with the trust necessary for intimacy. The less you've had reason to trust, the more courage you need in order to learn to trust someone enough to be intimate.

In an intimate relationship, the risk of loss of partner and loss of familiar identity are both *real*. The first is painful and sad, the second is frightening. The less you feel warm tender love for yourself, the less you feel yourself to be a deserving part of humanity and the more devastating the threats of loss are.

With severe self-doubt you may easily interpret loss of the person you love as evidence of personal inadequacy. And the less you trust yourself, the harder it is to trust anyone else enough to let go of the only identity you've ever known.

These are the major fears that stand in the way of risking intimacy. But if intimacy is an end product, how does one get there? The answer is easy to relate, but hard to do: Expose to your partner *exactly* how you are feeling about yourself and about him or her.

If you share that, if you share your private thoughts and feelings and listen to and care about your partner's as well, you *will* become intimate. And by exposing yourself you will step off into the void. You will be in less control, but you will be confronting the two losses.

So we have come full circle. To love intimately, you must be willing to love yourself. Only if you can compassionately love, understand and cherish yourself despite your weaknesses can you have the courage to let others know you as you truly are.

And the more you have the courage to let others know you as you truly are, the more you will find yourself comfortable with the experience of loving yourself. Loving cycles (like vicious cycles) feed off themselves and have their own momentum. No wonder it's frightening to let yourself go.

Many love partnerships in trouble fall into this basic style: "We never fight." Pleasant, polite and passionless. The dissatisfaction and resentments are never openly acknowledged. How can each feel they are cherished, despite (or even better, *because of*) their imperfections, if problems are ignored?

The relationships of these "diplomats" are careful, superficial, and civil. They avoid direct confrontations; an effective attitude if battles are to be avoided at any cost. But how many real-life diplomats feel profound love for one another? Passion just isn't part of their game. Protocol and tact are great for the State Department but lousy for love.

Love relationships force you to juggle the chance of being rejected against the chance of losing your autonomy—a delicate balance indeed. Stay too far away, you'll be lonely; too close and you might become hopelessly dependent. That's the problem—fitting liberation and intimacy into one lifetime.

Every day we see people who want magic, who want to love and be loved but don't want to risk hurting or being hurt.

But
loving
is
risky
business.

Another "sick couple" pattern is: "We never stop fighting." This style of constant warfare is dramatized powerfully in Albee's *Who's Afraid of Virginia Woolf?* Each partner in the play operates from a profound sense of guilt and low self-esteem. Terrified by loving intimacy, they use each other to brutalize themselves. ("Nobody could love me unless they were *even more worthless!*") Their passionately hostile interaction feeds the secret feeling that "It's all my fault." What can be gained from this behavior? Torment—which to many is far preferable to loneliness.

But having faults does not justify enduring abuse from oneself or others. Chronic guilt is a poor excuse for avoiding responsibility. It's a cop-out, pure and simple. You feel badly, so you act ugly, then abuse yourself for doing so, thus doubly demeaning yourself.

Living together or marriage so often becomes an escape from personal responsibility. It can become an escape from the responsibility for everything you think, feel and do . . . for loving and caring, for your needs for love, security and self-respect, despite your "failings."

Your partner may become a prop in the plays you devise, a character you create from past dreams. "Only a parent could love someone as defective as I feel. So I find a spouse to love me as a parent would. Then I treat that person as I treated my parents." Ironically, your partner might be feeling and doing the same. "Well, that's all right, we can take turns parenting each other, unless we both want to be children at the same time!" And, if you want to, you can observe and categorize what you're doing without bothering to change. Indeed, Transactional Analysis (TA) provides convenient labels for every imaginable parent-child interaction. Unfortunately, you remain unhealed, hopelessly stuck at a dead end. It's little wonder that intensity and intimacy fade in such cases. The more you make your partner over into a parent or child, the more difficult lovemaking becomes. It's hardly surprising that sex becomes perfunctory for couples who act in this way—how many healthy people can be enthusiastic about incest?

Okay, what alternatives do we offer? Try these for starters:

- Your well-being is your own responsibility.
- You can't have intimacy unless you know you can do well living alone.
- Every relationship is unique.
- Frequent explicit negotiations are needed to keep you on course.
- You may change; so may your partner.
- You can't assume anything.
- Nothing is permanent.
- Love shouldn't be taken for granted. It must be appreciated and demonstrated in words and gestures.
- Learn to feel who you and your partner are at this moment—not who you were, will be or wish you might become. Share the NOW.

The MORTAL ENEMY of any relationship is taking YOURSELF and EACH OTHER for granted.

Yet that's the usual tendency. Over time people begin to assume things. Why? Again, habit. You get used to what you see the most. Soon you get into a rut, usually putting up with the parts you don't like. "For better, for worse, in sickness and in health" never works well when it's out of balance with the commitment "to honor and to cherish." Despite the evidence of recent divorce rates, commitment for many people is still easier than tenderness, respect, fairness and consideration. It's just so much easier to hang in there, even if it means a life of contempt and hatred. And, it's easier to expect good treatment as your due, rather than to give and risk losing respect in order to receive it.

If you do not feel cherished and respected, who is responsible? Why, *you are*, of course! You must make certain you get what you need by asking, explaining and offering what you want in return. "You scratch my back, I'll scratch yours! I'll give you love and respect—if you give it to me in return!"

And if all that doesn't work—use leverage. Apply sanctions *after fair warning.* No laundry, no eating together, no sex, whatever will get their attention—not childish retaliation, but a show of force to emphasize that you are serious about your demands. If you don't get paid, stop working. Only slaves work for nothing. If you prize yourself, you will demand what you want. You will use what power you have. You will negotiate, compromise and give more than fair return for what you get. But you won't be cheated. There is no substitute for respect . . . and no love without it!

"My God, that sounds so cold, so businesslike."

Yes, we know. But if the business part of love isn't healthy, the spiritual side gets sick too. No one knows better how to take care of you than you. Wait for the other person to "see the light" and you've got a long wait. You have the responsibility to offer, earn and require respect, understanding and caring.

Choose a partner to whom you are attracted and with whom you feel compatible. Every day give some kind of feedback about what's going on within and outside of you and about how your partner is doing in meeting your desires and needs. Have your partner do the same. Keep educating each other ("Here's how I like to be loved") for as long as you are together.

Firmly demand and you'll get action; patiently wait and you'll probably keep on waiting. With practice, the work of love may become easier. But the work will always be there. Everybody knows the easy parts of love—the eager beginnings, the first flows of passion. But the hard parts—the painful confrontations, the tough negotiations—are just as important. If you want good relationships that last more than a year or two, the difficult work must be done.

1 Reveal your discomfort immediately.

As soon as you sense discomfort in the relationship, share your concern, even if the cause remains uncertain. Don't save up resentment. That does no one a favor (with the possible exception of headache and upset-stomach relief medicine manufacturers).

Ralph and Nancy used to do it this way: if she felt he wasn't talking to her enough on Monday, she would wait until Friday, allowing the anger to build, documenting her case . . . then wham, like this:

"Ralph, you never talk to me! You're always working, watching TV, or playing tennis, but you always want your meals on time! You've made me into a prostitute housekeeper!" (She didn't stop there. By Friday she had plenty to say.)

Had she expressed herself on Monday, she wouldn't have been nearly so angry, nor as willing to blame her discomfort on him: "Ralph, I'm feeling distant from you today, and I'm not sure why. Let's talk about it, okay?"

Principles:
- Stay current.
- Remember, nobody's at fault, nobody's to blame—so no animosity builds up.

2 Show your feelings.

A fight without revealing honest feelings, especially anger, is just a pallid mockery of real interaction. Shouting can help make confrontations productive. On the other hand, physical violence makes a constructive, satisfying end to any problem almost impossible.

Ralph and Nancy went out to dinner. He felt hurt by something she said while they were being served. He was angry, but only buttered his bread, coldly retorting, "Darling, making fun of me in front of the waiter won't help matters." He felt she was cold and unfeeling, but making his point without emotion was so dishonest that he made as little impact at dinner as he had in bed the previous evening. Why fake being calm when you're mad?

Principles:
- Love doesn't mean anything when strong feelings aren't felt or demonstrated.
- Anger is always secondary to pain and fear.

3 Contract for mutual change.

What does your partner do that you don't like? What would you prefer? What would you do in return for the preferred behavior?

The worst way to fight is to complain without offering a plan for change.

For example: He comes home at a different time each night and expects supper ready and tasty. You'd like him to call just before he leaves the office, and to appreciate the effort and creativity involved in meal preparation.

Or: You'd like her to build you up in front of others once in a while instead of carving you up. You'd love her to brag about you to her friends and parents.

Decide what change you'd most appreciate and ask for that. Make it something that can be done starting now. Ask what change in your behavior your partner wants in exchange. This way, you both assume the risk of changes, and you both receive the rewards.

Principles:
- Don't waste the gift of language.
- I'll scratch your back if you'll scratch mine.

4 Give and demand feedback.

Is what you're saying really what they're hearing? Is what they're saying really what you're hearing?

How can you both know for certain? Are you perhaps just talking (yelling, screaming) to score points before a real or imagined audience? Are you simply stomping on your victim? Is that what you really want to do?

Remember Nancy's line from our example: "Ralph, you never talk to me." What could Ralph do? He could curse. Or retaliate. Or bitch back with an itemized account of the times he had talked, starting with the time when he asked her for their first date all the way to that very morning, when he asked her to pass the coffee.

But, if you want to fight constructively, make sure that you are understood.

Ralph could repeat whatever Nancy said in their argument word for word. But when he asked her whether or not she seriously meant that he never talked to her, he was surprised by her answer. She told him tearfully she felt like he thought she was never worth listening to and that what she wanted most was to feel that he respected and admired her.

The more frequent the feedback, the better you'll understand yourself and your partner.

Principles:

- Fight about real differences instead of assumptions.
- It's hard to be understanding, if you spend all your time defending yourself and trying to win.

5 Stick to the present.

Historical anecdotes, as in "I still remember when you hit me two years ago," or amateur fortune-telling, as in "You'll never change, you'll always put the children first," are obstructive maneuvers. Fight about the present and keep off the past and future.

Principle:

- Here and now is more frightening than then, but it's the only thing that can be changed.

6 Be explicitly understanding.

This is most difficult when you're angry, but you move into the expert category when you can pull it off. Don't hide your anger. Show it clearly. After you get it off your chest, you'll have room for understanding. Show the other person that you understand (not necessarily agree with, but understand) how they see it. From time to time, as you give and receive feedback, try to put yourself in the partner's place. How would it feel to be in the other person's shoes and to be relating to you? Would you risk reversing roles in the argument? Take a chance by playing your partner's role and letting him or her play you for five minutes. If nothing else, you should get a good laugh out of viewing yourself from the other side.

Principles:

- In relationships, understanding works better than winning. Winning converts a partner into a loser.
- If you don't understand each other, you aren't even friends.

7 Allow enough time to finish the fight.

Walking out in mid-argument is destructive. If you must stop because you're about to slug him, or Mother Nature is calling, then stop temporarily. But make sure to schedule a time to continue.

Avoid quick jabs like those Ralph used as he left in the morning, "If you call that 'being together' at breakfast, I'd rather you'd slept in!" (Exits, slamming door.)

These parting shots leave a lingering poisonous fallout. If you're going to fight, then make sure you fight. Arrange time for arguments, to be interrupted only by mutually agreed-upon recesses.

Remember, the following are lousy reasons to stop:

(a) crying
(b) yelling
(c) "the kids will know we're fighting"
(d) one of you is getting a headache
(e) the phone is ringing

Principle:

- Never let a fight end or fade away without generating some hope. Eventually you have to create some alternatives that could solve your problems.

8 No audiences! No grandstanding!

A good fight is a partnership session to work something out creatively for mutual benefit. Open arenas encourage playing to the crowd, taking sides, pyrotechnics, and keeping score—none of which helps in the least.

Audiences have their place at sporting events, plays and politics. They don't belong in intimate relationships. In order to improve from your interaction with someone, avoid an audience. Your battles should be honest, so they had best be private.

Principle:

- You can't prove you're a good person or anything else in a relationship. Being better than your partner (whatever that means) or trying to look good is terrible abuse of a relationship.

9 No labels! No name calling!

Remember your goal: to change how you behave toward each other. Pigeonholing, condemning, insulting—all such manuevers block progress toward change.

Ralph and Nancy would come up with many vicious and probably accurate insults. But their fights were little more than name calling:

"You're just like your mother."

"You're a nagging bitch."

"You're a selfish bastard."

"You're a self-centered egotistical shrew."

Principle:

- Enduring a relationship without mutual respect is like walking continuously barefoot on a bed of hot coals.

10 Silence is vicious.

Using silence is the same as walking out of an argument. It will destroy a relationship when used consistently. Avoid it.

Principle:

- Sometimes silence isn't golden, it's just base.

11 If necessary, agree to disagree.

Occasionally, you'll reach an impasse. So what! If you disagree use mutual feedback to clarify exactly what the disagreement is. Repeat what you understand your partner to be saying, and have the other show you he/she knows what you're saying. Agree on understanding each other, but, if necessary, agree to disagree.

She feels that your friend, Sam, is a bore. You feel he's brilliant. Two thousand hours of discussion and a nation-wide opinion poll won't necessarily change your minds.

Neither will the two of you be brought together dragging out that old argument. It's time to agree to disagree, and to move on.

Principles:
- A good relationship requires mutual understanding, NOT agreement in everything.
- Your truth is your truth and you have a right to believe it and express it—but it isn't THE TRUTH.

12 Your feelings and your actions are your responsibility.

As you argue, remember that what you think, what you feel, what you say, what you do—all belong to you. You have a right to your feelings, you have a right to speak your piece. But, you can't make anyone else responsible for what you think, feel and do.

He or she doesn't make you think ill of yourself. Oh, you might react in certain ways because of what the other person does or says. But that's your choice. Efforts to place responsibility for your thoughts, feelings or actions on others lead to endless accusations and recriminations.

Principle:
- Making someone else responsible for your feelings and behavior is as useful as making them responsible for your bodily functions.

13 Avoid empty "nuclear" threats.

Leaving, divorce, murder and suicide are all "nuclear" threats. Sometimes the first two are necessary. All four are extremely painful. It isn't fair for either of you to use them as threats in combat.

Principles:
- Don't play with fire or you'll get burned.
- Only superb relationships are worth dying for. None are worth killing for.

CREATIVE COMBAT

the follow-through

Pay close attention to the following principles. They're necessary to assure long-term payoffs from creative combat.

EMPHASIZE THE POSITIVE

You've had the combat. You've contracted for mutual changes. Your partner is obviously trying to make the changes you've asked for or even demanded. But habits are powerful. Your partner is not perfect. (Are you?) He or she is going to slip back to the old ways from time to time.

What do you do?

Accept the backsliding so long as you see some positive efforts. Change is difficult. Reward efforts. Demonstrate your appreciation by word and deed. If you both keep trying to change, keep rewarding each other for fine efforts and allow occasional slips, you're well on your way!

Some people are so afraid of disappointment and so afraid to hope that they latch on to their partner's slips. They magnify any failures, clutch at any evidence of old behaviors that bothered them in the past. They emphasize the negative and ignore efforts at change.

Their game is: "Prove you're a changed person and I'll relax and enjoy you. If I reward your efforts too soon, you'll just disappoint me. I'll feel foolish and hurt all the more for having hoped and tried."

These people have made an important and unfortunate choice. They'll never risk the tension that occurs when one dares to try and hope. And they'll never achieve greater satisfaction either. We understand their fear but regret their choice.

What if your partner refuses to engage in creative combat? What if no real efforts at cooperative change occur? Then remember:

USE YOUR LEVERAGE

Ask yourself: How much do I value my self-respect? Do I have as much right to satisfy my needs as anyone on earth?

It's easy to spot people who choose to remain victims: they whine and complain; they bitch and nag; they moan. They shake, look defeated, walk slump-shouldered, lack energy, are easily irritated, readily catch colds, miss work or school, suffer constantly from an endless variety of non-critical infirmities.

Why?

Often because they will not use the leverage they have with others. They'd rather bitch than have the courage to fight openly.

First, you must *ask* for what you want.

Why? Because loving you does not necessarily mean being able to read your mind.

And if the asking doesn't work?

DEMAND! Demanding (as opposed to nagging, bitching, and complaining) implies a creatively selected and escalating sequence of pressures that you will bring to bear until your needs are met. Demands apply psychological leverage.

Should you be willing to negotiate, compromise and discuss alternatives? Of course! But remember: Only the willingness to demand can get you more than you've got. Demands are only bluffs if you are unwilling to impose sanctions. Bluffing will not work for long. You should never threaten nuclear war (like "leaving for good") unless you're really prepared to resort to it. Otherwise tactical weapons (demands) won't work.

You say you'd never use nuclear weapons? Don't be so sure!

Ask yourself right now: What behavior on his or her part would provoke me to end this relationship (leave the marriage, quit the job, end the friendship)? Will I risk imposing sanctions knowing he or she might leave (fire, avoid) me in retaliation? What would cause me to risk living without that particular relationship?

"Till death do us part," you say? Then you have chosen slavery, or maybe just suicide or homicide. Is that really what you want?

Unless you set limits to compromise, you are a slave. And the condition of slavery can become so painful that you will eventually attempt to escape through illness, alcohol, drugs, hypochondria, breaking the law, or perhaps some other form of invalidism.

If you can't survive without your partner . . . if "peace at any price" is your game . . . if your self-respect and needs are not worth the trouble, then you have no leverage. You are doomed to remain forever dissatisfied, envying those who have mastered the methods of successful living.

Ellen, a whining housewife, nags, bitches and complains about her "male fascist pig" husband. She suffers from recurrent back pain which makes her life miserable. It also punishes George by adding financial burdens (doctor bills) to his already sex-deprived existence.

"George treats me terribly," she complains. "He's never home. He's selfish, unloving. In bed it's "Wham, bam, thank you ma'am!", with foreplay restricted to a "How about tonight, Honey?"

Poor helpless Ellen . . .

Has she ever considered forcefully stating her unsatisfied needs? "George, I want love and respect . . . I want to feel precious to you." Would she be willing to deprive him of things he gets from her and apply direct, up-front sanctions? Would she stop cooking his special meals? Would she take a vacation by herself? Would she be willing to deprive him and say so, honestly and directly, warning him that unless he changes his behavior she *will* retaliate? Would she have the courage to leave if he doesn't?

Ask yourself. If demanding, rewarding real efforts, and application of effective leverage all don't work, would you continue to put up with your dissatisfaction? Are you betraying yourself in some relationship at home or at work right now?

Many people, lacking the courage to fight, suffer (with or without obvious complaint) for years. Then, suddenly, they quit the intolerable situation (marriage, job, friendship). But they never give the other person a chance to work out a solution. They use their ultimate weapon first and never try the tactical arsenal of asking or demanding. What a waste!

"Can't people just get along without having to hassle, in order to lead a satisfied self-respecting life?"

Want the answer straight?

No!

No two people and no situation can be perfect enough to allow that kind of permanent peace on earth.

In summary: In a relationship, loving warmth breeds intimacy; occasional loving anger invigorates. Intimacy is a marvelous but risky business.

Love does not
hold people together
. . . rather, like a
garden of delicate flowers,
love needs nurturing to thrive.

Are you willing to risk it?

Exercises

- Sit down with the most important person in your life (besides yourself). Go over the 13 points for Creative Combat. Discuss how well each of you feel you're both doing. Which points could you work on? Remember, no blaming.
- Next, ask yourselves: "Despite whatever fears I may have, would I be willing and able to leave this relationship if I'm not treated with love and respect? Would I be willing to use tactical weapons if my words aren't heard and don't seem to make a difference?"

Courage: Parents and Children

What about kids?

To those who need to understand how they become the way they are . . .

To those who want to live differently from their parents yet find themselves repeating the same old ways . . .

To all children who naively look to all adults as models . . .

To all, we devote this section about children—their nature, their nurture, but most of all, their spiritual growth . . .

Conventional Child Upbringing

We see most children being raised to survive life's turbulence as though the world were but a battlefield:

"Beware of strangers, foreigners, the unknown. Don't offend lest you be rejected. You'll get our love only if you behave in defined ways. Achieve what we didn't or we won't feel fulfilled. Do as we say, don't do as we do. Safety first. Work first, enjoy later. It isn't nice to fight. Be honest, unless it hurts others. Tell him you're sorry even if you don't mean it. It's a sin to be angry, especially at Mommy or Daddy. Sex, drugs, and alcohol are bad for you, but okay for us. Don't think, question or argue. Be a 'good' kid and do what you are told. If you act or believe differently than we do, it means you don't love and respect us. Crying is weak. Handle your feelings. Don't upset us. Our religion is best, our values are correct. Trying hard is nice, but success counts more. Winning is everything.

"How would *that* look to the neighbors? Bad thoughts are as bad as bad deeds. No, don't! You should! You shouldn't! Look at how you look! See what you did! Look at *me* when I talk to you. I'll love you someday when you do better. I'm busy. Don't bother me. I'll pay attention if you're naughty or sick. Look how I've sacrificed for you. Be friends with, date and marry your own kind. Don't talk to strangers. Beware of the dog. Keep off the grass.

"Men don't hug and kiss other men. Men are smart, tough, fight and compete—the hunters! We killed 315 of the enemy today and lost *only* 50 of our own, so you see, we're winning! Women are soft, sensitive, warm and gentle—the caretakers. Why? Don't ask silly questions."

Extraordinary Child Upbringing

Imagine instead a childhood of: "I love you" while hugged to the sweet smell of your mother's breast, or the rough, but immensely strong, safe grasp of your father's lifting and swinging you through the air; not because of some exemplary performance, but simply because you exist and they love you.

Imagine instead parents who say:

> "What do you think? How do you feel? Life is often painful—will you let me comfort you? I'd really like a hug from you. We're going, would you like to come along? We're doing this for you because we want to, not because we have to. Here's how I do it—I'll teach you if you'd like. I like it when you do this and I don't like it when you do that. If you cooperate with me, I'll reward you with my respect and friendship; if you don't, I'll feel less close to you and want to please you less. Treat me and yourself with respect and I'll reciprocate. Please share with me how you think and feel. I want to understand and know you. I hope you're interested in my feelings and ideas too. Even if we don't agree, we at least feel understood. I understand how you see it, but as your parent, I won't let you do

that now. It may not be completely fair, but we'll do it my way unless you've convinced me otherwise.

"I realize if I'm brutal, mean or unfair, you'll retaliate against me or take it out on yourself or others. I know you can punish me by hurting yourself.

"I'm responsible for how I act, but I'm not responsible for how you behave. That's up to you. It's wise not to offend others but far more important not to betray your own sense of worth. I'll try to be open and honest with myself and you in the hope that you'll do the same.

"I want you to succeed, but more importantly I want you to be proud of who you are. You don't need to accomplish anything in particular for my sake; I take care of my own needs to feel meaningful. I recommend you not to live off my accomplishments either.

"Even though we love you very much, we must make sure we take care of ourselves too. Unless we feel satisfied, we'll resent taking care of your needs. We need to get away by ourselves regularly.

"If you feel angry or resentful, please let me know directly. If you feel loving and warm, be open about that too. I won't hesitate to do the same with you.

"You and I are going to be with each other for a long time. We're going to have to work through a complicated transition. At first I'm going to have to take a lot of responsibility for you. But, by the time you're twenty, the responsibility will all be yours. It won't be easy for either of us.

"Once you've grown up I'd like to be your friend and that's not likely unless I try to understand, try to be warm, try to stand for what I believe, try to respect me and you. I don't want to be your boss or your servant.

"I want you to know that I believe nothing is more sacred than living with a sense of worth and self-respect. Without it, it's hard to feel meaningful. God lives inside each of us, if anywhere; to live for or obey God outside of you is but a pathetic step from the worship of false idols. It's in you. Learn from us and others but rely on your own inner sense of right and wrong. Pay more attention to artists, poets and novelists than politicians and evangelists. Beware of leaders lest you become a follower and lose your own direction. Please consider what I say and do, but don't swallow it whole.

"Experiment, take calculated risks. Make life an adventure, not a cocoon. Death will give you peace and safety soon enough. Life feels more precious when you sense how fragile and fleeting it is.

"Many people and things can seem ominous until you understand them. To be wary is wise. But don't let fears rule. Not to risk exploring is a foolish waste of life."

CHILDREN model themselves after what they see, not what they are told.

CHILDREN learn to love and respect themselves for what their parents love and respect in themselves and in their children.

CHILDREN will do anything to be noticed. Give them loving attention when they're well or they'll become sick, crazy, or self-destructive in order to get the attention they need.

CHILDREN learn to speak as their guardians speak and see what their guardians see.

Adults act as lenses which filter and focus the world for children. Parents define their children's reality with labels, which structure and organize the world and make it manageable. In so doing they inevitably reduce and distort the grandness of reality.

Parents' responsibility is first to themselves and then, by choice, to their children. It behooves adults to be willing to reconsider their biases, priorities, definitions and world views in light of their children's opinions.

To spoil a child with too much understanding *(which is, after all, the essence of love)* ***is not possible.***

Do for children that which they cannot do for themselves. But, do it so they can learn for themselves. Allow them to make reversible mistakes. Protect them from irreversible ones. The distinction isn't easy. Have the courage to struggle with it.

Ideally a parent is more a teacher and a coach than a guardian or a servant.

A child's respect and love cannot be bought. But, with courage, patience and understanding, it can be earned.

Many people are programmed in their youth to make choices out of habit and fear. But fear of what? Failure and rejection. Can you blame them? But what about the possibility of gaining self-respect, understanding, love, growth, excitement and fun? Loneliness, boredom and meaninglessness seem far too high a price for safety.

PROBLEM CHILDREN

It has been said that children are both a temporary gift and a responsibility, but not a possession. We in the United States, Canada and Western Europe make far too much of the distinction between children and adults.

"Problem children" or, far more accurately, the children we see from dysfunctional families, reflect their parents' belief that *their* children, (i.e. the kids that they *own*) are something essentially different from *them* the parents; as though children are not quite human.

Basically, kids with psychological problems are strangers to their parents. Somehow the family slips into seeing the child one way: "Billy is a brat." "Mary is selfish." Single versions ignore all the other possibilities. For example, Billy may act unruly, but also be scared and lonely, afraid his parents might divorce. He feels worthless and worries that his parents wish he hadn't been born.

As with couples, it's the same old trap—you only see one aspect of that other person. Out of the infinite possibilities, you pick on a few. The person may do the same to you and then the rut gets deeper. Sure, a kid may be born difficult, irritable and not as good-natured as others—but if you withhold basic, open love, which allows you to see the unique beauty of a child, he or she will only get worse. Problem kids may be born with problems, but how adults act can determine whether the child will get better or progressively worse.

Consider the various ways problem kids develop. They may have either been ignored, allowed to come and go as they pleased, or, on the contrary, they may have been ruled, regulated and protected with the parents assuming almost all responsibility for day-to-day decisions in their lives.

(We know the trap we fall into when we dare to pontificate on the raising of children. But we want to share our views on "an ounce of prevention" in addition to our "pounding" away at cures.)

John, an Eagle Scout, with no history of any misbehavior, murdered his father, mother, sister and dog. Jane ran away from home and became a "masseuse," convicted twice for prostitution before her nineteenth birthday. Both came from upper middle-class homes. Both had extremely concerned, protective parents with strict rules and discipline. Both had to clear their choice of friends, use of free time, curfew and bedtime with their parents.

Other kids who get into trouble have parents who neither protect nor control them. In fact, their parents have little to do with them at all. Some of these growing-up-on-their-own kids get everything they could ask in the way of material goods, others get nothing.

Some problem kids are overprotected, and others are ignored. There would appear to be no rhyme or reason, no pattern. Is it all genes? Or is it the terrible influence of their "good-for-nothing friends" or the failure of the schools or television violence?

Yes, no, maybe, all of the above, none, a combination . . . who knows for sure?! We certainly don't.

But one thing we do know. We have never seen a troubled kid (without some physical brain disorder) who felt that his or her parents:

- were honest and direct
- were proud of themselves
- asked nothing more from the child than they demanded of themselves
- demonstrated verbally and physically their warmth and respect
- spent a great deal of time and effort to understand the child
- could firmly forbid, refuse and discipline and yet be able to accept their child's anger.

While it is crucial to make certain that you understand what your children feel and think, it's important to share not only your point of view, but the reasoning and uncertainty, the deliberations and the agony, which make up your thinking. After all, you don't *know* with absolute certainty what's right or wrong; rather you can guide your children, like yourself, with glimpses through the fog.

Part of the information you use to make decisions ideally comes from your child's point of view, the rest from your own experience. At best, you have biased data. You're just human, remember? As a parent, you have the responsibility of the final decision when agreement is lacking, and you will make it—not necessarily the best decision (only time will tell that), but the decision you can best live with whether the children like it or not.

It's interesting that the more insecure people are of their motives, and the more opposition they face for their points of view, the more stubborn, inflexible and certain they try to seem about their position in any disagreement.

Scott, my oldest son—tall, athletic, but definitely overweight at the time—had agreed not to eat sweets in our house. I had suffered from being fat at his age and wanted to discourage him from overeating junk food. If he wanted some he could use the money he earned to buy his own.

One day we noticed that some ice cream had disappeared. Clearly, from the circumstances, we knew Scott had eaten it. No big deal, until he denied it!

I confronted him. "I love you, Scott. You're one of my closest friends. But, I don't lie to my friends and I won't tolerate your lying to me. It hurts to see you feel you need to lie to anyone. I hate feeling that distant. I love you too much to live this close together and be lied to. If you want me to be just your father and not a friend, okay, we'll try it out right now. I don't want to see you, eat with you or talk with you for two days. See what that feels like. Good luck finding someone who treats you better than I do. I'm as loving a friend as you'll ever meet." Separated by pain and resentment, we wept thirty feet apart. He seemed to feel as lonely as I.

"Hey, Dad, the Cincinnati Reds are doing it to the Dodgers again, come look at the TV!" My guts tightened with the pain of hurting him and the fear of losing his love, but I stood my ground. "Damn it, two days, not before. I need to respect you and me. I won't if you lie. I won't if I retreat so soon. You have to learn how strongly I feel. I hope you don't lie to me again, because I miss so much being close to you." The tears wouldn't stop, my throat ached. This may have been the most important experience we ever had. The hug and kiss the next evening felt so good. The increased closeness we've had ever since was worth the price of a very painful weekend.

Relationships seem to work much better when the love is unconditional, but the friendship is not!

GIFTED CHILDREN

Tremendous inborn intelligence and talent is associated with great sensitivity, perceptiveness, stubbornness and an unusual way of seeing things. Gifted children with these attributes often feel they are strange, and they get hurt easily. They soon develop a false sense of being defective and unlovable.

All children need a great deal of understanding and comfort from adults. But exceptionally gifted children need more than most. Otherwise they misinterpret their tendency to get hurt easily and to see things differently as evidence there's something wrong with them.

This understanding and comforting is rarely offered. It is no wonder so many geniuses lead such tortured lives.

Exercises

- Compare and contrast your childhood with both the "conventional" and "extraordinary" child upbringings described in Chapter 20.
- Do you see a correlation between conventional upbringing and self-doubt later in life?
- If you have children, are you raising them in a more extraordinary way?
- Here's an ambitious exercise. If your children are teenagers, ask them to read this chapter and discuss it with the family. You must all know that there will be no punishment for respectful and honest opinions.
- Conventional child upbringing might be labeled "outside-in" or "material" style child rearing, while extraordinary child upbringing might be labeled "inside-out" or "spiritual" style child rearing. Can you see why?

Freedom: An End and a New Beginning

PART ONE

Philosophy, Biomedicine and a Tirade on Drugs

"A perfection of means and confusion of aims, seems to be our main problem." ALBERT EINSTEIN

In the earlier parts of this book, we tried to show specific approaches for changing, several paths for getting around roadblocks that stop many people. Now we are at the outskirts of our domain and can only gesture at the countless paths that lie ahead. This takes us to the limits of our knowledge about change—psychological, biochemical and spiritual. The beginning of this book is relatively simple. Some books may oversimplify to make a nice neat ending. This one doesn't. Nobody can really say what life is about. Ultimately, what you do is up to you.

PSYCHIATRY CIRCA 1978

The mind-healing arts have a tough time as it is without grappling with something as vague as happiness. Health is their goal, and that's vague enough. What is mental health? No definition can be given that does not invite argument. While therapeutic techniques can be defined with relative precision, the exact aims of treatment often go undefined. Worse yet, many approaches—electroshock, implosion, high-dose tranquilizers—seem like attempting to repair a fine Swiss watch by banging it on a tabletop. Psychiatry is, to say the least, a flawed enterprise.

One of the basic problems in therapy is the fluidity of the internal world. Emotions and feelings are in constant flux. And, like all the other parts of the human psyche, emotions and feelings are not things that can be weighed and measured. They are concepts, names for the unseen. Dealing with the psychological requires an act of faith, a belief that this invisible stuff really exists.

Yet physicists report that even seemingly solid objects, bars of steel, rocks, planets, and stars, are comprised of particles that are as intangible as the mind. The electron, for example, never has a specific location; even at rest, it remains a blur without definite outline or position. Its position depends on how you look. Indeed, a physicist would insist that much of what one can know of such particles is determined by how one looks at them. A strange paradox to be sure—everyday objects seem real, but what they're made of is as insubstantial as the mind.

How can the world be so unruly? Because it is deceptive. People made up rules based on everyday life about how the world was supposed to be. The human species evolved to deal with earth-size entities—animals, plants and people. But stars and atomic particles, also a part of the world, are of such different order of magnitude it's difficult to grasp their reality. Likewise, the reality of one's own mind is hard to grasp. At the atomic level and at the mental level, the rules are different from the everyday material reality we all know. You can avoid these hidden places if you wish. On this planet there are always enough distractions to keep you from looking in the mirror.

People outside the psychiatric field often believe that someone, somewhere, is on the verge of discovering a breakthrough which will make it easy for everybody from here on out. Popular magazines love to foster this myth by pandering to an appetite for science gossip. But there aren't any miracle cures. At least, not the kind that people often hope for. Sure, psychotherapy and drugs help many of the problems that people have with their lives, but, as far as we can see, the truly basic questions of existence will never be resolved that easily.

Research has provided many wonderful, new drugs. Thousands of people whose lives would have been crippled by profound disorders before can now lead lives of relative productivity and peace. Probably the first major effective chemical tool in psychiatry was the tranquilizer, chlorpromazine, also known by its brand names, Thorazine or Largactil. This drug and its relatives don't cure psychoses such as schizophrenia, but they do allow a lot of severely impaired people to leave the hospital and return to active lives in the community. Before these tranquilizers were produced, the procedure was to use ice packs, straight jackets and worse.

Later, the discovery of anti-depressant drugs undoubtedly helped prevent thousands of suicides. Anti-anxiety drugs have helped some whose lives would have otherwise been constant suffering. Of all the new psychiatric medicine, lithium carbonate seems to be the first to offer anything approaching a cure. It is a compound as simple as table salt, yet able to arrest the devastating cycle of manic-depressive psychosis.

The non-drug approaches to psychiatry, the social and "talk" therapies, have also been making significant advances. Behavioral modification has helped healthy as well as severely ill people. Approaches to curing addictions have been applied to abuse of food, cigarettes, alcohol and drugs. Innovations in family therapies have directed attention to the family unit as a whole rather than isolating one member as the sick one. Therapeutic approaches from psychoanalysis to more radical therapies have been refining old tools and inventing new ones. For example, cognitive therapy is now combined with behavioral approaches into a cognitive-behavioral therapy that emphasizes healthier attitudes. Most significant of all, attitudes towards care itself have changed. People expect more. We support this psychiatric consumerism and believe that the tools of mental health should be available to the public at large. For what are self-help books, if not do-it-yourself psychiatry?

Unfortunately, mental health progress has also brought about a dangerous backlash—over-reliance on medications. There seems to be an increasing tendency for people to turn to chemicals—from herbalism to tranquilizers—rather than to rely on themselves.

Probably the most ominous force in this regard is the academic research-drug industry complex. By and large, those who study new drugs and their applications are responsible, careful people. But more than a few are so wrapped up in the idea of drugs as a solution for human ills that they misread the impact of their new discoveries. Even with the best of intentions, they sometimes unleash substances with serious detrimental effects on the public.

The supply of money for supporting research is limited. Obtaining funds is an extremely competitive enterprise. Academic promotions are often geared to the results of research so that there is a not-so-subtle pressure to discover something or be out of the game. Researchers in these areas may feed the news hunger of the media by hinting that drugs allowing precise control of moods, increased creativity, and extrasensory perception development are being perfected.

Perhaps some day such drugs may be discovered, but it hasn't happened yet. So far, all that's been produced are chemicals that seem to have one common effect—they make the people who take them less bothersome to others. Doctors know that prescribing tranquilizers, sedatives and even anti-depressants can cause unhappy patients to become pleasantly quiet. Addictions to these legal drugs is extreme.

Valium is a good example. Its generic name is diazepam, but the drug has been so successfully marketed, its trade name is far better known. Next to alcohol, it, and drugs closely related to it, are probably the most widely abused in this country. They make people feel relaxed, dissolve anxiety and give a high reminiscent of a stiff shot of booze. For treating certain psychiatric conditions where anxiety is truly debilitating, these "minor" tranquilizers can be helpful. But that's not how they are used much of the time. Valium eaters, like the lotus eaters of Greek mythology, use the drug to forget, to get by, to cope, to slide though . . . instead of waking up and doing something. It's one of the most popular ways to avoid psychological pain—why change when you can simply escape? And once again busy physicians often use Valium and drugs like it to get patients to be quiet. Patients complain of this or that and a widespread tendency is to give medications until they stop complaining.

The doctors, scientists, and drug companies are not the only culprits in this game. This is a drug-using society. Prevailing cultural values flatly assume all problems have material solutions: "Live better chemically." "A drug for any ailment." Such attitudes aren't really new. Back in the time of the Pharaohs, medicines for every conceivable illness were concocted and consumed. But even the builders of the pyramids lacked our dedication to preparations and pills. Modern Americans are chemical freaks. It's hardly surprising advertising industries constantly coax consumers to ingest remedies for every ailment from aching heads to hemorrhoids.

The crazy thing is that it's not that people love drugs so much as they love the idea of fast relief. Life is complicated and impossible to grasp fully. It's so much easier to reduce everything to one problem that can be cured by some special pill or medicine. Some users graduate to the elite addictions of alcohol, cocaine or opiates. After extensive use, an addict no longer experiences any real euphoria. Instead, he takes each to avoid the pain of withdrawal. At that point, relief is guaranteed—a drug cure for a drug-induced problem.

Most people will probably never develop full-blown addictions, but subtle dependencies may often occur. Using tranquilizers even "just to get through a crisis" may cut back one's ability to learn how to handle problems. Who knows? Many people who frequently take Valium may be undergoing a gradual shift towards permanent dullness or chronic fearfulness. The slow decline may not become obvious for another decade. As a nation, we overuse food and chemicals so habitually that subtle destructive effects can go unnoticed for years. Other beneficial drugs have later proved to have devastating, unexpected side effects. Diethylstilbesterol (DES) was widely used by gynecologists more than thirty years ago and only in the last decade have its long-term hazardous effects been fully appreciated. Women whose mothers received DES have an usually high incidence of cancer of the vagina. Major tranquilizers like Thorazine and Stelazine can cause permanent and disabling involuntary movements.

We are not suggesting that drug research should stop. Unquestionably, it has provided substantial benefits for millions of people, but, as with the proliferation of nuclear energy plants, safeguards have not always been thoroughly scrutinized. Discovering drawbacks to drug therapy is rarely as glamorous as discovering promising new drugs. Government grants to universities and medical schools for drug research are often far more lucrative than grants for projects as mundane as developing community clinics. The incentive to make new drugs is also high in industry. It's far easier to package and distribute chemicals than develop innovative social programs. Drugs are not only easier to make, but the margin for profit is invariably higher.

No one really knows how drugs work, but one fact is clear: if a medication makes one feel good (or more accurately a little numb) or if it tones down the intensity of life enough so that one can simply float through, many people will take it. What will happen to this tranquilized, docile or artificially high population is anyone's guess. And every year, more new drugs are discovered.

It is against this backdrop of our society's overuse of chemicals that we view biological psychiatry. We don't discount the idea that some individuals have an inherited biochemical disorder which might be corrected by some specific drug. Insulin, although it doesn't cure diabetes, can certainly make it easier to live with. The trouble with pills is that they are such quiet, easy comrades. They can betray you before you even know it.

"Depression" is the catchword now. It's been called "the most common undiagnosed disease." But applying the disease concepts of medicine to psychiatry (the "medical model" approach as it is often called), has significant shortcomings. Feeling bored, fatigued, empty and sad may, indeed, be signs that you have a familial disposition towards depression. But, as we said earlier, these feelings may also be a *message* you're giving yourself that it's time to do something about your life. Taking drugs for depression can be like using an anaesthetic because your hand hurts . . . without bothering to notice that you're holding it in a fire.

Some psychiatrists who like the medical model approach have picked up some of the worst habits of medicine. They become aloof, mechanical and rigid in their approach to their patients. Instead of displaying compassion, they go through check lists, looking for "target symptoms" or "diagnostic criteria" for psychiatric diseases. Some medical model psychiatrists approach patients in ways that help keep the patient sick. Some may have disorders that are primarily biochemical. But even if many of their problems are biochemical, other troubles may be psychological and social. In face, more often than not, it's a combination of several problems rather than any one alone which brings people into treatment. Yet, many healers tend to treat only one area, referring the other problems elsewhere or simply ignoring their existence.

In Chapter Eight we mentioned that some people may be born with a predisposition towards getting depressed. They may find it relatively easy to get depressed, such as, "If you feel bad enough nobody will demand anything from you." And it's easy to stay depressed once you begin.

It's almost like there's a switch inside of them that turns the depression on and off. While it's not possible to turn the switch voluntarily by simply snapping fingers, they may learn, through experience that certain kinds of dissatisfactions or thoughts can trigger the switch and flip them into a depression. The whole process is a lot like banging on a television set in a certain place and finding that the picture improves. And, as in the case with a lot of learning, it can take place unconsciously. If there are social or psychological rewards for getting depressed at certain times, and if a person has any degree of biochemical predisposition, it "greases the skids" for a depression to happen. When there's an *advantage* to being sick, as with Ellie in the beginning of the book, it just often happens.

In our opinion, the best use of drugs is minimum use. If there's some way of "flicking the switch" by changing experiences, habits or relationships instead of using a drug, encourage someone to try it. The less you have to rely on something else, the better. Depending on a drug might make you dependent out of habit later. Try different ways of expressing feelings to see if something will work better than being depressed. Try exploring ways to get your needs met rather than giving up and hiding. Step back from the problem to try something new, even though there are no guarantees in this world.

In some cases in our practice, a depression is so severe, and the probable degree of biochemical contribution so large, that drugs are helpful to get people going. As soon as possible, however, we stop the chemicals. Ideally, we'd like to teach people how to modulate chemicals and use them properly for the briefest possible time in order to get the job done. Drugs, even the best, still tend to make one dependent on things outside oneself. They limit human potential for growth and insidiously produce a shallow, irritable crankiness. We prescribe drugs only when all other methods would be too slow, ineffective or dangerous.

If chemicals really got the job done, it wouldn't be so bad. Ideally, as with anti-depressants, drugs can work well enough to flip the switch and allow the person to bounce back. Then use can be stopped.

But, usually, they're just another halfway solution. They may lower the pain level but they also tend to keep people frozen in old habits. That's why we insist that if Valium, alcohol, marijuana or any other drug helps you feel good while you're living a meaningless, dissatisfying existence, then it's also helping you waste your life.

In a sense, the debate about whether or not to prescribe drugs in a mental health practice comes back to the old philosophical arguments of free will versus determinism. The free will side says, "You do what you choose to do," and the determinism faction insists, "What you do is the result of internal and external forces operating on you at that instant." Each point of view is ultimately pretty limited, and oversimplification of a whole that is profoundly complex. But drugs often get used in the materialistic and deterministic belief that what you do and how you feel is mostly the result of some chemical machinery within you. Even psychoanalysis, which is almost anti-drug in its orientation, tends to assume that behavior is merely the end product of instincts, childhood experiences and current situation. Deterministic extremes seem far-fetched to us. On the other hand, we wouldn't take the extreme free will position that you're able to do anything you want, but we would say that you can come close. We choose to believe that life is a game in which we are dealt a hand of cards at each moment (the determinism). How you play (the free will) is up to you.

Everyone owns a biochemical device (the physical body) and an information processing device (the mind). Many capabilities and limitations are inherited. Some go through life with equipment that is in good running order, while others have to struggle by with hardware that is inherently defective. But, in any case, what you do with it is still largely up to you.

GOING NUTS

Please be aware that our use of a label like "crazy people" reflects the familiarity and friendship we feel with some who are insane. In more formal psychiatric literature, these people are labeled schizophrenic or borderline. We mean no disrespect. Each of them is painfully aware of their uniqueness. Indeed, their uniqueness is at the heart of their agony. Somehow the use of formal labels tends to denigrate and isolate them even further, denying the human truth of how people actually talk. After all, a psychotic episode in plain words is simply "going crazy."

Craziness, in part, is bred of loneliness and the fear that no healthy adult would ever understand or care. Being crazy in the sense of hearing voices or seeing visions isn't necessarily bad; it's the isolation that brings the agony. Maybe the crazies are in touch with some higher planes of existence that others miss. Yet when they speak of their mad visions, they are rejected as though they've got the plague.

Whatever craziness means in its everyday usage (unusual behavior, peculiar thoughts, noisy outbursts), those people who experience it often inflict even more problems on themselves *by trying to be like everybody else.* That is not too surprising when you consider anyone with an oddity in our society is trained to apologize for it. People with severe mental aberrations are ostracized with particular vigor, as though their problems might be contagious. Yet many crazy people aren't crazy all the time. They are much like everybody else between their nutty episodes. Their madness fluctuates in response to external or internal events. A relative dies, they get in trouble in school; a friend rejects them, or just some internal biological alarm clock goes off and, once again, the switches that turn on their craziness start the cycle running again.

Crazy people have the same problems as everyone else, beginning with the most basic one in our society—not enough self-love. They can't love themselves because they're crazy. Indeed, that's usually how they start to be overtly nuts. They begin by devoting themselves to a rigid set of high standards and aspirations: "I have to be perfect." And by perfect they mean the way everyone else *appears to be.* These impossible standards begin a process of inescapable self-torture. Every thought becomes grounds for punishment.

Everyone thinks terrible, vicious, homicidal, bizarre or obscene thoughts at times. But when crazy people think these thoughts, they panic and try to hide them in some mental closet. An occasional nightmare or bizarre daydream, for most people is just a reminder that there's a lot of weird stuff in the mind. The soon-to-be crazy has a weird thought and gets into an argument with it, pleads with it, tries to hide it, panics about it, and ultimately uses it as a reason for self-punishment: "I'm sick and no good." After years of such wholesale self-destruction, the crazy loses grip on the selves at the center. Full-scale riot ensues.

Margot, a pale and lonely girl in her early twenties, used to carve "secret names" on her arms and legs with a knife. She tried to hang herself several times and even set herself on fire once. She heard voices telling her how worthless she was from the age of ten. Although her parents regularly complimented her on how "considerate" and "charitable" she was, Margot felt bad and ugly inside. She believed she had to do "one good thing" every day or evil beings would kill her or members of her family. Margot was fourteen when her younger brother died in a boating accident. The next day she tried to hang herself after slicing up her arms and legs a few hundred times with a razor blade.

For the next five years she cut herself, burnt herself with cigarettes and bit her arms until they bled.

"The voices would order me and I would resist them as long as I could, but finally they built up a pressure so bad I couldn't stand it. When I finally cut myself, it brought such relief, it didn't even hurt at all." By the time she was twenty-one, she had spent four years in a hospital, most of the time pacing around, staring at the walls and mumbling to herself. Her once pretty face, scarred with self-inflicted injuries, had long since frozen into the mask of chronic insanity.

Some people feel so overwhelmed that they fear they're about to go crazy. But, if you are like most people, you don't have to worry about getting to such a point because you couldn't become psychotic if you tried. You might feel so anxious or depressed that you would try to kill yourself, yet, even in the worst imaginable crisis, it is unlikely you could flip out for more than a few days. But, if you are like Margot, born with the right heredity into the right family, and grow up in such a way that nobody ever notices how desperate you are or shows you how to love yourself, you might be able to make it into full-blown insanity.

Margot truly got better. Eventually, she was lucky enough to be placed in a treatment center at a large university. She received the best drug, psychological and social treatments available. With modern treatment involving drugs, counseling, environmental support systems, education of patients and family, at least half of all schizophrenics attain a good level of functioning. Margot dramatically improved. She learned how to deal with her craziness, fixed what she could and lived with what she couldn't.

Pain most people find inconsequential can completely engulf crazy people. They feel so intensely that almost anything can overwhelm them. They become rigid, isolated and finally break down when they attempt to calm themselves. They must learn how to develop buoyancy from self-love and support from their relationships in order to keep their bearings in a stormy life.

In therapy with patients similar to Margot, we would try to show that we understand what it must be like to live in a world where one's vision, hearing, memory and feelings play constant tricks—and how much it must hurt to live in such constant chaos. Crazy people suffer from an extra dose of what hurts all humans. Next, we would try to get them to love themselves and take care of themselves as much as we would with anyone else. We would give them drugs carefully, prescribing the minimum effective amounts; amounts which would not anesthetize all the emotional pain, only slow their craziness to a manageable level. We would try to teach them how to keep from tripping over their mental quirks, as well as to form and use relationships for feedback rather than to rely completely on their own faulty circuitry.

That's what Margot learned to do. She improved to a point where she educated her friends to look for the signs that meant she was beginning to lose her grasp on herself. And, most importantly, she learned how to love all her selves and her madness too. She learned not to be terrified by the voices when they came, but to extend to them the same love she would to any part of herself. She learned how to use tranquilizing drugs during her episodes. Over a period of a year she rarely took more than a few weeks' worth of medicine. The old horror show would return now and then, and she'd be crazy for a few days. Once in a while she'd check into a hospital. But overall, she learned to let her madness go by instead of fighting it and sinking even further. She saved herself.

Maybe she just grew out of it. Maybe something in her diet changed, and she "magically" got better. Who knows? One thing is certain, though. It is uncommon for someone so severely impaired to ever get that much better, so when we do see it happen we are infinitely more enraged at moderately healthy people who let habits rule them out of fear and self-doubt.

PART TWO

Psychotherapy and the Judo of Ideas

"Words are the most powerful drug used by mankind." RUDYARD KIPLING

IDEAS ARE DRUGS

Now, after all our ranting and raving about society's overuse of drugs, we'd like to look at the whole thing from a different perspective.

Part of the business of being a person is to maintain a physical body. It's a marvelous factory: It takes in and metabolizes food, repairs itself, and, most importantly, gives us a place in which to live. All business at this physical level of being follows the commerce laws of chemistry and physics; our physical self is a series of biochemical reactions.

There is also a psychological level of being, a level where people are thoughts, feelings and memories. The psychological selves at this level have no tangible existence (you can't see your mind) but they live inside your physical body in the same way data is stored in a computer.

These two very different levels overlap. For example, when you think, a chemical change takes place in nerves responsible for sending messages from one part of your brain to another when you think. If you change your brain's chemistry with drugs, you also alter the psychological level. It's a peculiar overlap, to be sure, and its consequences are profound—drugs, in a very real sense, are thoughts within your body's chemistry. Conversely, thoughts produce chemical changes too, so in a sense, one might say that they are also drugs.

The physical and psychological do not exist independently—people are *at once* chemical and psychological beings. The two are but different ways of seeing. Chemistry influences how people think. What people think influences how their chemistry works. Simplistic approaches to this mind-body problem are exactly that—simplistic, and, therefore, useless. If people approach themselves as just a mind, or just a body, they are bound to get stuck.

Practitioners in the healing arts have often tended to focus on one level of existence and ignore the other. This is unfortunate since some problems are best dealt with by approaches on both levels at once. The story of Margot is a good example. She was treated with major tranquilizers for her psychotic episodes and with individual and social milieu therapy for her psychological problems. Each level influences the other. For example, Thorazine is a chemical molecule but it is also an idea—a packet of information about how electrical charges and molecular configurations can be arranged. In this way, it promotes a different chemical attitude in the brain. Changes at the physical level can be used to manipulate the psychological level.

Ideas are drugs too. They approach from the psychological side and set up a pattern of chemical changes that transmit information. Like chemical compounds, ideas may have widely varying effects. Some may be ignored, drifting into the mind and making a quiet exit. Similarly, a chemical without pharmacologic effect—(like cellulose, for example) can be eaten and excreted with the body barely noticing the passage. (Though, interestingly enough, cellulose does seem to have a function at yet another level—a mechanical one. Evidence accumulates that roughage, especially food with a high cellulose content, mechanically massages the lining of the colon, thus reducing the likelihood of colonic and rectal cancer.)

Part of the psychotherapy process is the presentation of powerful, upsetting ideas in ways that help a person change. Some ideas can be transmitted by the spoken word, others are carried by new experiences and some get through at a biochemical level in the form of drugs. People tend towards habitual behavior and the inertia of longstanding problems can be impressive. Despite one's efforts to change, it's possible to stay stuck in the same rut for years. Even apparent instabilities can be frightfully stable. Some people can be about to have a nervous breakdown for twenty years and yet never quite slip over the brink. Bad relationships are another common example. The same arguments can occur over and over again almost verbatim.

It seems to us that much of what happens in psychotherapy is the careful insertion of ideas that disturb the patient's ability to continue screwing him or herself up in the same manner. It works sort of like judo, where the person's momentum and preconceptions are used against him—not to defeat him, but to upset him enough to induce some change.

Theresa was bright, verbal, in pain and, as such, the kind of person most likely to benefit from the reshuffling psychotherapy can provide. She was in love with Jim, a man in prison for tax fraud. Theresa missed Jim dearly and felt more depressed every week. Jim had already served six months and still had a year to go.

Even nice people get busted for tax fraud. Jim was an ex-tennis pro trying just a little too hard to scrape together some money for his new club. Theresa came from a well-to-do family who probably would have helped Jim had he asked. But he was much too proud to take such assistance. He wanted to do it without any help from anyone, so he tried to stretch out his funds until the club got on its feet. Theresa was devoted to Jim and visited him regularly. He seemed to be doing well even though he was in prison. He spent this time catching up on novels, playing tennis and volleyball. Jim felt fine while Theresa felt worse and worse.

It seemed obvious that she was depressed, not only by the pain of living without Jim, but by her feelings of guilt because she was free while he was in prison. Although she had never discussed it with him, she felt that he had cheated on taxes for money to impress her and make her happy. Theresa's worries festered into an abscess of fears.

Ideas can cut like scalpel blades. Sometimes fears create painful boils of guilt that only a knife can cure. I gave her a viciously sharp idea.

"Theresa, what would it be like if, while Jim is in prison, you still visited him, but instead of being depressed you enjoyed your life and really had a wonderful time? If instead of looking sad when you visit, you looked vivacious and exuberant? If, while Jim is locked up, even though he *might* have done it for you, you still had the guts to let yourself have a great time?"

She was speechless. Red with astonishment at the heresy my question implied, Theresa tried to stutter out a reply.

I didn't give her a chance to talk. "Think about it for a while, Theresa. Don't give an answer just yet. Let the thought sink in for a moment . . . just *feel* what it would be like if, instead of dressing in the drab, dull colors you're wearing today, you'd let yourself be attractive again. You'd let yourself have a good time, an exciting, satisfying life . . . just *feel* what that would be like!" I was asking her to try a drug, the drug of a new idea to cure her self-imposed sickness, a thought that would induce chemical changes in her brain to make the stability of her misery suddenly unstable.

"You're picking on me! It's not fair!" Theresa wasn't kidding. She genuinely resented the idea-drug I had given her. And yet, almost as quickly as she complained, she relented. It was like half-pushing away a dentist after he touched a sore tooth. At first one might push him away, but finally give in; after all, drilling the tooth now would prevent a worse pain later.

I began to lean harder. "What would it be like? *How miserable do you have to be* in order to maintain your self-respect? Could you love yourself even if you had a good time while Jim is in prison?" It was time for Theresa to face her fears.

The idea was beginning to work its effects. "But, if I just enjoyed myself and didn't care whether he was in prison or not, wouldn't that mean that I can't establish closeness with anybody? That he really doesn't mean a thing to me . . .?"

"That's *ridiculous!* Certainly you care that he's in prison. You've shown him how much you love him. If you have a good time while you're not with him, how does that mean that you're not capable of love, that you can't establish a closeness with anybody? *How much* pain do you have to suffer on a daily basis? *How much* do you have to torture yourself to prove to yourself that you care about him? *What percentage of your time has to be spent being miserable?"*

There's something about judo and all such "combat" approaches that seems unfair, because they turn people's own force back on themselves. So unfair . . . but so effective. She took the bait.

"Oh, I don't know . . . five percent, maybe . . ." She thought about it for a moment.

"Okay, five percent of sixteen working hours . . . sixteen hours a day . . . that comes up to forty-five minutes a day, and you can have fun the rest of the time."

Theresa jumped upright in her seat. "What are you doing to me? I don't understand what's going on. I don't want to think this way!" She seemed to explode with contradicting emotions.

"Wait . . . I'm feeling the strangest sensation right now. Over the last few weeks I've had an odd, prickly itching on my skin . . . and right now I feel that it has suddenly been ripped off. I can't believe it. It's true. I don't have to feel bad. I *can* be free." The idea-drug hit its target.

"Well, Theresa, with Job it was boils. With you it's a prickly blanket. But I want to know how you're going to spend the other ninety-five percent of your time. How are you going to have all of that fun and satisfaction you've been denying yourself? Let me hear about it."

We both laughed, but I was quite serious. We then continued our conversation with Theresa planning some specific ways she could take better care of herself. Theresa changed after an idea upset the stability of her old habits. The upset was therapeutic, not because it was done by a therapist, but because she used it to live more flexibly and to grow. There had been something she was afraid to look at and think about. Yet, by deliberately thinking it, she became strong enough to address the question, "What am I going to do about it?"

She decided to take the chance of having a good time, even though Jim was locked up and to take the chance that she might even feel worse if she would dare to have a good time. An idea, within moments during our session, had changed her chemistry. She seized the opportunity to make the thought permanent . . . "I *can* be free . . ."

HOOKED ON BELIEVING

If ideas are drugs, then can you get addicted? Yes. Many average-appearing people are secret belief addicts, thought junkies, or closet concept freaks. They waste their lives trying to prove and reprove some useless point. Rather than look for multiple perspectives, they get locked into a single, narrow view.

One basic warning we'd give is *avoid addiction*, even to ideas. Ideas feed different selves within a person and some selves can become hooked. Like a fat twelve-year-old child whose closeness to the refrigerator exceeds all other attachments, selves can be hungry creatures. They grow fond of ideas and situations, and can set you up to prove something. Lots of people grow up with the idea that they're not good enough and spend the rest of their lives secretly creating situations in which to fail, get rejected or be humiliated, over and over again, just to confirm their hidden belief.

Others fear physical destruction so much that they seek to stare it down by a life of constant danger. Some are so afraid of dying that they avoid living life fully or rush into death by taking their own lives.

And, of course, idea addicts, like social drinkers or clandestine pill freaks, usually deny they've got the beginnings of a severe problem. It's always somebody else who's the junkie.

Most people have never had close contact with alcoholics or junkies. Addicts may seem alien, as though they were not like the rest of us. But it's often only a difference of degree, not of kind. Getting hooked on harmful ideas is frighteningly similar to getting hooked on dangerous drugs.

Some people can't see their addictions and claim they don't get high from their thoughts, so how could they be hooked? But who said anything about pleasure? Junkies aren't addicts because it feels good. There is some initial euphoria when one starts using drugs, but pretty soon it's just a question of taking the dope to keep from getting sick. Often the high is really just relief from the pain people are feeling about themselves and life. It's not pleasure they get hooked on as much as the numbness. In the beginning, the thought isn't even, "I felt good the last time I took heroin. I think I'll get some more." No, most of the time it's more like a light comes on somewhere in their head, saying, "Get heroin." Very robot-like and mechanical.

Thought addictions work the same way. If people get hooked on feeling bad, they become robots and respond to doses of thoughts like "You're a failure." It's not that they really like telling themselves they're failures; they become addicted to the routine. That's both the attitude and the problem. Drugs and ideas are never bad; it's simply that people use them poorly. No instability means no growth. Rather than using their ability to invent and grow, people often settle for the stable routine of being hooked.

Insidious preconceptions can color one's thinking. People often don't notice their own habits. It is only when they stop taking the dope that they realize how badly they're addicted. Otherwise, they may stay hooked on beliefs and never know it.

Words are the currency of mental commerce. They define beliefs and subtle preconceptions. Although personal philosophies are rarely clear statements, repeated use of certain key words reveals what one believes. For example, a person may not openly state, "My personal philosophy is that I'm not worth very much. Therefore, I *have* to do everything possible to take care of all the people around me." Still, that entire statement may be contained within one's habitual use of "should," "ought to" and "have to."

Words are just tools which have evolved into certain standard shapes and sizes. They can be quite a help with some tasks. But there are times to use tools and times to put them down. You wouldn't walk around carrying a screwdriver all the time, so why get hooked into using the same words constantly? The trick is to learn how to grip the tools tightly enough to use them, and how to put them down when you're done.

A few months ago Kay came to my office. Before I even saw her I had my own habitual idea, the theory that anybody coming into my office is probably hurting in some way. I try not to get hooked on that idea, but so far it has been a good tool. Kay had a different idea. She couldn't understand why she came in.

"I don't know why I came here . . . I just can't figure it out . . . I feel sort of blah, so I called up to make an appointment after your lecture last week. Maybe I'm bored?"

Another idea popped into my mind. That Kay had that sweet-sour pain so loved by intellectuals, that morass called existential neurosis, that feeling of emptiness and despair amalgamated with contempt for anyone "stupid" enough to feel good.

"I don't understand. Should I tell you why you came here?" I decided to point out that I didn't know the rules of her self-imposed game. Playing dumb can be an effective tool.

"I don't know . . ." Kay avoided the attempted humor of my response. To her life was grim. "Whatever I do, it seems I have the same empty feelings . . . blank . . . nowhere . . . Look, I know it's not unique to me . . . I know it's just the human condition." She waved her cigarette in a gesture of sophisticated boredom, seeming to emphasize that this was no everyday misery. Her suffering had been cultivated through years of college education.

"Ummm . . . *heavy*." I nodded my head as if congratulating her on the completion of her Master's thesis. The effect was immediate.

"What!" She snapped in a tone of righteous indignation, as though she came to my office prepared to play this human misery game by the official international rules, and somehow I was cheating.

"Well, okay, that's deep, isn't it? Very phi-lo-*soph*-i-cal . . . eh?" I raised my eyebrows and straightened back in my chair as if taken aback by her penetrating analysis of life.

"You're making fun of me!" Kay was no longer indignant. She was enraged. She had given me a chance to come to my senses, and here I was escalating my impropriety.

"I'm not making fun of *you*, Kay, but of your ideas, your theories, your beliefs. You've got yourself boxed in by them."

"Hey, I didn't make this up!" Kay screamed, "I didn't invent this role. Look . . . we all live and die . . . and what *difference* does it make! WHAT DOES IT ACCOMPLISH?!!!" Her palms were held aloft, her fingers spread wide in a beseeching gesture to some power above us.

"Kay, who are you talking to?" I asked in such a quiet whisper, Kay seemed shocked for a moment. She had been screaming, beseeching someone—a deaf god or an uncaring universe. She seemed startled momentarily, surprised by the extent of her own hunger.

After my question, she stumbled as if she lost her track for a moment. She seemed confused by her own thoughts. Up to that point, she had been carping like a person in a political argument, mindlessly rerunning old complaints. Now for an instant she seemed to be in touch with a raw experience of her inner pain.

"Why is the world like it is?" Not a bad question. But Kay had asked it to herself at least ten thousand times. Even worse, she was expecting a straight answer. She had never thought of philosophies, ideas and words as mere tools. This oversight was peculiar, especially since she had attained her Ph.D in philosophy and was aware (intellectually, at least) that throughout history old philosophical ideas have always been replaced by new ones. Yet she was still caught up in trying to figure it all out. (Maybe I'll get it by next week . . . maybe a new workshop would help . . . maybe . . .)

Many intellectuals get hooked on believing life can be solved. Thinking can be fun or useful, if you've got a particular job which requires thinking. But, if you're thinking in order to try to figure it all out, you'll never even get started. The fundamental premise behind Western-style linear human logic (that one thing at a time can be considered) doesn't apply to the big issues of life. Sooner or later, such fallacies catch up with you.

Kay's formidable intellect, Ph.D degree, excellent job and all her other assets weren't enough. While Barry, her boyfriend, would tenderly whisper, "I love you," Kay's mental gears kept on grinding, "Does he *really* love me?" "Do I *really* love him?" "What good does any of this ever do?" The doubts raged on; Kay had developed an addiction to a poisonous group of ideas:

First premise—No matter what you do, you eventually die and fade into oblivion.

Second premise—No matter what anyone else says about love, the fact is that everyone ultimately cares more about themselves than anyone else.

Conclusion—Love and all related sentiments are a sham. Nothing is worth doing because nothing makes any difference.

The bondage of logic. Like straps and chains, logic can become perverse sport for those who like that kind of thing. But to be hooked on self-torture, addicted to it because you think it's right, is really just a game in which you pretend to be in control to hide from facing the uncontrollable. Logic can be a useful tool; when carried too far it becomes an implement of suicide.

Kay was slipping into a pit of despair because she tried to think too much. I pushed her to feel the overwhelming intensity of her emotions. In the few sessions we had, I tried to help Kay live instead of only think about living.

It didn't work. Kay didn't change. Why? Maybe she wasn't ready. Maybe I pushed too hard. Maybe she was too in love with her problems. Maybe I couldn't see the approach she needed. Maybe . . . who knows?

But there's little doubt about the results: Kay stayed stuck. She was just as cynical and bitter when we stopped as when we began. Her last words to me showed how trapped she remained: "I think I've finally got it figured out. Nobody ever changes. We all just get worse."

Ultimately, there isn't any such thing as a single logic. There are an infinite variety of logics. There's the classical Aristotelian logic so beloved by St. Thomas Aquinas. But there's also the schizophrenic logic only really known by lunatics. And there is computer logic, the species of reason based on electronic switching. There is no one perfect reason we humans can ever use. It just doesn't work that way.

We may smugly laugh at prehistoric tribesmen who worshipped their flint arrowheads. Yet are we more enlightened when we treat reason as deity? Rigid devotion to one system of making sense is dangerous. Reason, ideas and words are man-made tools, never the final truth. The craziest thing about this world is that *it doesn't make sense.* Life is not a rational process. The real world is obstinately paradoxical. The big truths in life, the profound experiences and intense emotions are always far beyond the meager capabilities of human reason.

Such sentiments are not simply anti-intellectualism. Precision and clarity are vital to some areas of human endeavor. Without the logic of applied mathematics, for example, modern agriculture would be unable to feed as many as it does. But the nagging, frightened, homesick voices within are not silenced by common sense. Feelings move people more than any other force. Reason alone cannot meet the biggest challenges of life.

As children, Americans are taught that somebody somewhere knows what's going on. "Reasonable," "logical" and "rational" are words used by parents and teachers to suggest good, safe and under control and social myths continue. The stories of Achilles or Hercules are no longer revered. Tales about logic and science are concocted in their place. Such tools helped put a man on the moon. But don't think for a minute that you can logic your life out. Finding your path demands *both* mind and heart.

It's ironic that, while the application of scientific knowledge has often been shortsighted, its development has always been squarely based on a balance of head and heart. People would be better off were they to develop the vigorous evolutionary approach to knowledge that science uses. In general, the scientific community rewards creativity and new ideas. Science itself is an adventurous enterprise, constantly exploring and searching for ways to incorporate new thinking. Final answers are never found; rather the task is to refine the "state of the art," constantly.

Isaac Newton, for example, developed a theory in the seventeenth century about how things fall to the ground. He called his ideas the "Laws of Gravitation." His theories worked beautifully for everything from pendulum to cannon balls; that is, until the late nineteenth century. Then it became evident that his tools only work well on average-sized objects moving relatively slowly. Newton's tools had some serious limitations for understanding tiny, tiny things like atomic particles which move almost as fast as light itself.

So Albert Einstein had a better idea and produced a workable, relativistic theory that did a better job of explaining such phenomena. Is Einstein's theory true? What a dumb question! Is a screwdriver true? The question is: "Is it useful? Theories, like tools, may be useful, but they are never *the truth*. Some people get so attached to their tools they worship them as the only way to do it. Little wonder they find the changeover to new tools painful. A few theoretical physicists went to great lengths to figure out some ways to keep the old tools working even when it became obvious that they couldn't do the job. And now it becomes apparent that Einstein's tools may have some serious limitations too. Nothing lasts forever.

Evolution is at work. The evolution of scientific knowledge follows the same process of trial and error used by the evolution of living things. Nature herself has been designing life on this planet in a continuing process of constant improvisation and innovation. Some of the species that walked, swam or flew over this planet have been extravagant experiments to find out what works best. If individuals follow the same fluidity, the same eagerness to try new things that science and nature use, they might begin to grasp one of the most precious secrets of growth—change is proper, change is natural, change is inevitable. Everything is in constant flux. If you cling to habit, you're futilely swimming against the flow.

PART THREE

Spirituality and the End of the Line

"We are what we think. All that we are arises with our thoughts . . ." GAUTAMA BUDDHA

FREEDOM FROM YOURSELF

Of all the freedoms, probably the most precious is freedom from the traps you create for yourself. To be sure, there are countless forms of bondage caused by environments, people and diseases. Yet what one does to oneself is always far worse. Shakespeare, who had something wise to say about almost everything, points this out so well: ". . . there is nothing either good or bad but thinking makes it so."

But how can you get free of self-imposed bondage? Life can be seen as a game played on ascending levels. You begin life's game on the biological-needs level of food, shelter and clothing: "Eat or be eaten." Much of the world is still struggling at this basic level. Next are psychological needs: love, significance, security, fun. Most of this book deals with ways to meet these needs. But, after you satisfy biological and psychological needs, there's still more to do. Just when you make it on one level, it is time to go to the next.

Those who struggle their way up from poverty may get to experience the whole scenario in one lifetime. Starting in abject deprivation, they long to satisfy simple biological needs. "Someday . . . I'll be able to eat a meal whenever I want!" If you go to bed so hungry that you dream of food, the prospect of guaranteed meals can be a laudable goal. You can say the word "food" and it rings with deep meaning and significance, as though food means finally making it. But after you gain the financial security to ensure an adequate diet, you may find a thick juicy steak isn't the promised land it once seemed to be.

Most of the people we see in therapy have long since passed this level of struggle. Seeing a shrink doesn't usually cross your mind when you're starving to death. We get called in when people have met all their biological needs and are struggling with the psychological ones. "I just want to feel good. I feel so empty." Yet, like having a full belly, meeting psychological needs is not the end. Even with self-respect, love, security and fun, you might find a longing for the next step. It's back-to-school time again.

We think part of freedom, indeed the most essential part, is being free to be the imperfect, striving creatures that human beings seem to be. One's task is to learn to be the paradoxical mixture of perfection and chaos, of pain and peace, to be all the extremes without slighting the possibilities that lead to growth. Meeting psychological needs doesn't end the story. Instead, it teaches you to see your hunger as natural and proper. It sharpens your taste for the continuing turmoil that is growth.

At times, however, the endless succession of levels can be maddening. It's like finally becoming a big shot in high school only to experience the degradation of entering as a college freshman the following year. Each step up brings one to the bottom of another ladder. The cruel truth is you never get finished; as long as you breathe, life is an endless series of graduations and re-enrollments.

Endless growth can be upsetting. There's no way around it. Living things seem to want to work out a familiar routine; it's the hope of living with minimum effort. Dig in, get comfortable and change as little as possible. This approach has worked well for creatures like roaches. They worked out their formula of how to make it in the world back when fern trees were turning into petroleum. Fortunately, for the rest of us, some of the monster roach varieties died out. Nevertheless, the basic model has been unchanged for millions of years. Other creatures that tried staying the same didn't fare as well. Dinosaurs are the favorite example, but from trilobites to dodos, countless species have made an appearance for a time, then slipped off or were pushed into the dim void of extinction.

Humans do the same sort of thing in miniature. People who struggle up from the primordial muck of poverty often continually try to prove they made it. ("And I can eat *steak* every night!") For others, such amusement eventually wears thin. People who begin their lives in emotional poverty, where they never feel very good about themselves, can spend the rest of their existence trying to impress somebody with something (incredible *tennis game*, beautiful *Gucci shoes*, outrageous new *girlfriend*), but that also wears thin. In fact, anything wears thin after awhile. It may take a long time—cockroaches are still going strong after millions of years, but, eventually, they'll be gone too.

There is wisdom in the message from Ecclesiastes, "to every thing there is a season . . ." People should learn how to tell when something is wearing thin, learn how to tell when something isn't right for them, learn how to tell when something is eating at them; learn how to tell when to let go. Regardless of what you do, sometimes in this life you will feel happy and other times you will feel sad.

At best, people are all wandering around in the dark. But like a blind man who's looking for a warm room, it is possible to detect currents of air that have a slightly higher temperature. It is possible to sort of feel one's way out. Sure, once you give up the familiar you might walk into walls and stumble over things, you might fall down, but, if you keep trying to feel for the warm areas, you will move on. You can learn. You can become growth itself.

To go beyond your biological and psychological needs, you must play in a game that is far more complex. At the biological level, there is struggle—you against "them." At the psychological level, there is room for some cooperation and mutual understanding. Yet the belief that each person is a separate entity remains a fundamental premise. It is possible to entertain some liberal notions such as "we're all in this together," but the consciousness of oneself as a separate being is etched into each human's psychological hardware.

NOW WE GET SPIRITUAL ON YOU

Although the two of us don't have a clear view of the next level up, we can share some glimpses of what we see. The task of the next level is losing one's self. Losing everything: all the things you thought were true, all the clever tricks you acquired, all the experiences you saved, all the polished nonsense you worked so hard to perfect. You don't have to change your name, give away your possessions or eat only vegetables. It's a more subtle shift. You begin to loosen your grip on "proving anything." You flow into seeing a profound sense to life, even the contradictions, the hidden ecstasies, the inevitable suffering. What used to sound like gibberish begins to take on deep meaning: you don't exist, nothing exists, and everything exists. Gradually, you refine the intuitive part of your being, develop that "creative action" phase we spoke earlier. In time, you are not the you who was born one human being. You wake up to the connectedness of all life. You are everything. You no longer see distinctions between the essential nature of you as opposed to everything else. You understand that bad people no more exist than bad trees bo. You become freedom itself.

What we're talking about is a spiritual level of existence. We're almost afraid to use the words. Over the centuries, some of biggest conmen on earth have been preachers or crusaders. They cheapen the spiritual and give deity a bad name. They exploit God, riding His coattails as though He were a president campaigning to help re-elect some local official. "God has spoken to me and He wants to tell you that . . ." or worse "I know God wants you to . . ." People with that kind of message make one tense, waiting for the inevitable request for donations. Money and power, Hallelujah!

Yet there is some kind of upward direction, some kind of spiritual way out that your heart will reveal. The advice we're offering is to listen to your intuitive sense. If you find it leading you into yoga, vegetarian diets, joining a church, or even just playing a guitar with all your heart, go try it out. Then take a break after a month on your new path and ask yourself "Where is this getting me?" Listen with your heart. Just because someone else says it's spiritual doesn't mean it's right for you. Be like the blind man who feels his way towards the warmth. You're playing on a new level now and old rules won't apply. Apparently opposite ideas may simultaneously be true. Never rely solely on your rational mind. Use both head and heart.

It's no wonder that most people shut out the spiritual level entirely. It's far easier to remain like the roach. And there's probably nothing wrong about staying in place. If you want to be a roach and are perfectly happy being a roach, then remain a roach forever. But if you aren't happy with the insect life, take a step upward. Without fanfare, without public display, seek a taste of spiritual growth.

Maybe the word "God" reminds you of fakes and Holy Rollers too much for you to ever be comfortable using it. Okay, don't use it. Words are just words. For "God," like "love," has suffered heavy abuse over the ages. If so, ignore the words. "God" is much bigger than words could ever say. "Peace," "the flow," "the oversoul," "the force," call it as you see it. It's the experience that counts. Go outside. Feel the trees, feel the sky, feel the great world turning. Work, play, rest, create, live each moment as fully as possible. Look around, look within, feel the presence of overwhelming love.

If you're uncomfortable with religions, churches and hordes of believers, then take a walk in the woods or sit on the beach. Make your church portable. Make your heart your center. Look for what gives you deepest joy. The next level adds spiritual fulfillment to your list of needs. Your task is to find it.

Spirituality isn't really supernatural or unbelievable. It's simply another reality. If you had talked about electrons a few hundred years ago, people would have laughed. Now people take these little particles for granted, channeling them through wires to make things work. The more believable spiritual truths become, the more you see them everywhere you look. But like sub-atomic particles, you have to look for them, you have to open yourself to seeing before you know they're there. It's a choice. You can open your eyes or keep them shut.

We often hear people say they want something to believe in. Yet they seem to have a habitual reluctance to believe in themselves. "Something to believe in" often means "Won't somebody give me a break?" Begging when the heat is on—that's the closest many get to the spiritual. Their prayers sound like deals rather than devotions. "Look, God, I know I've been bad, but if you get me out of this jam I swear I'll do better." And once the danger passes, you guessed it, they slip back into the same old habits.

Our culture tends to conceive of the supreme deity as an irritable old man who is hidden away in an administrative office in the sky. By this vision, He is like a high school principal. You're sent to Him when you've been had. This version of seeing God as outside yourself makes you feel weak, lonely and isolated.

Unless you love yourself, you can't feel God within you. God wouldn't live in shoddy quarters. Love of self and God are one and the same. That doesn't mean humans are gods—they're simply part of it all. Selfishness, of all things, can open your eyes to your own lovability. True self-love is not done to impress anyone else, for approval or recognition. It's an intimate act between you and yourself. Self-love seems to unlock a storehouse of divine love. You find compassion for your human weaknesses and tenderness spreads to others. You become immersed in love's flow, and can feel the truth of such paradoxes as being part of all life.

Other visions of deity then become possible; God sits for many portraits. One God is the whole of it all, greater than the sum of the parts, the male and female of all relationships, the both and neither of every paradox, the focal point of all living energy, the light that leads us on.

Seen this way, the ancient benediction, "may God shine His face upon you," has subtle meaning. Life often seems to be a jumble of kaleidoscopic images. God's shining His face on you may be the gift of showing you the divine sense in the contradictions you see. Kind faces calm humans under stress. God's face may be the vision of profound order in this living universe.

Look for whatever brings you awe and peace. That's awe and peace, not stability and security. Spiritual paths help you refocus your purposes. They lift you so that you don't get locked into everyday existence. To be sure, this can go to an extreme. You could like merely for some pie-in-the-sky afterlife. The key, again, is balance. The biological is real, the psychological is real, the spiritual is real. Everyone can live on all levels at once.

THE BUSINESS OF BELIEVING

People worry about how the spiritual might conflict with their established habits. "What will I have to give up?" And that's not such a bad question. The "cost effectiveness" of embarking on a more spiritual path needs to be looked at thoroughly before one goes off the deep end. Many people don't take such an open approach. Rather than weigh the pros and cons of a spiritual path, they choose to dabble lightly in religions—a little lip service to Jesus, a sneak look at the day's horoscope, a browse through a story on mysticism.

Religions are maps to guide one along a spiritual path. *They are not the path itself.* Religions are any organized belief system from Catholicism to communism, from psychoanalysis to est. There are many aspects to religion. There's the "vision" side of it, an experience an inspired few tried to share with everyone else. Mohammed, Moses, Jesus, Krishna and Buddha each had a picture of "what it's all about." But religions also have social and business aspects—"The Church, Inc." Religious organizations construct buildings, give people jobs, print holy books and make converts. These organizations are manned by the "employees," the individual people who follow that particular faith.

It's easy to confuse these different aspects of religion and misjudge the true cost effectiveness. For example, you may know someone who's regarded as a devout follower by others, but seems like a total jerk to you. The person in question may be confined by an idea about his or her faith which is too narrowly defined. (Some Christians are devious about expressing anger because they're afraid to admit such feelings openly. This is odd, since Christ himself put on some marvelous displays of rage.) Or the individual might be an essentially false person; false in the relationship with himself or herself, with other people, with his or her God. It's also possible that you may misperceive that person, allowing your own bias to color your view. Whatever your conclusion, though, it's fair to say that a religious message should never be judged by its church or followers alone.

In a sense, religions are like styles in dress, clothing or music. As the world changes, styles change. Ideas on "how to do it" either survive or vanish. Church, Inc., organizations don't approve of this view. They pretend to be the only permanent thing in this world of changes—the Official Word. But all things must pass, and religions, like everything else, are born, flourish, and die.

Each person is a religious consumer trying to decide if it's worth it to buy a particular way. Each person may long for a higher sense of purpose. Which way should you go? The answer is pretty simple: choose religion in the same way an enlightened consumer would choose clothes, cars, food or anything else. They hear about it, investigate it, try it, and if they like it, buy it.

Whether you're an agnostic, atheist or believer, the tests for the product are exactly the same:

- Does your belief in something (or nothing) help you love yourself or others?
- Does it help you find meaning in life?
- Does it help you respect yourself?
- Does it help you find peace, love and joy?
- Most of all, is it right for you?

Check regularly; what's right for you today may not be right for you tomorrow. If the answers to the above are "yes," hang on to what you've got. If not, then it's worth looking for some new tools. The journey begins within.

BYE-BYE

Our book ends where it began—inside you. We started by urging you to take better care of your psychological needs. Now we're saying that when you've got that together, look at some of the other levels—spiritual, cosmic, divine, whatever you wish to call them. We've taken you as far as we can.

a few afterthoughts

WHICH IS THE BEST THERAPY?

It has no name. It transcends all schools and theoretical divisions. The best analysts, behaviorists, gestaltists, cognitive-behaviorists, medical modelists—the best therapists of any persuasion—use it as their basic approach. It is the key to how humans help each other heal.

These are strong words. In the world of therapy, vigorous partisanship is the rule. Therapists label themselves and each other by their differences. Similarities are usually ignored or denied. Yet we would insist that there is a general approach, a broad common way, that embraces all healing despite the superficial divisions.

We wrote this book primarily for the mental health care consumer, the "patient" or "client" as this person is called in the trade. But after presenting our ideas on change and self-help, we decided to also share our views on therapy itself. General readers are by no means excluded from this section if a bit of "psych jargon" can be tolerated. Indeed, we would welcome the discerning consumer-patient in this review of the enterprise of therapy. If the field is ever to make progress in the quality of care *actually delivered* it will only come from vigorous consumer pressure. When the public demands little, it gets less.

Therapeutic approaches begin life through the creativity of their originators. Initially, the new approach is simply "what the therapist is doing." Study and research may refine the approach but all too often, a morbid process also sets in. Devout followers appear. Rather than see the specific approach as a tool, these followers rigidly apply it as the official word. Movements begin. Apostles, true believers, and institute certification gradually kill the spirit of the new approach—what began as an idea about doing therapy gradually becomes corrupted into a fundamentalist religion.

It happened to psychoanalysis. It happened to behavior modification. It happened to Gestalt therapy, transactional analysis, and transcendental meditation. Rigid behaviorism has been saved from its black box, people-are-like-rats orientation, by amalgamating with cognitive therapy into a highly useful cognitive-behavioral approach. When good ideas become reified into fixed formulas, robot technicians are the usual result. Yet ironically, even when the originators deliberately foster the development of a therapeutic religion, they keep one special privilege to themselves: *the originator can break the rules at any time.*

Is such a privilege dishonest? We don't think so. For whether they admit it or not, the inventors know that each approach is just a tool. Even Papa Freud once said, "There's a time and place for psychoanalysis." But devout followers miss this vital point. They seem to think salvation lies in the words themselves, rather than the spirit they carry. Little wonder that a therapy which is dull and dreary when applied by a narrow-minded technician can still sing brilliantly in the hands of a true master. Therapy is not different from any of the arts—mere technical repetition can never produce a fine performance. Something more subtle is needed.

The best therapy is firmly founded on this subtle something. The best therapists, regardless of how they label themselves, have all mastered this essence. Yet it cannot be named or adequately described; it is an entity that the puny technology of words fails to grasp. It is an intuitive, internal experience that can be learned but never told; as Louis Armstrong once said of jazz, "If you have to ask what it is, you just don't know."

To some, such assertions may seem like preposterous gibberish. We confess they sometimes sound that way to us. But the practical business of doing therapy is not a wholly logical venture. Therapy is not a science. It is an art, like the making of fine wine. Such subtle crafts reluctantly yield their secrets to the scientific method; science makes bland wine and poor therapy. Perhaps some day, if science extends its reach, it may be able to embrace therapy and all the other arts as well. But for now, science's love of reductionism, logic, and precision excludes it from areas where the answers can be many and contradictory. Each human interaction involves such a vast number of variables that no formula or set of rules can be rigidly applied. Moreover, since boundaries in the lands of emotion are frequently indistinct, the variables themselves often escape definition. No one can say just how a person changes. Exactly how the best therapists work escapes rigorous definition.

To be sure, science does have a place. Even master vintners use scientific tools to check their crops. The best therapists, likewise, apply scientific knowledge in areas where it works well. For science is simply *one* way of knowing about the world. Like the doctrines and theories of the various therapeutic schools, it is simply a tool. As in any field, something else comes first—the master's feel for each tool's uses and limitations. Masters may choose different tools and work in different styles, but some indescribable excellence links them all. Indeed, this is just what makes them so good—the best therapy is simply what all the masters do.

Oddly, most writings on therapy focus on the tools themselves and overlook the crucial issue of how to use them well. This is hardly surprising since it is relatively easy to describe a tool and almost impossible to share a glimpse of what it takes to gain mastery (FIGURE 1). In this brief section, we shall attempt the ambitious goal of conveying some of what we think makes the best therapists so good. We shall accept the limitation that some indescribable essence, some touch that makes therapy art, cannot be captured in words. Nevertheless, it seems to us that many common elements in the way the best therapists work have gone

FIGURE 1
SOME PARTS OF THE BEST THERAPY ARE EASY TO DESCRIBE, OTHERS ESCAPE WORDS

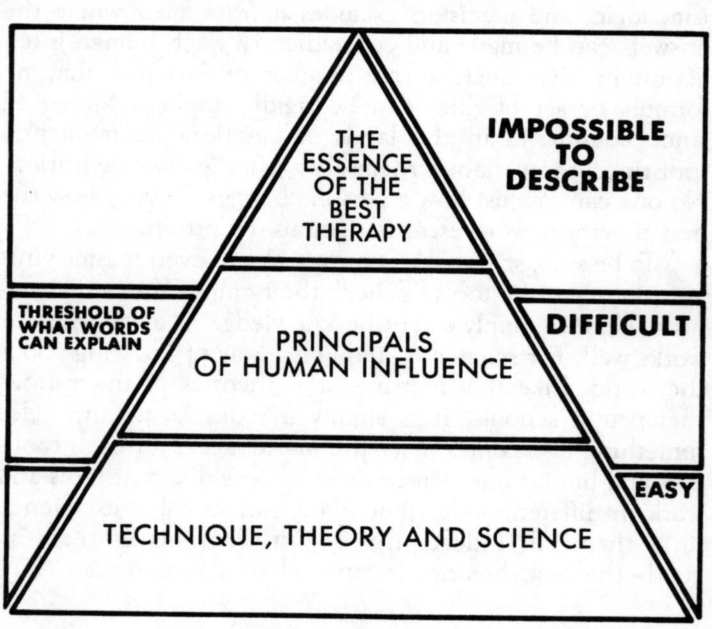

undiscussed because of undue emphasis on differences in their tools.

We have been fortunate enough to view the therapy performed by many superb clinicians. Videotape, film, and one-way mirrors do produce some distortions, but we have found the experience of watching quite illuminating. At one time, we both believed that one of the major therapies must be inherently superior to the others. After what we have seen, however, we have become convinced that some overriding process guides all the masters. Now we hope to focus some ideas about this process into a framework that might help the novice therapist learn faster and the consumer-patient evaluate therapy more wisely. We are not offering these ideas as scientific proof or irrefutable arguments. Rather, we hope simply to share a view of this paradoxical enterprise called therapy. Such a broad agenda demands a format the size of a book rather than a chapter. We know that. But we couldn't let this opportunity go by without at least a brief discussion on the subject.

To help us clarify our opinions on therapy let us divide therapists into three hypothetical groups: "the best," "the worst," and "the middle of the road." The best therapists are those who are most effective and efficient as judged by their clients. The worst are the least effective and efficient as well as the most frequently destructive. We shall describe these extremes in some detail, as they best illustrate the significant features. The middle of the road therapists can, for our present purposes, be ignored. While they may occasionally be brilliant and occasionally destructive, they generally remain safely mediocre.

PLANNING WHERE TO GO—THE GOALS OF THERAPY

THE BEST THERAPISTS, REGARDLESS OF THEORETICAL ORIENTATION, HAVE THE SAME GENERAL GOALS.

Depending on one's point of view, this statement may seem absurd or self-evident. When one considers therapy in its broadest sense (psychotherapy, behavior modification, chemotherapy, etc.) the most salient feature is the extent of disagreement on what it's all supposed to do. "Outcome measures," that is, criteria for measuring patient improvement, have yet to be devised in any way that has gained wide acceptance. Everyone has their own idea about what "mental health" looks like.

Still, it seems to us, that the best therapists intuitively understand when a patient is getting better. Their more rigid colleagues could argue the definition of "better" indefinitely—for devoted behaviorists, it's observable changes, for Gestaltists, emotional centeredness; for analysts, insight gains, and so on *ad nauseam*. The best therapists seem to have a gift for rising above the nomenclature squabble and seeing the hidden truth within.

It may be that the truth isn't all that hidden. Patients often seem to grasp "better" through that marvelous facility of common sense. Indeed, patients know far more about their care than most therapists seem willing to believe. While patients may lack a clear idea of what they want, and may resist attempts at help, they almost always know when they're getting better. Yet patient opinions are generally viewed with skepticism, condescension, or plain contempt by the therapeutic establishment.

Unfortunately, patients tend to enter therapy with low self-esteem, looking for relief from the *qualified expert*. As a result, they are generally content to play the role of obedient, respectful recipients of the therapists' magic (interpretations, reinforcements, etc.). If the patient is to leave therapy more competent to run his life, then he must move in the direction of being a responsible, active partner in the therapeutic enterprise itself. The best therapists encourage exactly that.

By helping the patient become actively involved, the therapist gains valuable input on where to go. This does not imply that the best therapists passively follow the patient's whims. Rather they seem to combine what they see and understand with what they have learned and know, then add this complex mixture to an intuitive sense of what "better" means.

WHILE THE BEST THERAPISTS ARE EXQUISITELY SENSITIVE TO PATIENT CHANGES, THE WORST THERAPISTS FAIL TO PERCEIVE WHETHER PATIENTS ARE IMPROVING OR DETERIORATING. This shocking assertion was suggested by what we have seen on videotape of therapy sessions. Of course, recording therapy on tape makes it easy for anyone to be a "Monday morning quarterback." Tape stops action, replays what really happened and clearly shows many micro-exchanges that went unnoticed during the therapeutic session. Yet such revealings help us all learn. Tape, more than any other medium, lets us see how good therapy works.

The best therapists seem constantly alert to the patient's mood and thinking. The worst therapists, on the other hand, get so wrapped up in their theoretical assumptions that they miss much of what's happening with their patients. Novice therapists are also prone to this malady, for they often feel so self-conscious and awkward ("*Now* what do I say?") that they miss half of what they would have seen were they safely protected video spectators. Learning to do therapy is a painful process.

Of all the worst therapists, the most destructive are those whose ethical posture might best be described as "loose." They ignore signs of patient improvement, subtly undermining any process in an apparent effort to keep the patient in therapy. Were efficiency a more important concept in the consumers' mind—time and dollars spent vs. therapeutic change achieved—these grossly inefficient and unethical therapists might not survive in the marketplace.

But how can even well-intentioned therapists be so blind to the patient's reality? The answer is inherent in human nature; we are all partially blind and see only what we are ready to see. Our expectations weave a subtle web of bias and prejudice. In time we become blind to our own blindness; our perceptual distortions become so automatic that they are invisible. If a person wears prismatic spectacles that invert all images, in a week or two the inversion is no longer obvious. Removing the distorting lenses *then* makes the world seem upside down. If lenses worn for a few weeks can cause such confused vision, it is hardly surprising that years of bias can distort what we see in patients.

274 SINCE NO SINGLE THEORETICAL STRUCTURE CAN ADEQUATELY DEFINE PATIENT IMPROVEMENT, THE BEST THERAPISTS FLEXIBLY USE SEVERAL PERSPECTIVES JOINED BY AN INTUITIVE SENSE OF "HEALTH."

Multiple images give the fullest picture. Almost everyone has seen photographs of the NASA command center with its rows of TV and computer consoles. Radar, radio, and video equipment follow each spacecraft as it takes off. The multiple image composite comes closest to telling the full story.

Using multiple images is not a new concept in psychiatry. Eclecticism was a movement in the 1950s that attempted to get a fuller picture of human behavior by combining the various theoretical schools of the day.[1] It was, however, like the Edsel automobile of the same decade, a less than stunning success. Eclecticism borrowed from here and there but seemed to lack a cohesive direction. More often than not its approaches were lumpy mixtures of incompatible techniques.

We believe the fundamental problem in previous "ecumenical" attempts has been a misperception of the place of therapy in doing therapy. While lip service is generally paid to the importance of rapport or "listening with a third ear," far greater emphasis is focused on seeing the patient through biochemical, analytic, cognitive or behavioral theories. "Conceptual" is a favorite word in such discussions, while "practical" almost never appears. Even the behaviorists, who would probably consider themselves "practical" in spirit, tend to focus so narrowly they ignore any issues that fail to neatly fit the behavioral paradigm. From our point of view, the existing schools all seem to overlook the practical issue of an *intuitive sense of improvement* that makes it possible for the best therapists to link the confusing array of patient images into a meaningful whole.

The images are confusing because we can never see all of the patient. Indeed, the observed patient is not the patient who is actually there. For whatever is actually there is unknowable—it's impossible to pick which reality *is the* reality. A therapist sees a patient through sensory apparatus that filters, extracts and analyzes. The act of perception emphasizes some features and glosses over others—what reaches consciousness is a biased image as though the patient were viewed through tinted glass (FIGURE 2). We could postulate a "ground reality" of the "patient who is actually there," but we can never see this phantom. All we see are our perceptions; these *observations* can never be the same thing as *that which we are observing.*

The use of theory interposes yet another layer of tint, for it filters the already filtered perceptions (FIGURE 3). Thus theories, even the best, are *reality twice removed.* In their highest use, theories are voluntary, interchangeable prejudices. By reducing what we see to a simplified model, theories emphasize important points that might have otherwise escaped our attention. Yet mismanaged, theories can become the invisible biases that blind the worst therapists to patient improvement.

FIGURE 2
OBSERVATIONS OF THE PATIENT ARE NOT OF THE PATIENT WHO IS ACTUALLY THERE

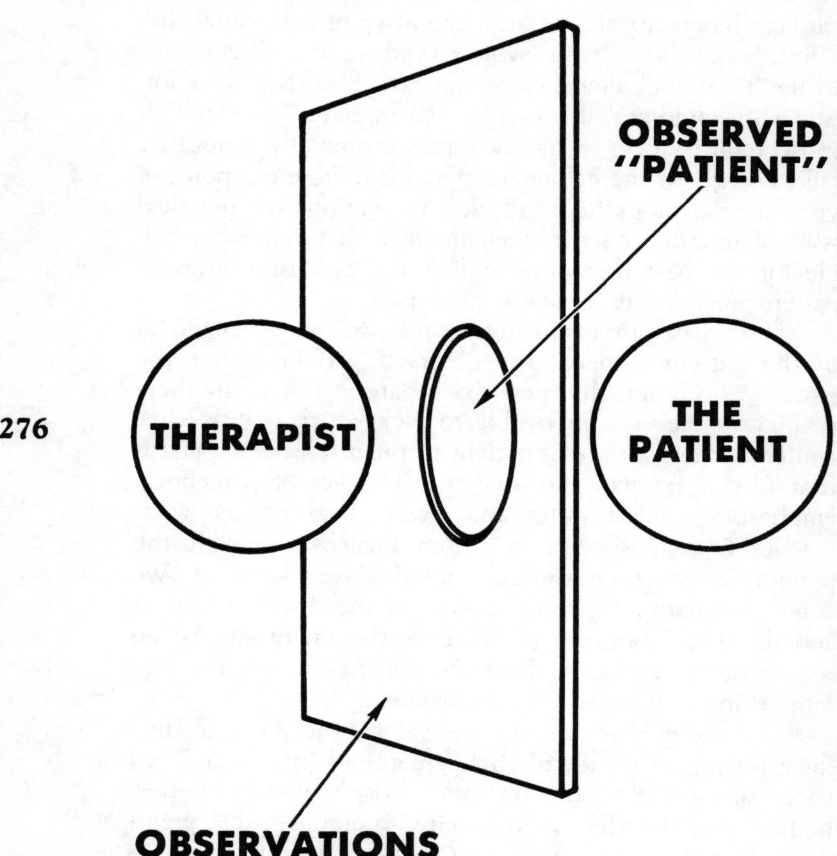

FIGURE 3
THEORIES ARE REALITY
TWICE REMOVED

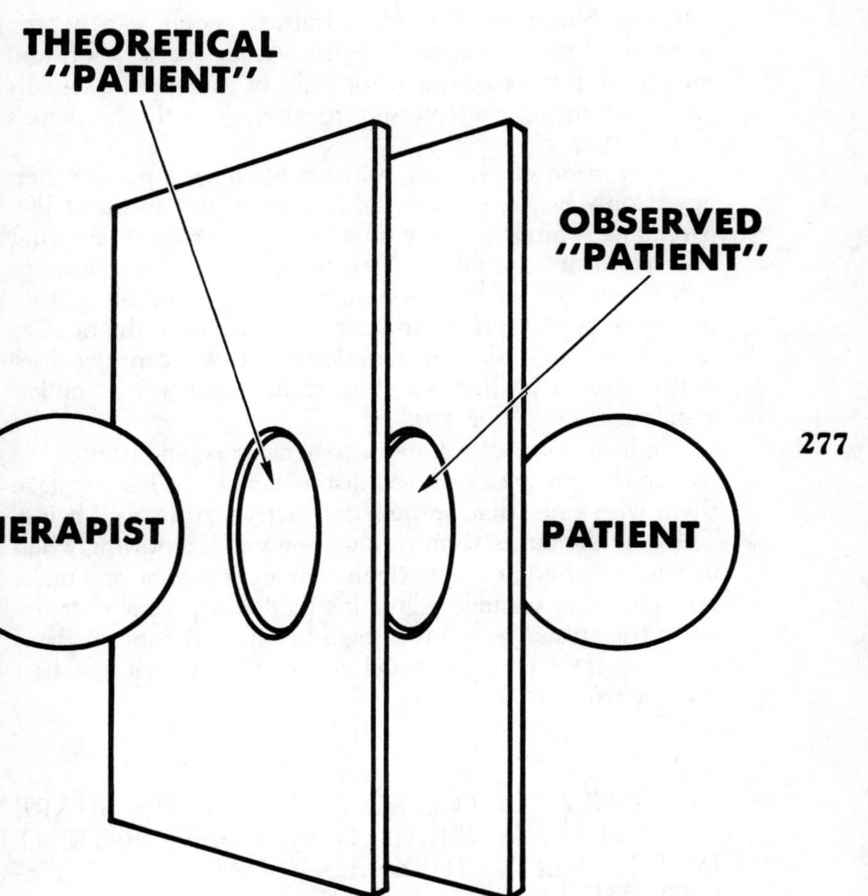

One might hypothesize that training and experience make one less susceptible to such severe distortions. Unfortunately, observations of psychiatric academia do not support this conclusion.[2] Training is often indoctrination in selective blindness. The most trained people can be the most blind to the patient's reality. Academic position and membership in professional societies or therapeutic schools can exert strong peer pressure to always see the Emperor's new clothes.

Distortion of perception inevitably plays a part in therapy if only because it inevitably plays a part in all of life. We humans produce perceptual distortions so regularly that they permeate the fabric of everyday life. In our efforts to survive, we reduce the "booming, buzzing, confusion" into manageable perceptions and concepts. We have the need to understand in order to function. But we can get into destructive ruts when we cling to any one way of understanding as the "true way."

Indeed, one could define therapy as an attempt to reduce the patient's own self-distortions, or at least replace them with ones that are less destructive to his well-being. The best therapists seem to have the gift of knowing when to relax their grip on a particular theoretical view and move on to another vantage point. It's hardly surprising that the worst therapists, locked into rigid beliefs and habits as they are, find it so hard to model the flexibility that the best therapy teaches.

NOT ONLY DO THE BEST THERAPISTS SHARE INTUITIVE GENERAL GOALS OF "PATIENT IMPROVEMENT," THEY ALSO SHARE SOME SPECIFIC THERAPEUTIC GOALS.

The difficulty in discussing therapeutic goals is primarily one of language. Each therapeutic school dictates its own criteria for successful treatment. In general, these concepts are non-intersecting with those of other schools. Yet we believe that the best therapists, regardless of what they say in professional meetings, seem to work towards more or less the same specific goals in actual practice.

We came to this conclusion after seeing therapists of purportedly antithetical schools say and do very similar things with patients. We saw renowned behaviorists reward the development of insight with a smile or nod. We watched as legendary analysts encouraged behavioral change with precisely timed questions. When questioned, each of these therapists usually explained their actions in the language of their specialized schools. More than a few however, shared our suspicion that apparently alien therapies have striking similarities.

The common maneuvers that we observed suggested that the best therapists might have similar specific therapeutic goals. Yet isn't the caution of this statement almost absurd? To the lay person, *of course* therapists try to do the same things. It is simply the overtrained professionals who exaggerate the importance of language and labels. Nevertheless, while many authors have proposed some reductionistic lists,[3,4] the pervasive assumption seems to be that irreconcilable differences exist between the various approaches. We disagree. All therapies are linked. The best therapists employ goals and principles that transcend the individual schools. The most meaningful division that is borne out by observation of videotape is not related to the theoretical schools at all: the best therapists do it one way and the worst another.

"BEST THERAPISTS" GOALS Goals for the patient (therapists for patients, and to varying degrees, patients for themselves)

DEVELOPMENT OF SELF-SUFFICIENCY *(autonomy, independence, self-directed planning) Patients usually wish for increased satisfaction and control. Therapists seem to focus on development of self-mastery and self-reliance necessary for the patient's goals.*

AVOIDANCE OF PERMANENT HARM *(counter-therapeutic relationships, over-dependence, exploitation) Therapy is not without risk and the best therapists seem to follow the medical dictum* primum non nocere: *"first, not to harm." Stress to the patient is widely used as a therapeutic tool, much as the cutting edge is used in surgery. Nevertheless, sanctions against permanent harm—especially exploitation of the patient psychologically, financially or sexually—seem fundamental to good therapy.*

RELIEF OF SYMPTOMS *(psychological pain, depression, anxiety, marital discord, alcoholism, etc.) This is the primary reason why patients seek therapy. While some therapists de-emphasize this goal, the best keep in mind that for patients, symptom relief is usually central.*

BALANCING OF CONFLICTING NEEDS *(intimacy vs. independence, work vs. play, security vs. excitement, etc.) External forces and internal pressures threaten to overwhelm individuals and groups. Learning how to take care of one's needs in the midst of conflict seems to be a key lesson for the patient.*

ESTABLISHMENT OF A POSITIVE SELF-IMAGE *(self-awareness, self-respect, compassion for deficiencies) Most therapists tend to foster psychological awareness. The best seem also to teach self-respect and self-compassion.*

FOSTERING OF THE INHERENT CAPACITY FOR SELF/HEALING *(growth, personal courage, honest self-evaluation, careful risk-taking) Ideally, the goal of therapy is to dispense with any further need for therapy. The best therapists seem to focus on this autonomy-related issue early and encourage patients (implicitly or explicitly) to take responsibility for their decisions and actions.*

"BEST THERAPISTS" GOALS Goals for the therapists (therapists for self; the best therapists usually explicitly share these goals with their patients)

SENSE OF PERSONAL SATISFACTION AND MEANING. *The best therapists all seem to want this goal but doing therapy is rarely their only source of meaning in life. It is as though periods of "not doing therapy" (play, vacations, hobbies, rest, etc.) are vital to doing the best therapy possible.*

INCOME AND PRESTIGE. *The best therapists seem quite open about the fact that doing therapy is also a business and their way of earning income. Yet they manage these financial aspects without becoming crass. These therapists usually admit that they enjoy the prestige and honor our society affords its healers. Yet they rarely succumb to the pomposity that afflicts much of the profession. In brief, the best therapists are open enough about their motivation so that they are not dominated by their own desires.*

"WORST THERAPISTS" GOALS Goals for the patient (therapists for patients—almost never openly discussed)

WHILE THE WORST THERAPISTS MAY PAY LIP SERVICE TO THE EXPLICIT GOALS OF THE BEST THERAPISTS, THEY COVERTLY PURSUE ENDS DESTRUCTIVE TO PATIENT IMPROVEMENT.

This is a serious charge. Anyone who has worked in the mental health field has seen the proof. Therapists who harm more than help are not rare. For many of these worst therapists, such covert goals may be, in psychoanalytic jargon, "unconscious." Just as often, they are deliberately deceitful. Little wonder that such "healers" tend to see the general public as adversaries.

GENERATION OF MORE BUSINESS *(more frequent visits, more hospitalizations, more referrals) The worst therapists regularly exploit their patients financially. Frequent patterns include billing for more time than is spent and unnecessary prolongation of outpatient therapy or hospitalization. Incompetent treatment often leads to the delivery of more care than is necessary, a trend which allows the worst therapists to reap financial benefit, even if they are not deceitful in their motives. A mixture of the two seems far more widespread—dragging out the therapeutic process with partial incompetence and occasional cheating. A strong financial incentive exists in that a few extra visits here and there soon add up to considerable therapist income. It is an abuse that is almost undetectable by the patient or insurance carrier.*

CESSATION OF COMPLAINTS. *This is not the same as symptom relief, for the worst therapists are mainly interested in having the patient stop complaining. Rather than seek genuine change, these therapists tend towards palliative drug treatments. It's hardly surprising that minor tranquilizers are the most widely prescribed drugs in the United States.*

DEVELOPMENT OF PATIENT DEPENDENCE. *By making decisions for the patient, often under the guise of "supportive" therapy, worst therapists foster increasing dependence. Patients succumb to this opiate with surprising frequency—having someone else "be responsible" is a temptation many find hard to resist. Third party payment (insurance and government sponsored programs) probably helps make this abuse so widespread. When the patient doesn't bear the expense of care, the usual consumer pressures for quality are absent. The result is occasionally as extreme as ten years at five visits per week, without any patient improvement.*

FOSTERING A NEGATIVE PATIENT SELF-IMAGE. *The worst therapists perpetually assault the patient with perceived and imaginary defects. The emphasis is on the negatives which, of course, are easily found in everyone. This is probably in part due to the financial incentive for keeping patients sick. It may also be the result of excessive reliance on theoretical models that emphasize pathology over health. Rather than teach patients how to live with inevitable flaws, the worst therapists perpetuate the myth of obtainable perfection.*

JUSTIFICATION OF THEORETICAL BIAS. *The worst therapists, even if they do not exploit the patient financially, almost always use the patient to confirm their own beliefs. Patients are often taught theoretical jargon, so that even if they don't improve, they can have magnificent "insight" into their continuing chaotic behavior. The worst therapists blame patients for all therapeutic failures—"too little motivation," "too many characterologic problems," etc. Special contempt is reserved for patients who improve too rapidly. "Flight into health" or "transference cure" are the smug predictions of doom, even though many patients maintain such gains.*

INCOME AND PRESTIGE. *The worst therapists share this goal with the best, for they desire to make money and be admired. For the best therapists, this is* **a** *goal. For the worst, it is often* **the** *goal.*

SENSE OF PERSONAL SATISFACTION AND MEANING. *For the worst therapists, doing therapy may be the only source of satisfaction and meaning, since their personal lives are often a mess. Many are so socially awkward that they have no intimate relationships outside their work. Some "worst therapists" become devoted to financial adventures, but many others exploit the therapeutic relationship itself, using patients to satisfy their needs for power, intimacy, and even sex. Generally they fail to obtain full gratification and seem instead to suffer more than their share of missed appointments, uncollected fees, and malpractice suits.*

BEING RIGHT. *The worst therapists worship this goal. While these therapists may feel profoundly defective as people, they use their patient as a handy dummy—"someone who is always wrong." They play "I know all the right answers" and through subtly timed sniping, erode the patient's marginal self-confidence. Rather than ever display genuine warmth or empathy, the worst therapists show their love of being right in a manner that could best be described as aloof, arrogant, and smug.*

BEING BLAMELESS. *While the best therapists try not to harm, the worst therapists are more concerned with not getting caught. While they claim to be protecting themselves from ungrateful patients and grasping attorneys, their behavior suggests instead a desire to never be blamed for anything. Rather than take responsibility for their own actions, they seem to need some "accepted precedent" to justify everything they do. They pose as scientists (wearing long white laboratory coats) or deep thinkers (using a pipe as a constant prop) to suggest the magic mantle of great wisdom. Often they are but technicians who mechanically repeat standard formulas, papering their files with carefully worded notes to "protect the record." "Defensive medicine" is a phrase often used to excuse their attitude. "Covering your ass" is another.*

THE ESSENTIAL VEHICLE—THE THERAPEUTIC RELATIONSHIP

THE BEST THERAPISTS TAKE AS A FIRST PRIORITY THE ESTABLISHMENT AND MAINTENANCE OF A RELATIONSHIP THAT SERVES THE GOALS OF THERAPY.

An effective relationship between the patient and therapist is the *sine qua non* of therapy. Without it, therapeutic sessions are only expensive conversations. The more ambitious the goals, the more drastic and difficult the changes desired, the more profound this relationship must be. Patients come into therapy because they hurt; their pain, along with the relationship, provides the leverage for change.

The worst therapists may deliberately seek a relationship which serves their particular goals. More often than not, they seem to ignore the issue altogether. The worst therapists tend to put excessive faith in specific maneuvers such as making interpretations, giving medications, or following behavioral modification protocols. Such mechanized approaches to therapy almost always fail. These worst therapists, regardless of theoretical orientation, are often described by their patients as "remote"—and the patients respond in kind by never becoming fully involved in the therapeutic process.

THE BEST THERAPISTS RAPIDLY DEVELOP AN INTENSE RELATIONSHIP WITH THE PATIENT—EMOTIONALLY CHARGED, TRUSTING, RESPECTFUL, CONFIDENT.

They do so by closely monitoring the patient's behavior and explicitly displaying their own reactions—resonating with what they hear, see and intuitively sense from the patient—in a way that shows the patient they care and understand.

The best therapists seem to have an unspoken maxim: "If it doesn't get across, what good is it?" Therapeutic approaches may sound wonderful on paper, but if they don't work *with the patient at hand*, they are useless. Careful observation of the patient on a moment-to-moment basis, seems the best way to tell if a particular approach is working. What the patient feels shouldn't necessarily dictate the course of therapy, but it should *never* be ignored. A cold and distant approach almost always produces evidence that the patient feels demeaned or rejected. Likewise, bland acceptance of anything the patient says is too unreal to foster a strong relationship. The best therapists seem unafraid to stop at any moment and discuss or comment on the status of the therapeutic relationship when it doesn't feel right.

Empathy is the term most often used to summarize these aspects of an emotionally intense relationship. Ultimately, it is a statement that the therapist seems "in tune" or "resonates" with the patient's hidden thoughts and feelings. Empathy does seem crucial to good therapy[5]; experimental studies by Truax[6] and his associates have clearly shown that it increases therapeutic effectiveness. Empathy that is *explicitly shared* with the patient seems to have more profound impact than the silently and privately experienced by the therapist. Patients can't read minds and often desperately need vivid assurance that they're with someone who understands.

The worst therapists, on the other hand, fail to establish an intensely empathic relationship with the patient. Empathy is rarely avoided out of ignorance, since it is a natural human reaction. Rather the worst therapists have trained themselves to be peculiarly unnatural. Typically, they justify their bizarre parody of human emotions with grand sounding theoretical explanations. Some defend the diffident approach with claims that the patient (might be the therapist?) "can't handle" strong feelings. That may be so, but the best therapists seem to know that therapy is the place for the patient to learn how. Others may claim that intense emotions necessarily mean patient exploitation—as though feeling intimately understood starts a malignancy that must always culminate in over-dependency, unresolved transference or sexual intercourse.

Still others remain aloof because they are too frightened or incompetent (often as a result of poor training) to relate at an emotional level with a human being who was been designated as "the patient." They justify this rigid distance with such catch phrases as "blank screen technique," even if the treatment is not strictly psychoanalytic. Or they claim they must maintain "appropriate professional distance," and through such subtle coldness leave the patient feeling hopelessly inferior.

Empathy does not mean condoning all the patient does, nor is exploitation an inevitable consequence of empathy. Indeed, empathic therapists seem to have a deeper appreciation of what the patient feels and so seem far less likely to abuse. Yet the worst therapists hide behind cold myths. They are people who have drifted into a life of defensive cowardice and seem to have trouble ever being truly empathic with anyone. The best therapists know excuses for avoiding empathy are all rubbish. Showing the patient understanding gives that human a sense of dignity and helps begin the recovery of self-esteem.

Especially at the beginning of therapy, often what the patient needs most is some genuine warmth. *No school of theory demands that the therapist adopt an attitude of aloof con-*

descension. Even the best therapists who adopt the neutral stance characteristic of psychoanalysis show quiet respect and empathy. They do not seek to humiliate the patient—"blank screen technique" does not call for snobbish disdain. And the therapies that use non-talking modalities still require therapists' empathy for maximum effectiveness. Even if the therapeutic plan is primarily medication or behavioral modification, (or, for that matter, surgery) how the patient is approached before, during and after these maneuvers will dictate the degree of empathy felt and the patient cooperation obtained. Whatever the approach, if it is not possible for a therapist to feel and show empathy towards a particular patient, a referral should be made to another therapist. Without empathy, and the respect and dignity that it brings, therapy becomes a cruel parody of itself.

THE BEST THERAPISTS EXPLICITLY NEGOTIATE MUTUAL EXPECTATIONS WITH THE PATIENT.

Duration, responsibilities, frequency of contact, and professional fees are the subjects most often discussed. The best therapists also usually cover expectations of healing and mutual responsibilities (the "Therapeutic Contract"[7]). In general, ethical limits seem to be left implicit but are discussed if the issue arises in an individual case. The worst therapists seem to skip all of these areas (with the exception of professional fees, of course) and plunge directly into some habitual formula. The manner in which these points are negotiated also seem significant: The worst therapists seem rigid and uncomfortable in discussing mutual expectations, while the best therapists negotiate with an easy grace.

LEADING THE WAY—THE PRINCIPLES OF THERAPY

THE BEST THERAPISTS, REGARDLESS OF THEORETICAL ORIENTATION, USE PRINCIPLES DRAWN FROM THE BROADER FIELD OF "HUMAN INFLUENCE."

Some might cringe at our choice of words, but the fact is *therapists try to INFLUENCE patients to heal.* Indeed, patients present themselves for treatment because they want to be influenced—"helped" is the usual term—for they sense assistance is needed. The worst therapists refuse to meet this need, often reciting such homilies as "The patient must not be influenced by the therapist, he must only influence himself." But even if the patient could influence himself to change, his seeking therapy is clear evidence that he has not. It is also usually evidence that whatever the people around him have been doing hasn't helped him much either.

The worst therapists are mechanical in their approach. While they seek to influence, they often leave out their humanity in the attempt. Or they may confuse influence and total control and assume that an attempt to influence *anything* about a patient is, by necessity, an attempt to influence *everything.* The best therapists know the game is much more subtle. Therapy, even if its fundamental purpose is to help the patient become more self-determined, (i.e., self-influencing) requires the initial push ("help") of strong influence. And the best therapists never seem to lose sight of the fact that they are trying to move (influence) a human being.

We would define the general field of "human influence" as that class of endeavors where a person has a purpose in dealing with others. While this notion might at first seem absurdly broad, it emphasizes the connectedness of many apparently unrelated activities (FIGURE 4). Approaches to influence can readily be classified by their most obvious features: *Distance* is the most basic and ranges from the extremes of personal intimacy to mass communication. *Duration*, likewise has a broad range from the one-time question of a stranger on the street, to the lifelong interactions in a family. *Intensity* rounds out the three basic characteristics; it is somewhat related to distance, but occasionally even remote forms of influence (political maneuvers, popular music) can have extremely intense effects.

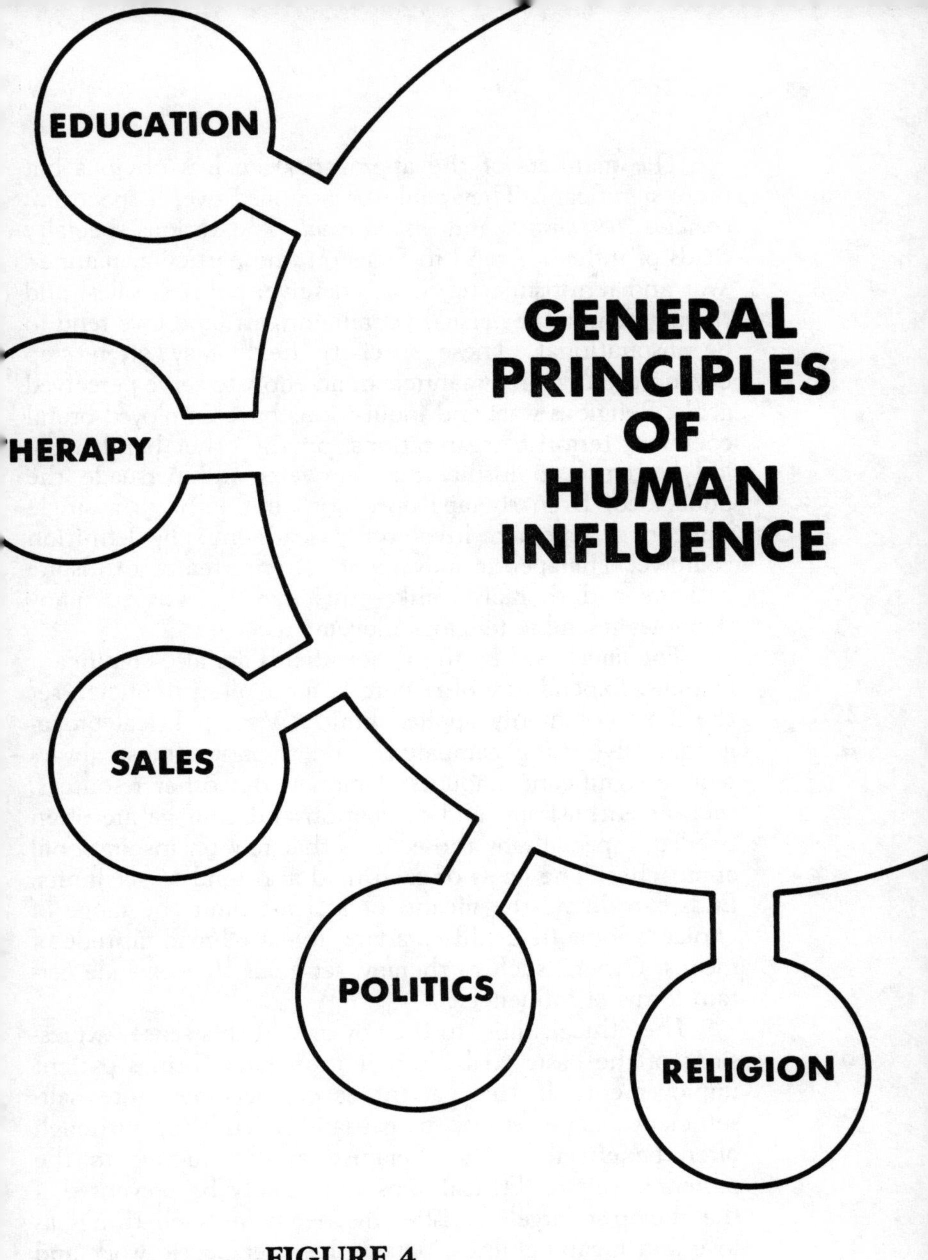

FIGURE 4
THERAPY IS A SPECIALTY FIELD OF HUMAN INFLUENCE

The manners of the approaches are less obvious but more significant. They could be arranged over a spectrum: *coercive, persuasive,* and *inspirational.* The various specialty fields of influence tend to focus on one particular manner. War and terrorism tend to be coercive; politics, sales, and therapy tend to be persuasive; religion, art, and love tend to be inspirational. These specialty fields may often step beyond their favored manners in an effort to serve perceived goals. Religious wars and inquisitions have employed brutal coercion; terrorist organizations, on the other hand, regularly attempt to inspire new converts and persuade the undecided. Even therapy does not limit itself to a single category of approach. Involuntary treatment is by definition coercive. Therapeutic movements often attempt to inspire patients and therapists alike—this may be why so many therapies resemble religious movements.

The *limits* used by the various fields are also significant features. Expenditure of resources, most often financial, set the most commonly applied limits. Wars, political propaganda, advertising campaigns, and therapy almost always require significant amounts of money. But other resources, such as enthusiasm, and dedication and courage are often needed, especially by those fields that rely on inspirational approaches. The goals of each field also tend to set limits. Ends can define the means, or at least limit the range of choices. Some fields, like warfare, tolerate broad latitude of means. Others, such as therapy, set goals that exclude certain forms of influence.

The ethical limits to therapy are, in this sense, expressions of the basic goals. Exploitation rarely brings patient improvement. If the patient is to become more self-sufficient, maneuvers to perpetuate dependency, although often beneficial to the therapist, are destructive to the patient's welfare. Ethical slips can usually be prevented if the therapist largely satisfies his needs for such things as love and meaningfulness outside his therapeutic work and thus minimizes having hidden agendas. When all goals are forthright, it's much easier for the therapy to be honest.

The best therapists freely admit they are trying to influence the patient. Keeping mindful of their goals, they draw approaches from the general field of human influence in vigorous pursuit of whatever best helps the patient heal. They find it easy to adopt a close, intense relationship with the patient, for they have nothing to hide. Once again, the particular theoretical orientation seems irrelevant. The best therapists, whether they use behavioral protocols or primal scream, make the purposes and techniques of their influence explicit. By explicit and implicit means, they persuade and even inspire the patient to try "doing it on his own," in the future. Even the psychoanalytic game, while delicate, is no exception—under the heading of promoting insight, an analyst *influences* the patient to see the way he allows himself to be *influenced.*

THE BEST THERAPISTS USE THE INFLUENCING APPROACHES THAT MAXIMIZE THEIR THERAPEUTIC LEVERAGE.

Patients usually come into therapy after all else has failed. They are often in deep ruts, and a firm grip along with powerful leverage is required to get them moving again. Influencing is essentially a kinetic process: efforts are made to alter a trajectory. Throughout the various fields of human influence, the first task is to get an adequate hold on the human in question. In therapy, this is achieved through a rapidly established, intense therapeutic relationship.

The "newness" in the first few sessions is a priceless commodity—delays in establishing an emotionally intense bond may create an insurmountable inertia later. Part of why therapy works is that it is "different" from everyday life. Patients, by their habitual behaviors, immediately and unconsciously try to make therapy the same as the rest of their lives. The "corrective emotional experience" proposed by Alexander[8] seems most likely to occur if it begins as soon as the patient and therapist meet.

The "stuckness" that brings patients into treatment can be profound in degree. While the patient may appear on the verge of losing control, this "instability" is often frightfully stable. Patients tend to cling to their problems. However unhappy their circumstances, they may find the prospect of change too frightening to view. Such "resistance" is rarely deliberate. Rather, a patient can be like the drowning man, whose fear and desperate thrashing fights off the very rescue he hopes for. This is the source of the ethical imperative to maintain a firm grip and strong leverage.

Thus, while the best therapists may share control of the therapeutic relationship, they know that giving up too much control is both unethical and potentially dangerous. They strive for balance, avoiding the traps of over-control on the one hand, and abdication of responsibility on the other. By building the therapy around a respecting, empathic relationship, they find ways to focus on the agreed upon goals to help the patient make the moves he couldn't do on his own. From a foundation of a strong therapeutic relationship, they apply the general principles of influence most relevant to therapy:

- Fostering *hope* and expectation of healing by explicit or implicit encouragement. Although the terms may vary—symptom relief, growth, meaning, increased satisfaction—the patient, nevertheless, expects some "benefit" from therapy and the best therapists use that leverage.
- Use of a *theoretical rationale* acceptable to both the patient and therapist, which serves as a framework for insight and behavioral change. A credible explanation enhances the patient's sense of personal control and makes cooperation more likely.
- Encouragement of non-destructive *emotional release*. Such catharsis may occur through confrontation in the "here and now" or through the creation of emotionally laden experiences through recall, fantasy or role play. The experience of tension relief seems to leave the patient eager to try alternative approaches to dealing with his life.
- Deliberate use of the patient's *discomfort* or *pain* to promote change. ("People don't change when they feel

good.") This non-specific feature is rarely acknowledged but is one of the most useful and universally applied. Pain may be harnessed when it is easily mobilized, but often intrusive, empathic confrontation is required to uncover hidden psychological pain.

THE BEST THERAPISTS ENCOURAGE PATIENT REEDUCATION.

Education is the fostering of learning. The best therapists, even if they do not openly endorse the notions of learning theory, try to reeducate the patient. Such experiences are the patient's key to learning how to do it differently next time. Education is provided by:

- Provision of *new information* by precept, example or self-discovery that broadens alternatives and thus increases the possibility of self-direction and hope.
- *Modeling,* either explicit, as in role playing, or implicit, as in the therapist's own personal style.
- Explicit or implicit encouragement to accept *moderate risks* in the pursuit of success experiences.
- Encouragement of frequent repetition or *practice* of revised thinking, feeling and behaving in and outside of the therapeutic sessions.

WHILE CONSIDERABLE VARIATION EXISTS IN CLINICAL STYLES, THE BEST THERAPISTS SEEM TO SHARE SOME COMMON APPROACHES TO THERAPEUTIC STRATEGY AND TACTICS.

Considerable variation exists in the best therapist's use of strategy and tactics, as these often follow the dictates of theory. Each school promotes the therapeutic stance it deems most effective. Tactical and strategic elements may be specifically prescribed by theory, or may arise when novices imitate their teachers. Voice tone and personal appearance are two of the most obvious features—indeed, the regimental uniformity of clothing, hairstyle, and smoking habits among therapists at professional conferences (who are presumably not doing therapy at that moment), would convince even a casual observer that healers too fall prey to fads.

Yet in spite of allegiance to subspecialty groups, the best therapists seem to share some approaches. Once again, the similarities are attributable to the nature of human influence itself. Those who excel at any art or sport follow the dictates of the discipline. For example, master tennis players try to control the opponent's ability to return a volley. That is part of what the game is all about. Likewise, the best therapists play the same overall game, regardless of the style of their individual strokes. Common strategic and tactical elements employed by the best therapists seem to include:

• The best therapists control the *tone* of the course of therapy. Regardless of the therapeutic stance—directive vs. non-directive, intrusive vs. passive—the best therapists choose a specific tone and adhere to it for a set period of time. They may skillfully change their stance during the course of therapy, for example, arranging to be more intrusive and available at the start, then more reserved and distant at the end. Yet the best therapists never thrash around. Even when they make dramatic changes in their roles (for therapy, in a very real sense, is theater), they carefully ensure that their audience is still with them. Getting through to the patient is what therapy is all about.

In practice this seems to mean that they best detach themselves from their personal lives while assuming the role of therapist. Human feelings are not discarded, but the worries and pressures of other activities must be set aside if therapy is to work well. The best therapists seem to set a tone of involvement serious enough to be truly empathic, yet just distant enough to maintain full perspective.

The judicious use of humor seems to help in this regard. The best therapists avoid pomposity by seeing the silly aspects of the grand enterprise of therapy. Likewise, they gently help the patient see the irony of his human predicament and encourage the mixture of tension relief and insight that laughter can bring.

• The best therapists maintain a clear sense of *direction*. Usually this is based on an intuitive sense of where to go next. But the best therapists also use "objective" signposts—reduction of symptoms, reported improvements, changes in observed behavior—to help guide the therapy. The therapist's observations of himself are also crucial bits of information—"do I feel anxious? bored? excited?" The best therapists mix these various observations and feelings and so evolve a sense of where the therapy should go next. The knack of doing so seems to be largely intuitive and experiential. For the best therapists all have it, while the worst—even if they do their therapy exactly "by the book"—never quite catch on.

• The best therapists develop interventions in a process that could best be described as *refined trial and error.*

Theory can't dictate what to say next. Even the most complete protocols for behavioral modification or chemotherapy ignore the arty question of what to do before and after the protocols. For the best therapy is an art that transcends theory. This is a direct consequence of the points we made earlier. All theories to date, and for that matter, all writings on the subject, (including this section) fail to fully apprehend how therapy works. Most are either too restricted, and thus useful only in a narrow area, or are too broad, and fail to provide meaningful guidance.

Even the best theories can't tell the therapist exactly what to do. When therapists use theories as recipes, rather than as suggestive guides, the results are generally dismal. Nevertheless, many therapists would insist that their pet theories describe all that is necessary to know. But the best therapists, even when they fanatically cling to habitual dogma in arguments with their colleagues, still tend to use the same basic process in actually doing therapy.

Trial and error. The phrase sounds ominous, for it implies that we don't quite know what we are doing. And that's the truth. Although some of the lay public may believe otherwise, the fact is no therapist really knows just how therapy works. From what we have seen, the best therapists share in this state of ignorance. If anything, they revel in it, deliberately avoiding a rigid plan of where each session should go. While the worst therapists attempt to build in steel and concrete, the best let therapy grow like a living tree.

The best therapy works by trial and error. This is our most shocking statement. We firmly stand by it. The "knack" of doing therapy, the subtle nuances of timing and touch are developed by experimenting to find what works best. This does not suggest wild or blind stumbling. Indeed, the best therapists rapidly review the effects of each action they take. After each intervention—even only a word or nod of the head—they quickly review its effects on the patient.

The best therapists use refined trial and error to develop a uniquely tailored therapy for each individual patient. Careful cutting, fitting, and adjusting are needed to develop a therapy that works best for that particular person. While the worst therapist may rigidly apply a single mechanical technique on one extreme, or dilute and bastardize a dozen approaches on the other, the best therapists find a way to tread the middle ground. But before each session arrives, even before each moment occurs, the best therapists refrain from planning *exactly* what to do or say next. They follow hunches and ideas and evolve the approach as they go.

One of the observations that prompted this conclusion arose during videotape seminars. In the course of the discussion about tape, a peculiar phenomenon became apparent: prominent specialists and academic faculty viewers, who usually judge therapy by theory, frequently disagreed about whether a particular moment on tape was good or bad therapy. Student viewers, unschooled in theory, had much higher rates of agreement. At first we thought this finding meant unsophisticated viewers judged tapes of therapy as though they were simply watching another TV program. Yet their opinions did not seem directed towards "entertainment value."

Student evaluations frequently contained phrases like "they're really talking now" and "it finally started moving again." Free to see without the rigidity of theoretical constraints, the students noticed something their teachers were missing. We believe the students saw an ambiguous emotional quality well known to actors, salesmen, and politicians. Good therapy, as with any human influence relationship, only occurs when there is a feeling that "something is happening." Without that feeling, the play goes unfelt, the product unbought, the voter unswayed, and the patient unhelped.

Living with ambiguity is hard, but the best therapists make it look easy. Intuitive feelings are, by necessity, ambiguous—if they were clear and precise, they could be subsumed under the rubric of rational thought. But therapy, like the rest of the arts, relies heavily on feelings. The best therapists combine the *rational* elements they observe and the *intuitive* elements they feel. Both are important and both must be balanced in order to do the best therapy. Yet the temptation for many is to ignore the intuitive elements and to focus solely on the rational dictates of theory. At such extremes, the crucial questions go unasked: "Is something really happening?" "Is the patient really getting any better?"

The best therapists know theories and techniques make excellent servants, but very poor masters. Doing the best therapy requires some indescribable commitment and concentration, some awakening that only comes with devoted practice. Just short of that indescribable realm, indeed on the very fringes of what can be put into words, is this process of refined trial and error. It is not at all unique to the process of doing therapy. We described it earlier in the book in terms of changing one's own life. For it is an amazingly commonplace phenomenon involved in any field where excellence is achieved. It is simply the way the best anything gets done.

First, action is taken in a state of intense intuitive concentration. We would refer to this as the phase of *creative acting.* In therapy this could be any action by the therapist—a statement, a question, a laugh, a shout, a nod, a silence. For it to work best, the action must occur in this deeply involved state of mind. Respect and empathy seem crucial, whereas self-consciousness, poor concentration or hidden agendas can destroy it utterly.

Second, at some point after the creative action—usually within a few moments—a phase of *critical reviewing* occurs. The effects of the action are reviewed both in rational and intuitive terms. "Is there any change in the patient's observable behavior (appearance, speech, affect, mood) or reported experiences (symptoms, thoughts, feelings)? What does the patient seem to be experiencing? What does it feel like to be him at this moment? What am I, as the therapist, experiencing right now? Which of my feelings are attributable to what's going on in the therapy? Is the therapy moving along well? Is the patient really getting any better?

The phase of critical reviewing does not necessarily produce a single answer of what to do next. Rather, as the therapist stretches through all the rational and intuitive points of view he sets the stage for the next cycle of intuitive action (FIGURE 5). This cycling seems to be present to some extent within everyone, since *thinking about acting* and *acting* are really alien states of mind. A switching between these states of mind seems necessary for the best therapy. Critical reviewing does a very poor job at empathy and is unable to ever come up with anything really new. The intuitive phase of creative action on the other hand, if entirely unchecked, can lead to dangerous excesses. Among therapists, some tend toward the overly rigid commitment to

FIGURE 5
REASON AND INTUITION BALANCE AND CORRECT EACH OTHER

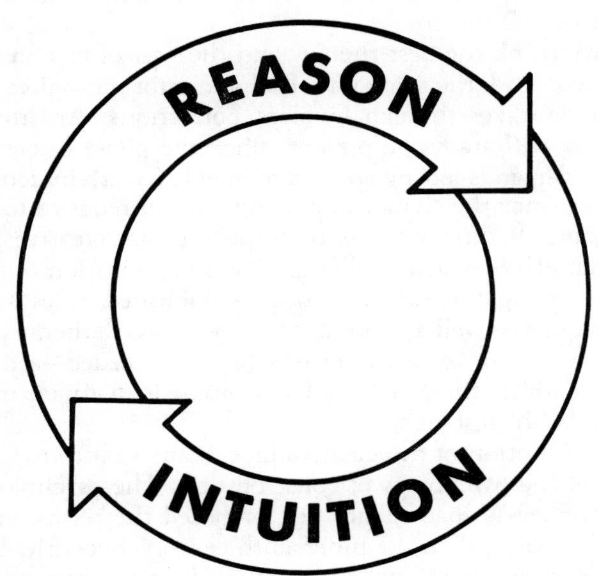

299

constant critical reviewing and they are often negativistic and punitive towards their patients. Others whose free-wheeling allegiance to any "gut feeling" makes them unbalanced, can become the potentially destructive "charismatic" therapists described by Yalom.[9]

Self-correcting cycles seem to be one of the most all-pervasive aspects of living things. Simple physical movements mimic the same feedback correction that is employed in grand acts of creativity. As one reaches for a teacup, continuous recalculations of trajectory through eye-hand feedback produce one apparently smooth excursion. But if one looks closely at the hand, a fine, but jerky tremor, present in all muscle movements, makes the trial and error obvious. One's hand doesn't really know where the teacup is; one's eye is unable to reach and grasp. Moment-to-moment corrections, feedback, and coordination are necessary to guide the course.

We think the best therapy and the best of any creative endeavor work the same way. Trial and error minimizes dangerous mistakes through frequent corrections. An irreducible risk will always be present, since the phase of creative action demands letting go for a moment. Creativity requires courage since the chance of making errors is required to play the game. It should hardly be surprising that creative therapy is much like creative living. Slavish application of technique or rigid adherence to pre-established rules never works quite as well as finding one's own way. Rather, a process like the stroke of the artist's brush is needed—a touch here, a touch there, reflect for a moment, a touch more, then, "Ahh! Just right."

This notion of the creative process fits well to the concepts of the psychology of consciousness. The psychologist-philosopher William James first proposed the term, "states of consciousness" in the nineteenth century. Recently, Tart[10] and Ornstein[11] have applied it in their investigations of psychological and neurophysiological phenomena. Elsewhere we have proposed a mathematical model of the creative process,[12] based on the phase transition "catastrophe theory" of Thom and Zeeman.[13]

We would model creativity as a cycling between non-intersecting states of consciousness. One state, "*the everyday state of consciousness,*" is largely made up of rational thinking and the semi-rational "common sense." The intuitive state of mind, on the other hand, is one of profound concentration, and brings a feeling of merging between the "one who is acting" and the "one who is acted upon." We call this "*the sense of union state of consciousness.*" These two states of mind are "parallel realities" so the transitions between them usually involve a leap or jump. Catastrophe theory neatly lent itself to mathematically describing this leap and helped firm our suspicion that creativity requires that one learn how to "let go."

Of all the qualities that make the best therapists so good, this use of trial and error seems to be the most important. It is how the great innovators developed the existing schools. It is how gifted clinicians have always practiced. Blending intuition and keen rational observation is difficult to learn, but the alternative is therapy of inferior quality. The worst therapists hope that their theories or techniques will save the day. They stretch and cut the patient's reality to fit their own notions and blind themselves to the subtle feedback required for trial and error tailoring. The best therapists, even when they consider a patient in terms of a theory's diagnostic category, keep alert for exceptions to the rules. In so doing, they maintain the gift for seeing choices where none were seen before.

Theories and techniques are, by necessity, *retrospective* accounts of what the best therapists did. Their frameworks made handy points of reference, good maps that can be checked during the phase of critical reviewing. But no theory or technique can direct the phase of creative acting. The best therapists, like creative masters in any field, often deliver their finest work without premeditation, reacting far more rapidly than the slow pace of deductive reasoning could ever allow. The best therapy is a living process that follows the scent of which issues are important and which are mere distractions. Indeed, it could be said that the best therapists don't "do" the best therapy. Instead, they simply avoid doing anything that would stop it from occurring on its own.

• The best therapists develop their own unique *therapeutic styles*. The best therapists do not act the same way all the time. For example, they may be somewhat subdued with one patient, yet almost raucous with another. Still, each best therapist tends to develop a style based on his or her favorite approaches. Personal differences among therapists are probably the crucial variable in this area. Some are uniquely suited to one clinical stance, while others may find that approach incompatible with everything they feel.

The range of styles is so broad that, rather than list several, we will describe only one—our own. We would like to think of ourselves as "best therapists," for we have deliberately attempted to follow what works best. Whether we make the grade remains to be seen, but for our purposes here, we will suspend that assessment. Rather than "one of the best therapeutic styles" let us simply call it a therapeutic style that we both share.

We have attempted to commit ourselves to a process of refined trial and error, and have over the years become progressively less attached to any specific body of therapeutic theory. We try to directly apply principles of human influence in our own practices. We also tend toward a therapist-consumer partnership model—to us the ultimate judgment of effectiveness lies in the combined opinions of therapists and patient. Both are inevitably biased. Either one alone can distort to a point where the assessment is worse than meaningless. But the combined judgment generally has high merit. To assess therapy outcomes we like to include anyone else who is directly involved in the patient's life—family members, social workers, government agencies, "third party payers"—all with the patient's permission, of course, in order to get the best overall picture of the results of therapy.

We have also grown rather fond of follow-up data. Ours is rather informal, derived from telephone calls and sporadic questionnaire letters, but they have greatly reinforced our belief in the general approach outlined above. We have also become taken with the notion of "therapeutic efficiency" for it seems to us that the principle of maximum results with minimum costs is too often ignored. Perhaps this is simply because it is so hard to show that any therapy is even effective, let alone to calculate its overall efficiency. Nevertheless, we avoid such things as the analytic stance since it is so grossly inefficient that we wonder if it is ever effective at all.

In our experience, the therapies that achieve maximum effect most efficiently have also tended to be time-limited. Research has suggested that even single session therapies can have profound impact.[14] While we both have in our practices a few patients whose biochemical problems are profound (such disorders as manic illness and schizophrenia) and some require long-term care, the bulk of our patients have the more general "problems in living" and are seen for about ten to fifteen sessions. We do not strive for brief therapy with brevity for its own sake, but rather a limited contact therapy, with widely spaced follow-up sessions, to search for the minimum contact necessary to get the job done.

One of our most prominent personal goals has been to keep therapy from becoming boring. So far, we seem to have succeeded. The overall mix has been a delicate balance of surprise and familiarity that keeps us quite involved. We have also found that writing about therapy is often as much fun as doing it.

In our clinical styles, we both tend toward the fanatical regarding empathy. In doing therapy, we first try to establish as powerfully empathic a relationship as possible. It seems to us that if one is cold and aloof, even for the first few moments, the patient remembers this hurt and finds it hard to trust. Explicit empathy for the patient's humanity—not bland acceptance for all his actions, shows that we care and understand, or at least try damned hard to. Empathy can't be faked, but oddly, with practice, it can be learned. All humans have some profound bond of common experience. Empathy taps this reservoir.

Empathy and respect seem to allow license for maximal therapeutic leverage. We strive to show our warmth and to sense just how much the patient wants to be pushed. We then push *slightly* harder. For some reason, erring on the side of pushing too little comes across as cold. For all but the most paranoid patients, we use intrusive empathic guesses as they seem to convey warmth and interest while exposing hidden thoughts, feelings, and beliefs. These largely intuitive guesses are often grossly intrusive, yet they allow the patient an easy exit. Empathic voice tone allows these statement-guesses to work: "Your voice sounds so sad to me when you talk about your wife." Delivering interpretations with a built-in sneer never works as well: "You seem to feel that your wife never loved you." Subtle changes in words or tone can profoundly alter what the patient hears.

In our styles, we avoid the passive "blank screen approach." While it may be useful in strict psychoanalysis, most people are not suitable candidates for such therapy, at least while in the throes of acute discomfort. And we also avoid the other extreme of a rigidly warm, non-judgmental approach. "Unconditional positive regard," a phrase developed by Carl Rogers to describe a respectful, compassionate attitude, is often used as an excuse for a mere affectation of warmth. To us, this is a perversion of Rogers's ideas; he is anything but insipid, yet many technician therapists invoke his name to explain why they act like smiling, nodding robots, uttering saccharine statements of what the patient just said.

Therapy must feel real. The underlying message to the patient should convey "Here we are together. I respect you as an essentially worthwhile person. I'm human, too; no better, no worse; I want to help you get the life you want." Hope is generated by the leadership and confidence of the empathic therapist. Empathy models the courage to feel intensely in a confusing world. In our styles, we strive for just that. Hiding behind being "clinical" or "maintaining one's professional image" often destroys the therapist's ability to converse and interact directly. The language of the heart is plain talk.

In dealing with patients, we also try to project an involvement that could best be described as "passionate." We are well aware that passion is a word that causes great concern for it is usually taken to mean sexual excitement. Such a narrow definition is absurd. For many, sex itself is boring, mechanical, and devoid of any deep feeling, let alone passion. We use "passionate" in its original sense—emotionally intense. Passionate is vibrant, involved, alive, experiencing the full range of contradictory human feelings. People often come to therapy because of their inability to deal with their own emotions. Either they are blown about by their feelings or bury them until they erupt into strange symptoms. Therapists who project the same fear of passionate existence offer little hope for modeling how to deal with intense feelings.[15]

We allow ourselves to experience our full range of emotions while playing the part of therapists. During the split seconds that we begin to experience a feeling, we ask ourselves a few questions: "What am I feeling? Is this feeling mostly related to my experience with the patient or is it left over from some other time? Would it profit the patient for me to show what I feel?" Usually we don't get a chance to ask ourselves all these questions. Instead, we get so tuned in to the patient through our obsession with empathy that what we feel is almost always a reaction to that specific patient. We try to become living barometers by intensely reflecting back what we feel and try to teach the enrichment that passions can bring.

We steadfastly maintain respect for the person's ability to rapidly change and so vigorously attack habits we feel are counter-productive. We freely confront self-destructive beliefs and behaviors, employing ridicule or even loving anger when the patient demonstrates lack of concern for him or herself or others. We make use of exposed emotions to help people enhance their self-awareness. Such a perspective shows that even "bad feelings" have a rightful place.

Passionate confrontation and intrusive empathy seem to create an "emotional resonance" that provides a controlled channel for releasing pent-up emotions safely. The patient, in learning the courage to feel hidden feelings, also gains the courage to experiment with new behaviors. While we attempt to influence the patient with our own value system, we also vigorously encourage him or her to develop his or her own. We focus most often on feelings, but also on the attitudes, thoughts, and behaviors that produce those feelings. We encourage self-confrontation and barrage the patient with feedback via multiple channels of input, often using such dramatic confrontive devices as mirrors, video tape, spouses and friends.

This direct, open, highly charged atmosphere accomplishes a variety of purposes. The patient's habitual style is rendered ineffective. He is, for a period of time, deprived of the usual social relationships which tend to perpetuate self-deprecating neurotic behaviors. Through passionate confrontation, we try to establish a controlled emotional instability and thus promote the fluidity that makes meaningful change possible. For our styles, at least, passionate confrontation seems vital for the patient's development of a loving, respectful attitude towards himself. It is a highly stressful experience, but one that helps make it possible to deal with the inevitable messiness of human life.

We also encourage *consciously adopted-behavioral change.* This is a concept that overlaps behavioral, cognitive, and Gestalt theories. It also seems part of the common sense assumption that "you are not really different until you act differently." We like to say "the fastest way to change how you feel is to change how you act." We encourage patients to set specific behavioral goals, establish reward systems, keep records of their changes, and in general, try to act in accordance with the way they would like to be.

Central to this process of change is the assumption of a new self-belief or self-concept. One must consider the possibility that one is not who one has always believed oneself to be, that one may be able to be more. In all learning, it seems at first that one must act *as if* one has already changed. Actors and artists of all kinds have long been familiar with the mysteries of immersing oneself in a new role. We try to teach patients ways to master this process of designing a new part for themselves.

This is an awkward and difficult maneuver. To act as if one is more than one has even been feels hypocritical. It creates an identity crisis that is necessary if one is to change. We consider consciously adopted behavioral change more crucial than insight or the reliving of early life experiences. (Indeed, depending on the current rate of inflation, it is true that "insight and seventy-five cents will get you a cup of coffee.") Understanding changes nothing, action does. We encourage people to face their fears and inevitable human defects, then focus on their strengths and sense of inner beauty. Believing you are well allows you to act well. Acting well makes it progressively easier to feel well. Lasting change seems to require both.

PSYCHOTHERAPY AND THE HUMAN SPIRIT

We therapists, in our desire to be scientific, have been wary of any emphasis on spiritual issues. Artists in every other field have not been so cautious. Quite the contrary. From poets to choreographers, from composers to painters, master practitioners of every art have plumbed the depths of their intuition for inspiration. They have sought the guidance of the muses, the voice of the human spirit. The best have heard it. They speak of being merely the vehicle, the medium of their creative efforts.

Likewise, the best therapy, as we've said, is an art. The best living is the same. Only if therapy and life are performed from the heart can they be the best we have to offer.

Only if therapists and patients humbly seek a harmony with universal rhythms, and only if we appreciate the limits of our control and influence and become the medium for a power infinitely greater than our own, can true healing occur.

Love is resonance, one human with another. The highest love is resonance with the vibrations shared by all that is. The source of all healing is that resonance.

In this section we have ranged far and wide in our thoughts on the best therapy. We hope we have stirred both thought and discussion. While we closed this section with some observations on our personal styles, we would emphasize that our way is not *the* best way. We have adopted a style that fits our beliefs and experiences, and who we are as people. Many other therapists, with radically different styles, achieve superb results. But our central thesis here has been that the best therapists ultimately do pretty much the same thing. Therapy is simply one specialized way that human beings try to influence each other. Therapists, after all is said and done, are all in the same business. Which is the best therapy? It is simply the best therapy that a therapist can do with that particular patient at that particular moment.

We have included for you here a questionnaire and consultation agreement which we use in our practice. We hope you find them useful and will adapt them to suit your particular practice.

the R&R PERSONAL AND FAMILY INVENTORY

Name ______________________________

Therapist ______________________________

Date ______________________________

As your therapist I'm asking you to fill out this questionnaire. It may be a tedious job, but it will give us both a baseline from which to consider possible changes. The ultimate goal is to find ways for you to improve your well-being and satisfaction.

The use of a questionnaire format for this kind of data allows us to make the best use of the valuable time we will spend on a person-to-person basis. Your identity on this inventory will be kept strictly confidential. Please mark an X beside the answer or fill in the blank where indicated. Thank you for your cooperation.

1. I am seeking counseling for help with

0 family or couple problems.
1 school problems.
2 job problems.
3 drug problems.
4 alcoholism.
5 sexual problems.
6 mixed-up thinking.
7 legal problems.
8 other ______________________________

____

2. I am

0 single.
1 married.
2 remarried (state number of marriages ________).
3 divorced.
4 separated.
5 a widow (or widower).

3. I have been in my current marriage for ________ years.

4. I have had ________ children.

5. The number of people living in my home, including myself, totals

1 1 person.
2 2 persons.
3 3 persons.
4 4 persons.
5 5 persons.
6 6 persons.
7 7 persons.
8 8 persons or more.
Of these, ________ are children.

6. The language spoken most often in my home is

0 English.
1 Spanish.
2 Italian.
3 Portuguese.
4 Other ________________________________

7. Have you ever received counseling, therapy or psychiatric care?
0 No previous care received.
1 Yes, as an inpatient only.
2 Yes, as an outpatient only.
3 Yes, as an inpatient and outpatient.

8. Total time spent in individual or group counseling:
0 No previous care received.
1 Less than one month.
2 1-3 months.
3 4-12 months.
4 1-2 years.
5 Over 2 years.

9. Who suggested you come to this office?

0 Physician or psychiatrist.
1 Friend or relative.
2 Clergyman.
3 Employer or school.
4 Judge or attorney.
5 Other ______________________________

10. In the past year I have received medical treatment for:
1. ______________________________
2. ______________________________
3. ______________________________

11. I take the following prescription drugs (state dose and frequency):

1. ______________________________

2. ______________________________

3. ______________________________

4. ______________________________

12. Have you had a physical examination within the last month?

0 No.
1 Yes.
By Dr. ______________________________
____
____

13. How many years of schooling have you *completed?*

0 8 years or less.
1 Some high school.
2 Graduated from high school.
3 Some college.
4 Bachelor's Degree.
5 Graduate school or other post-college training.
6 Graduate degree(s):

(Please List) ______________________________

____

14. My income is:

0 I have no income.
1 from family or relatives.
2 all or partly from welfare.
3 largely self-earned.
4 Other ______________________________

15. In the past year or two my income has significantly

0 not changed.
1 increased.
2 decreased.

16. Was this change expected?

0 No
1 Yes

17. In general, my current work (in or outside of home) is

a 0 very dissatisfying.
b 1 dissatisfying.
c 2 neither satisfying nor dissatisfying.
3 satisfying.
4 very satisfying.

18. During the last 2 months I have been absent from work or school

0 0 days.
1 1-3 days.
c 2 4-6 days.
b 3 7-9 days.
a 4 over 10 days.
5 Not been working or in school
a. by choice.
b. *not* by choice.

19. During the last 6 months, time that I have missed from work or school has been

1 by my choice.
b 2 *not* by my choice.

20. During the last 2-6 months of school my grade point average has been:

0 I am not attending school.
1 I have just entered school.
c 2 3.6-4.0
3 3.1-3.5
4 2.6-3.0
5 2.1-2.5
c 6 1.6-2.0
b 7 1.1-1.5
a 8 0-1.0

21. During the last 2-6 months I have been arrested and charged with: ____________________

____

0 I have never been arrested.
1 I have not been arrested in the last 6 months.
a 2 1-2 times
a 3 3-4 times
a 4 Over 4 times

22. During the last 2-6 months external stresses (death of loved ones, illness, job problems, divorce, home-moving, etc.) have been for me

0 very mild.
1 mild.
c 2 moderate
b 3 severe.
a 4 very severe.

23. During the last 2-6 months I have been able to express my feelings of love, sadness and anger (with words) to those who are important to me

a 0 never.
b 1 infrequently—once a week or less.
c 2 occasionally.
3 regularly.

24. During the last 2-6 months I've felt a sense of warmth and pride in myself

a 0 never.
b 1 infrequently—once a week or less.
c 2 occasionally.
3 regularly.

25. During the last 2-6 months I have thought of killing myself

0 never.
c 1 infrequently—once a week or less.
b 2 occasionally.
a 3 regularly.

26. During the last 2-6 months I have felt well enough to do what I usually do during the day

a 0 never.
b 1 infrequently—one day a week or less.
c 2 sometimes—two or three times a week.
3 daily or almost daily.

27. During the last 2-6 months I've been getting out of the house to do the things I enjoy

0 once or more per week.
c 1 once every two weeks or less.
b 2 once a month.
a 3 less than once a month.

28. During the last 2-6 months I have felt loved and appreciated

a 0 never.
b 1 infrequently—once a week or less.
c 2 occasionally.
3 regularly.

29. During the last 2-6 months I have felt significant or special

a 0 never.
b 1 infrequently—once a week or less.
c 2 occasionally.
3 regularly.

30. During the last 2-6 months I have had fun

a 0 never.
b 1 infrequently—once a week or less.
c 2 occasionally.
3 regularly.

31. During the last 2-6 months I have had sexual relations

0 never.
1 once a month or less.
2 once every two weeks.
3 one or two times a week.
4 three or more times a week.

32. During the last 2-6 months sexual activity has generally been

0 I have not had sexual activity.
a 1 very dissatisfying.
b 2 dissatisfying.
c 3 neither enjoyable nor dissatisfying.
4 enjoyable.
5 very enjoyable.

33. During the last 2-6 months my life has been

a 0 very dissatisfying.
b 1 dissatisfying.
c 2 neither fulfilling nor dissatisfying.
3 somewhat fulfilling.
4 very fulfilling.

34. My natural father is

1 ________ years of age.

0 deceased at age ________.

The cause of death was ____________________

____

35. My natural mother is

1 ________ years of age.

deceased at age ________.

The cause of death was ____________________

____

36. List ages of brothers and sisters (B for brother, S for sister). If deceased give cause of death.

____

____

____

____

____

____

37. My blood relatives have a history of serious depression or suicide.

0 No
d 1 Yes

38. My blood relatives have a history of psychiatric illness requiring hospitalization.

0 No
d 1 Yes

39. My blood relatives have a history of alcoholism or problem drinking.

0 No
d 1 Yes

40. My blood relatives have a history of criminal activity.

0 No
d 1 Yes

41. During the last 2-6 months I have had an alcoholic drink (beer, wine, or liquor) on the average

0 never
1 less than 2 oz. per day
b 2 2-4 oz. per day
a 3 more than 4 oz. per day

42. Drinking has been a problem for me during the last 2-6 months. It affected my work, family life, etc.

0 Yes
1 No

43. I smoke cigarettes

0 never
1 less than 1 cigarette daily
c 2 less than 1/2 pack per day
b 3 1/2-1 pack per day
a 4 more than 1 pack per day

44. During the last 2-6 months I have taken marijuana

0 never
1 once a week or less
c 2 less than once daily
b 3 once a day
a 4 more than once a day

45. During the last 2-6 months I have taken PCP (angel dust), LSD, mescaline or other hallucinogens

0 never
c 1 once every two weeks or less
b 2 once a week
a 3 more than once a week

46. During the last 2-6 months I have taken cocaine, diet pills, "speed" or other "uppers"

0 never
c 1 once every two weeks or less
b 2 once a week
a 3 more than once a week

47. During the last 2-6 months I have taken barbiturates, sleeping medications or tranquilizers (i.e. Valium, Librium, Serax) or other "downers"

0 never
1 once every two weeks or less

c 2 once a week
b 3 more than once a week
a 4 daily or almost daily

48. Drugs have been a problem for me during the last 2-6 months
0 Yes
1 No

49. During the last 2-6 months I have gained ☐/lost ☐ (check one) ________ pounds.

50. Eating and weight control have been a problem for me during the last 2-6 months.
0 Yes
1 No

51. During the last 2-6 months I have had difficulty with my sleep habits
0 never
1 infrequently—once a week or less
c 2 occasionally
b 3 regularly
a 4 every night

52. In filling out this questionnaire I have been
0 honest.
1 mostly honest.
2 mostly dishonest.

Please note that some of the answers were prefixed by A, B, C or D.

In order to score yourself on this self-assessment questionnaire, please give yourself **three** points for each **a, two** points for each **b** and **one** point for each **c** and **d**. Total a, b and c will be weighted in this way:

Total a __________ multiply by 3 = __________
Total b __________ multiply by 2 = __________
Total c = __________
Total d = __________

Total Score = __________

A, B, and C indicate how well you can take care of *you*. Each D indicates increased susceptibility to stress.

Your total score gives you an idea of how well you're doing with your life.

Total Score	You are caring for yourself:
0-4	very well
5-9	reasonably well
10-19	not too well
20-29	poorly
30-49	self-destructively

Life is like that rather perverse game, golf. The higher the score the worse you're doing. You can never get your score to the perfect level. There's just too much unexpected change and stress. But what you can do is learn to minimize the impact of the bad changes, to read the telltale signs in your life and take care of yourself as best you can.

We wish you courage in this endeavor.

CONSULTATION AGREEMENT PART 1 (CONSULTANT)

1. I agree to serve as your consultant to help you achieve mutually agreed upon goals which include:
   a) developing increased self-sufficiency and self-respect
   b) avoiding permanent harm to you
   c) relief from your symptoms
   d) balancing your conflicting needs
   e) fostering your ability to heal yourself

2. I see myself as a strong, confident, healthy, well-informed expert despite the errors I inevitably make.

3. Not being all-knowing nor all-powerful, I cannot guarantee results other than that you can increase your self-esteem just by having the courage to experiment with your life.

4. I will avoid using you to satisfy my needs except insofar as you help me feel that I contribute by helping you and to the extent that you have agreed to reimburse me for my services.

5. I feel the responsibility of striving toward the ideal of providing my services as efficiently as possible, that is the maximum service with the minimal possible expenditure of time and cost.

6. During the time we contract to spend together in our consultations, I will exclusively devote my interest and energy to you. In between those consultations, I will not be readily available as I will be attending to others, including myself. It's obvious but worth saying: I have the same responsibility for **my** life that you have for **yours**.

____

Signature of Therapist

CONSULTATION AGREEMENT PART 2 (CONSULTEE)

1. I want to accept full responsibility for myself. I realize that my health largely depends on how I conduct my life—how I think, how I feel and what I do. I'm aware that blaming anything or anyone won't help me.

2. I came here to improve my life and that means I may need to change how I feel and think as well as how I treat myself.

   I am aware that as part of my changing, I may decide to change friends, job, spouse or life-style.

3. I know that anything less than my full participation will lead nowhere.

4. I am willing to enter into open, trusting communication and will consider what you say in order to benefit my growth.

5. I understand that unrecognized thoughts, feelings and desires can profoundly influence my life and lead to or aggravate physical and emotional distress.

6. I understand that I must experiment with different ways of thinking, feeling, and behaving in order to find ways that suit me best. I know that no one way will work forever so I must learn to

experiment continuously to find the best way for me at any one time.

I realize that trying out new ways will at times feel awkward, artificial, and uncomfortable . . . even frightening at first.

7. I know you expect me to meet my financial obligations promptly and understand that I will pay for all time reserved unless cancelled forty-eight hours in advance.

I am consulting ______________________________ to assist me in my efforts to change.

Please initial to indicate you understand. This does not necessarily imply your agreement.

____

SUGGESTED READING

Cognitive Therapy of Depression by Beck, Rush, Shaw and Emery
New York: Guilford Press, 1929.

Existential Psychotherapy by I. Yalom
New York: Basic Books, 1980.

For Your Own Good by A. Miller
New York: Farrar, Straus & Giroux, Inc., 1983.

REFERENCES

1. Abrams G M: The New Eclecticism, *Arch Gen Psychiat,* 20:514-523, 1969.

2. Temerlin B, and Trousdale C, The Social Psychology of Clinical Diagnosis *Psychotherapy: Theory, Research, and Practice,* 6:24-29, 1969.

3. Karasu T B: Psychotherapies: An Overview, *Am J Psychiat,* 134, 851-863, 1977.

4. Goldstein A et al: *Psychotherapy and the Psychology of Behavior Change,* John Wiley & Sons, New York, 73-145, 1967.

5. Cartwright R D and Lerner B: Empathy, Need To Change, and Improvement With Psychotherapy, *J Consult Psychol 27:* 138-144, 1963.

6. Truax, C B: Effective Ingredients in Psychotherapy: An Approach to Unraveling the Patient-Therapist Interaction, in *Creative Developments in Psychotherapy,*A R Mahrer and L Pearson (eds): The Press of Case Western Reserve Univ, 267-279, 1971.

7. Berne E: *Principles of Group Treatment,* Oxford University Press, New York 1964.

8. Alexander, F: Unexplored Areas in Psychoanalytic Theory and Treatment—Part II, *The Scope of Psychoanalysis 1921-1961:* Basic Books, New York, 319-335, 1961.

9. Yalom, I: *Theory and Practice of Group Psychotherapy, 2nd ed.,* New York, Basic Books, 1975.

10. Tart C T: *States of Consciousness,* E P Dutton, New York, 1975.

11. Ornstein R E: *The Psychology of Consciousness,* W H Freeman and Company, New York, 1972.

12. Read R A and Rusk T N: States of Consciousness: A Two-Phase Model of the Creative Process, *Proceedings of the Eighth International Congress on Cybernetics,* Namur, Belgium, 1976.

13. Zeeman E C: Catastrophe Theory, *Scientific American,* 234:4, April, 1976.

14. Malan D H et al: Psychodynamic Changes in Untreated Neurotic Patients, *Arch Gen Psychiat*, 32: 110-126, 1975.

15. Bandura A et al: Psychotherapists Approach Avoidance Reactions to Patients' Expressions of Hostility, *J Consult Psychol*, 24: 1-8, 1960.